*Liberty is the right to do
all that the laws permit*

— Montesquieu

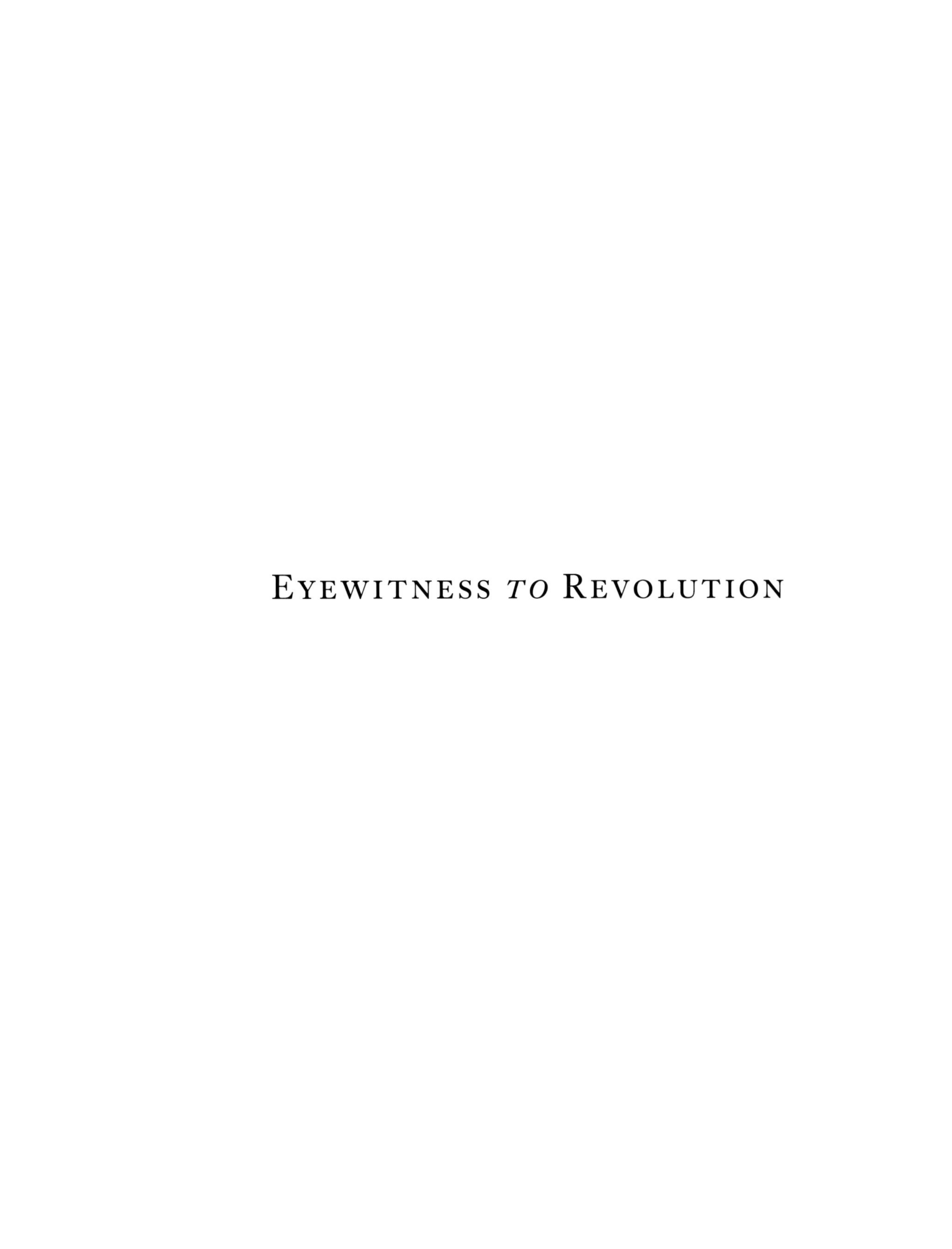

Eyewitness *to* Revolution

EYEWITNESS *TO* REVOLUTION

THE AMERICAN REVOLUTION COLLECTION *AT THE* CONCORD MUSEUM

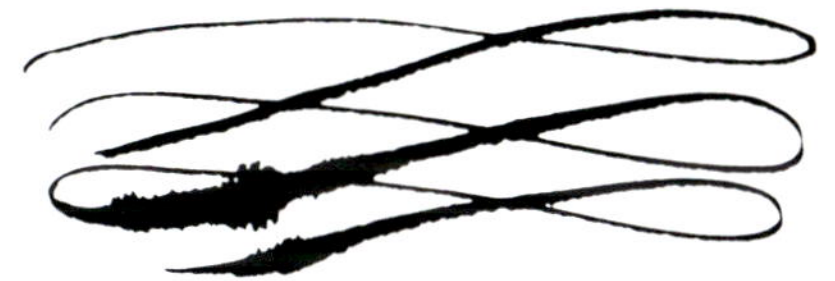

David F. Wood

CONCORD MUSEUM · CONCORD, MASSACHUSETTS

DISTRIBUTED *BY THE* UNIVERSITY *OF* PENNSYLVANIA PRESS

CONTENTS

FOREWORD

IN 1775, THE PEOPLE of Concord understood they were living through extraordinary times. David Brown, captain of one of Concord's minute companies, and his family carefully saved and passed through generations a looking glass broken by British troops on April 19, 1775. Today, that fractured mirror, with its single surviving shard, stands as a poignant witness to the Revolution, prominently displayed at the Concord Museum and featured in this book. It is objects like David Brown's looking glass that form the heart of the Concord Museum's American Revolution collection — artifacts that not only witnessed history but, in some cases, quite literally reflected it.

We owe the continued existence of these remarkable objects to the foresight of the families who preserved them and, a century later, to Cummings Davis, founder of the Concord Antiquarian Society. At a time when few saw value in everyday objects from history, Davis recognized the profound significance they held. His relentless collecting and the establishment of "Mr. Davis's Museum," as Henry David Thoreau referred to it, laid the foundation for what is now the Concord Museum's exceptional collection. Thanks to Davis's vision, the Museum can trace the story of the American Revolution with remarkable continuity — from the 1760 conquest of Quebec, through the pivotal events of April 18 and 19, 1775, and the Siege of Boston.

Just as Cummings Davis shaped the Concord Museum with his vision and dedication, another individual has profoundly influenced its development: David Wood, the Museum's Curator and author of this book. At the moment of *Eyewitness to Revolution*'s publication, David is celebrating his fortieth year with the Concord Museum. His name is synonymous with the institution, and there is no one who has done more to care for, expand, and delight in its collection. Through this book, you will experience not just David's deep expertise in the history of the Revolution, but also his enduring enthusiasm for uncovering new stories within the Museum's collection — stories he continues to share with joy and passion.

Eyewitness to Revolution is made possible by the Decorative Arts Trust who saw the merit in publishing a first-of-its-kind history of the American Revolution told through the collection of the Concord Museum and awarded the Museum their Prize for Excellence and Innovation. Significant support for this book came from Anna Winter Rasmussen and Neil Rasmussen whose dedication to the Concord Museum and David Wood are unparalleled. The stunning photography of the Museum's collection included in these pages was made possible by Martha J. Wallace and Edward W. Kane. We are grateful for additional support of this publication from Ryan and Kathryn Hanley and Gilbert and Susan Roddy.

Much like David Brown's looking glass, we invite you to reflect on the people and objects that shaped our nation, and to consider the lasting legacy of both the individuals and the objects of the American Revolution.

— LISA KRASSNER

Edward W. Kane Executive Director
Concord Museum

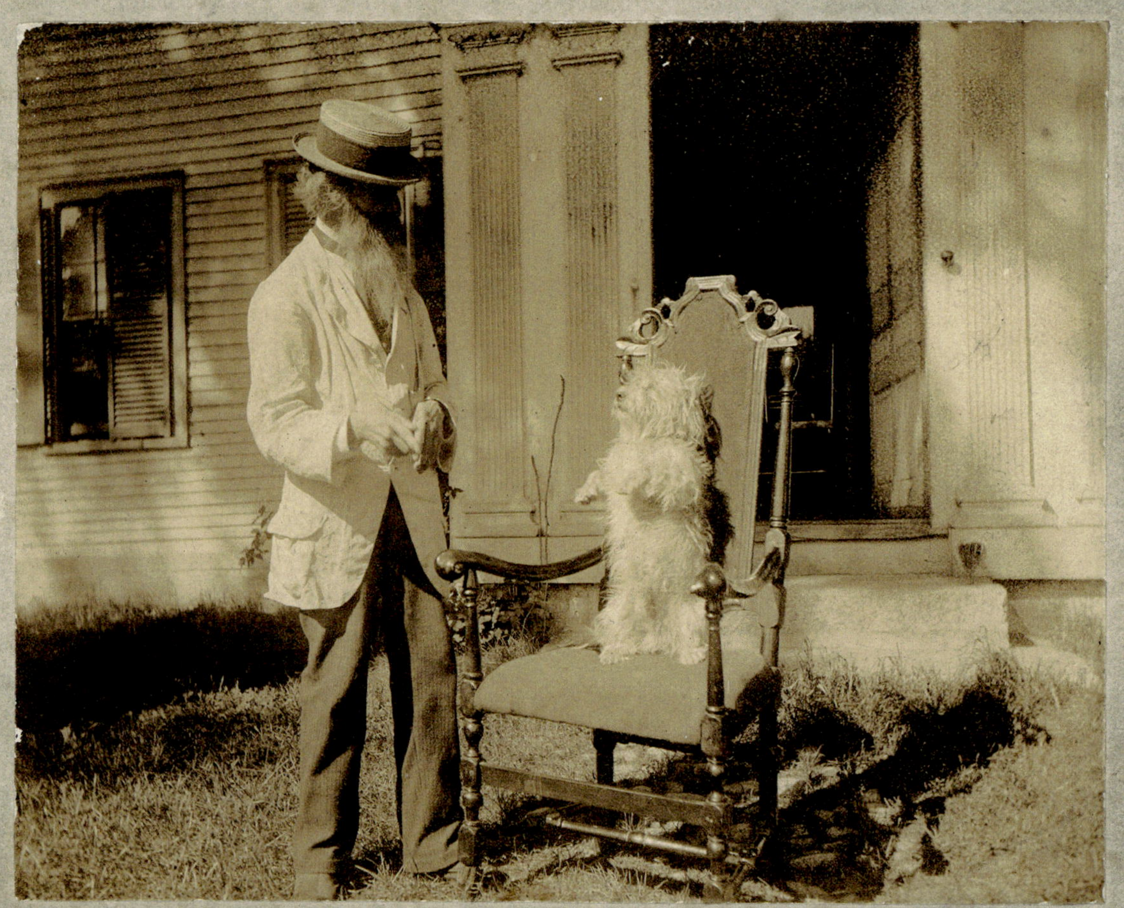
Pi -1164 a

**CUMMINGS DAVIS AND DON
AT THE FRONT DOOR OF THE
REUBEN BROWN HOUSE**

Attributed to Alfred W. Hosmer
(1851–1903)
Concord, Massachusetts, about 1890
Photograph on paper
Height: 4³⁄₁₆″; Width: 5¼″
Concord Museum collection. Pi1169a

"VERY NOTABLY GOOD" is how the great entrepreneurial proponent of American antiques Wallace Nutting described the Concord Antiquarian Society collection in 1921. "We know of no other Museum collection in a town the size of Concord of equal merit with this," Nutting went on, "or indeed in any public collection aside from the two or three greatest."

The collection that Nutting admired consisted principally of material assembled by Cummings E. Davis (1816–1896). Born in Brooklyn, New York, Davis was a descendant of one of the first English families to farm Concord's fields. Davis came to Concord in July 1850 and for the next forty years collected historic objects with an impressive energy and determination. Cummings Davis had left school in the ninth grade and in Concord sold confections at the train station to earn a living. While limited in education and limited in means, Davis evidently was not limited in inspiration. "Whatever belongs to the remote past has an unspeakable charm for me," the collector told the *Boston Transcript* in 1870. "Mr. Davis is a born collector," the Deerfield antiquary George Sheldon wrote in 1889. "To him there is little else worth living for."

Davis's inspired collection was on view to the public in rooms rented in the Court House in Concord center before the beginning of the Civil War. Henry D. Thoreau recorded a visit to "Mr. Davis's Museum" in 1860, which was neither the first nor the last visit the writer made. By that early date the collection was receiving additions from Concord families. "Miss Lydia Hosmer (the surviving maiden lady) has given him [Davis] some relics which belonged to her (the Hosmer) family," Thoreau noted of his visit. Apart from the few things that attracted Thoreau's attention that day there is no other account of what Davis was exhibiting in 1860. A list Cummings Davis later compiled gives an indication of what was of interest to the collector. Tellingly titled "Sacred Collection," the list includes fewer than two hundred of the perhaps two thousand items Davis had collected by the end of the 1870s. The variety of forms and media is evident, but it is also clear that the organizing principle of the collection is neither form nor medium nor even variety itself. Each object was selected for its history. It is for example the andirons *of* Doctor Cuming that Davis wanted, the worktable *of* Mrs. Gerrish, the chairs *of* Paul Litchfield, the snowshoes *of* Henry Thoreau, not just andirons, worktables, chairs, and snowshoes.

On April 19, 1875, the hundredth anniversary of the battle that began the Revolutionary War, tens of thousands of visitors came to Concord to celebrate the event in the company of President Ulysses S. Grant. The dinner tent, erected near Concord's historic North Bridge, seated 4,000. On a table set up in the tent were a group of relics of the famous battle, including three items from the Davis collection: a six-pound cannon ball [no. 30], a sword from a private in the British 10th Regiment [no. 51], and a cartridge box stamped "GR" [no. 38], the last a gift to Davis from Henry Thoreau in 1856.

The dignified attention drawn on the occasion of the centenary to the significant relics of the North Bridge fight between Massachusetts Provincial militia and minutemen and British Regular Army soldiers in the Davis collection may have been reflected onto the rest of the collection as well. In 1881 twenty-five inhabitants of Concord, Ralph Waldo Emerson among them, offered to pay to rent a larger room in the Court House at a cost of about $150 a year "for the purpose of securing a better place for the arrangement and exhibition of the valuable collection of Mr. C.E. Davis." This initiative led five years later to the establishment of the Concord Antiquarian Society whose mission was "to collect and preserve objects of antiquarian and historical interest." In 1887 the Society acquired the eighteenth-century Reuben Brown house, which in addition to deep historical associations had more than twenty rooms, enough to house an estimated two thousand objects insured for $2,500 (which would buy fifty acres of land in Concord at that date) and to provide living quarters for the collector. The Reuben Brown house came to be called the Antiquarian House and quickly became a destination for anyone interested in American antiques. Before the great urban museums established their American wings — the Metropolitan Museum of Art in 1924, the Museum of Fine Arts Boston in 1928, the Brooklyn Museum in 1929 — there were few places to go to see an assemblage comparable to the Cummings Davis collection.

The collection was initially installed in the rooms of the Reuben Brown house with little apparent regard to chronology or to the functions of the objects displayed. In 1907 the collection was reinstalled as period room settings, an innovative approach at that date that soon became a common mode for displaying American decorative arts. These were the rooms that so appealed to Wallace Nutting, who photographed them in 1912. Many of the early written works that popularized American antiques featured pieces from the Concord Antiquarian Society, including Russell Sturgis's *The Furniture of Our Forefathers* (1900), Frances Clary Morse's *Furniture of the Olden Time* (1908), Alice van Leer Carrick's *Collectors' Luck* (1919), and Nutting's own *Furniture of the Pilgrim Century* (1921). These writers tended to focus on the furniture and ceramics in the collection and did not feature the material associated with the American Revolution.

The Society erected a new purpose-built Antiquarian House, which opened in 1930, on land given by the Emerson family and with leadership monetary gifts from the Concord painter Elizabeth Wentworth Roberts and from the descendants of Colonel James Barrett.

The brick structure was designed by architect Harry Little (who had married into the Barrett family) and featured some advanced engineering, such as the plenum chamber in the basement intended to humidify the interior in winter and cool it in the summer. Russell Hawes Kettell collaborated with Harry Little and with Society president Allen French on the interiors, which were conceived as a series of a dozen period rooms representing the seventeenth, eighteenth, and early nineteenth centuries in chronological order. Allen French was a historian who specialized in the American Revolution, publishing among other books *The Day of Concord and Lexington* (1925). Russell Kettell was vice president of the Concord Antiquarian Society, taught art and art history at the Middlesex School, and collected and wrote about American antiques. Kettell acquired early interior paneling, none of it originating in Concord, from dealers who specialized in salvaging material from demolished homes. Little modified and augmented them with new millwork in period styles to create the new rooms. Kettell made a gift of the paneling to the Society in 1930 and in 1956 bequeathed more than one thousand other objects, ranging from early pine furniture (Kettell published a book on the subject in 1929) to lighting devices. Kettell's bequest was the most substantial addition to the collection since the acquisition of the Cummings Davis

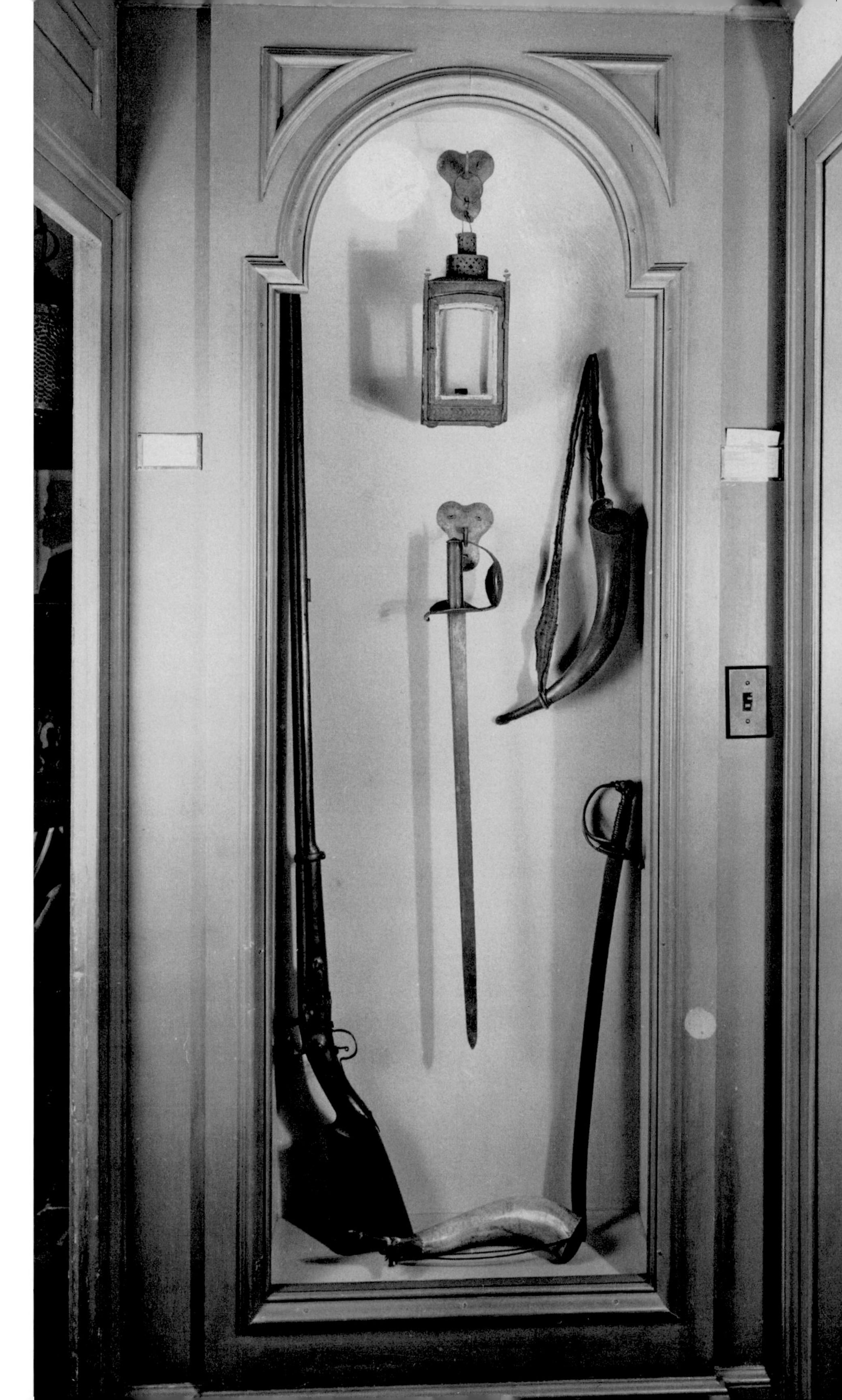

material in 1886. Included in the bequest was a significant group of documents related to April 19, 1775, among them an iconic *"BLOODY BUTCHERY, by the BRITISH TROOPS"* broadside with its grim rows of coffins [no. 58].

While still a favored way to present American antiques to museum-goers, the period room idiom was limited in its ability to present thematic topics outside the domestic realm. In the 1930 installation the only space dedicated solely to the subject of April 19, 1775 and the beginning of the American Revolution was the Lantern Case and the adjacent Relic Room.

Beginning with a project funded by the National Endowment for the Humanities in 1982 (*Two Towns: Concord and Wethersfield*, which did not address the subject of the American Revolution), the Society began to reconsider its total commitment to period rooms. In 1986 the Concord Antiquarian Society began doing business as the Concord Museum, and by 1991 had built an addition designed by architect Graham Gund. At the same time four period rooms were reinstalled and the rest repurposed as changing gallery spaces. Further grants from the National Endowment for the Humanities supported the planning and implementation of a long-term exhibition installed in one third of the former period rooms. Titled *Why Concord?* the project was directed by historian Robert Gross and opened in 1997. A chrono-logical consideration of the major topics of Concord's history, *Why Concord?* included for the first time a substantial gallery space dedi-cated to the subject of April 19, 1775.

In 2014 the Concord Museum opened *The Shot Heard Round the World: April 19, 1775*, a temporary exhibition in 1,000 square feet of gallery space. Co-curated by researcher Joel Bohy, *The Shot Heard Round the World* considered the events of April 18 and April 19, 1775, essentially hour by hour. When from 2018 to 2020 the Concord Museum reno-vated its buildings and reinstalled all its galleries, the 2014 exhibition provided the template for a 1,000-square-foot gallery titled *April 19, 1775*, in which more objects in the Museum's American Revolution collection are shown together than had ever been possible before. The stories that the individual objects tell unite to testify compellingly to the breadth of the response on that day, to the depth of the prepared-ness that underlay the actions taken, and to the entire commitment of the participants. This had to be a preconcerted action, as the royally appointed governor and military commander of Massachusetts Thomas Gage asserted of the event in an official report, and the Concord Museum installation tends to agree.

Eyewitness to Revolution includes seventy-eight objects dating from 1760 to 1790 that relate to the American Revolution. It includes all the items on view in the *April 19, 1775* gallery, as well as April 19 material not in the exhibition. Also included are some objects dating from 1760 to 1775 pertaining to the lead-up to the conflict, and another group dating from 1775 to 1790 that are associated with events from the Siege of Boston to just past the end of the Revolutionary War. The text is structured as a continuous narrative carried forward by the objects in the collection. A needlework picture, a smashed looking glass, a wooden spoon, a stair tread, a scattering of flints, a silver-hilted sword — each was an eyewitness to the American Revolution. In testifying to what they saw they testify as well to the power of material culture to improve our understanding of history. That so many aspects of the broader narrative of the American Revolution can be not only addressed, but even conditioned by these objects gives support to the opinion Wallace Nutting expressed in 1921: the collection is very notably good.

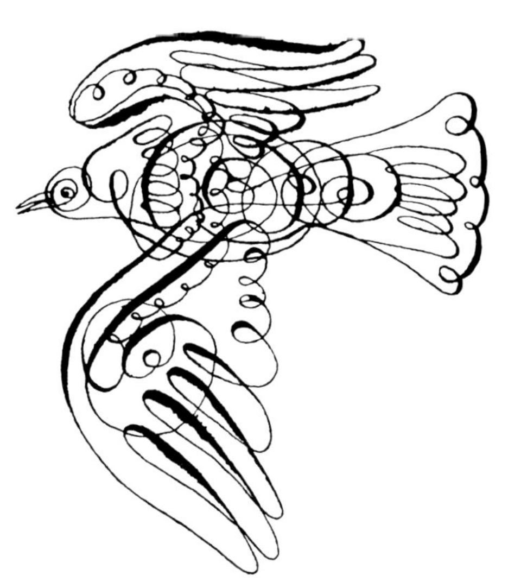

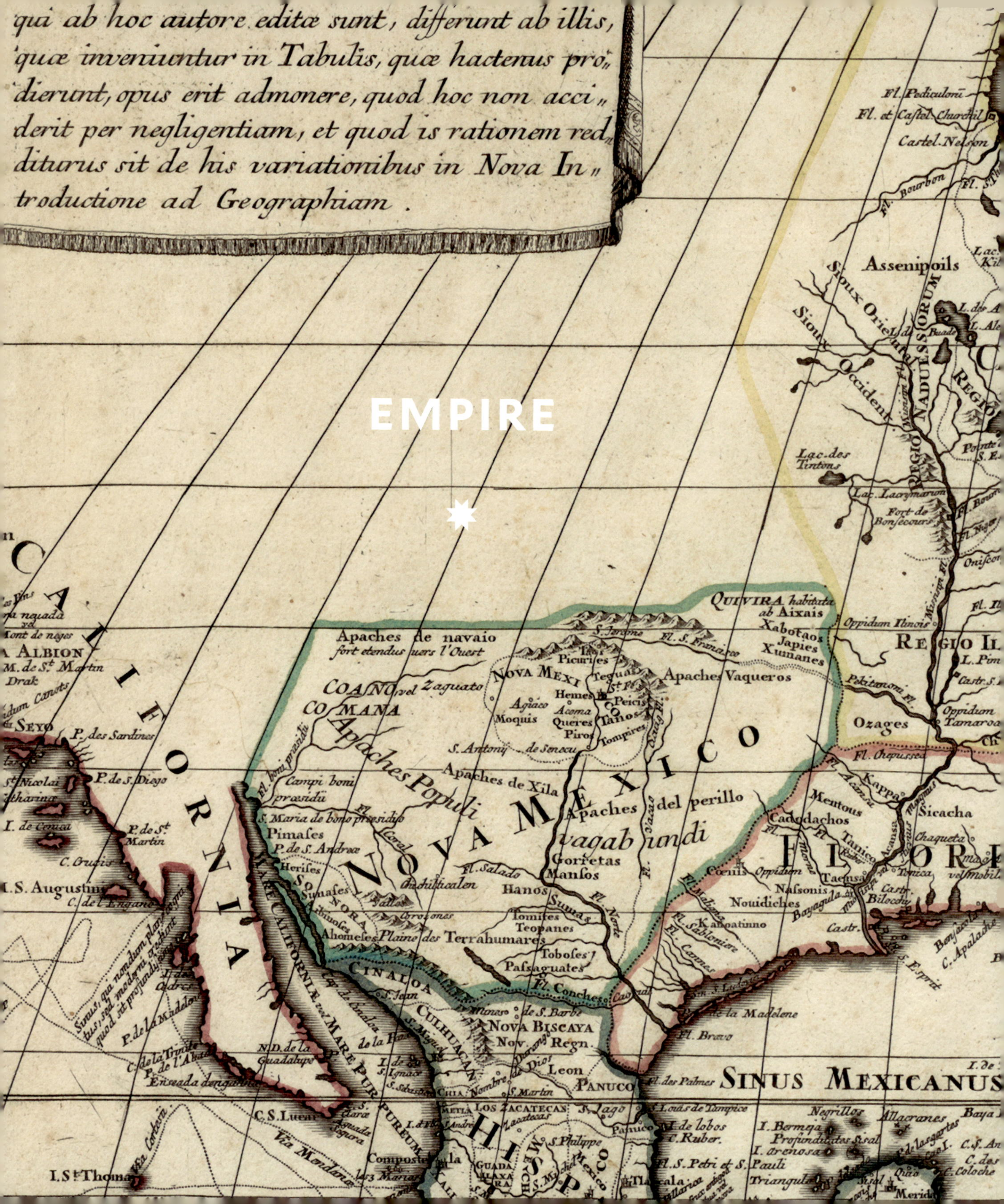

qui ab hoc autore editæ sunt, differunt ab illis,
quæ inveniuntur in Tabulis, quæ hactenus pro„
dierunt, opus erit admonere, quod hoc non acci„
derit per negligentiam, et quod is rationem red„
diturus sit de his variationibus in Nova In„
troductione ad Geographiam.

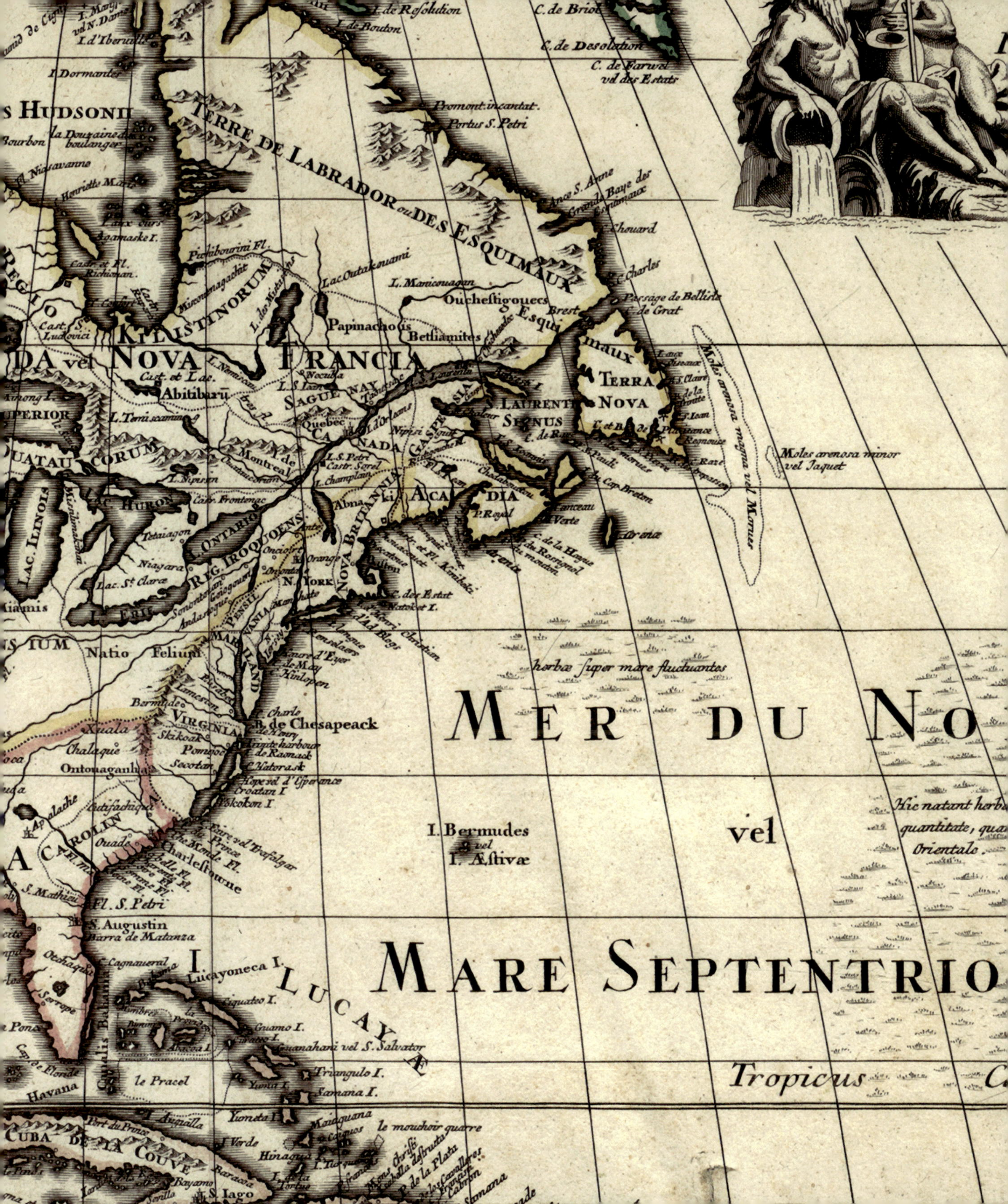

C. de Resolution
C. de Briot
C. de Desolation
C. de Farwel vel des E. stats
I. Mayn vel N. Danie
L. d'Iberuille
I. Dormante
s HUDSONII
Bourbon
la Douzaine de boulanger
N. Savanne
Henriette Marie.
L'aux ours
Agamache I.
Cast. et Fl. Richman.
Pechibonrini Fl.
Promont. incantat.
Portus S. Petri
Ana S. Anne
Grand Baye des Chaleaux
Thouard
Lac Outakouami
L. Manicouagan
Ouchestigouecs
Brest
S. Charles
Passage de Bellisle de Grat
REGIO
Cast. S. Ludovici
KILISTINORUM
DA vel NOVA
FRANCIA
Papinachous
Bethiamites
Esqui
maux
TERRA
NOVA
Cast. et Lac.
Abitibaru
Necula
L. S. Izar
SAGUENAY
L. Nemiscau
Quebec
L. Temiscamine
CA
NADA
L. d'Orleans
S. LAURENTII
SINUS
Lac aux Oiseaux
S. Claire
de la
S. Iean
SUPERIOR
Amoug I.
Montreal
L. S. Petri
Castr. Segrel
Nipisi
GASPESIA
S. de Ra
et B
Placentance
Remouse
QUATAU
CORUM
L. Sipisen
Castr. Frontenac
L. Champlain
C. de Rare
S. Pauli
Cap Breton
Moles arenosa magna vel Monte
Moles arenosa minor vel Iaquet
LAC. ILINOIS
LAC. HURON
Tetaiagon
ONTARIO
RIG. IROQUOENS
Oncaiort
NOVA BRITANNIA
ACA
DIA
P. Royal
Verte
Adrena
de la Haque
Niagara
Lac. S. Claire
Senonio
Onoiagou
Orange
N. YORK
Miamis
LAC. ERIE
Andaraque
PENSI
VANIA
C. der E. stat Natoket I.
Henry Christian
SIUM
Natio Felium
MARI
LAND
I. d'Eyer
I. de May Hinlopen
herbæ super mare fluctuantes
MER DU NO
VIRGINIA
Xuala
Skikoak
Pomejoo
Secotan
B. de Chesapeack
C. Henry
C. Natorask
Hope vel d'Esperance
Croatan I.
Roskokon I.
Chalaque
Ontonaganha
vel
Hic natant herbæ
quantitate, qua
Orientale
I. Bermudes
vel
I. Æstivæ
A CAROLIN
Apalache
Oschaqui
Serrope
Charlestowne
Fl. S. Petri
S. Augustin
Barra de Matanza
Cagnaueral
I. Lucayoneca
I. L U C A Y
MARE SEPTENTRIO
Havana
CUBA
DE LA COUVE
le Pracel
Guamo I.
Guanahani vel S. Salvator
Triangulo I.
Yuma I.
Samana I.
Mariguana
le mouchoir quarre
de la Plata
Tropicus
S. Iago

T HE CONQUEST OF QUEBEC in 1760 was a European imperial event, though it happened in Continental North America. Both France and England had laid claims to the traditional homelands of the Huron-Wendat, Wolastoqiyik (Maliseet), Innu, Mi'kmaq, and other nations 150 years earlier. As a result, there were North American theaters of war during several of the costly dynastic wars that overspread Europe for over a century.

After 1600, England tentatively at first, but ever more forcefully began claiming large areas along the Atlantic seaboard as, essentially, detached pieces of the parent state. By 1760 there were thirteen English colonies along the Atlantic, from Massachusetts in the North to Georgia in the South. England also claimed and colonized islands in the sea between the North and South American continents, islands that had been the homelands of the Taino and Kalinago (Caribs), and other nations. France too claimed and colonized some of those islands. With few exceptions these colonies were principally commercial ventures.

Quebec had been a strategic wartime goal for England several times in conflicts with the French over the troubled course of the eighteenth century. During the Seven Years' War, with the aid of some 6,500 New England militia soldiers, the British Regulars, foot soldiers of the British Army, tried again to conquer it. The British Regular Army was comprised of professional soldiers, but the militia was comprised of civilians, men over the age of sixteen who were by law required to train annually (September was a common time of militia musters in New England) and to serve militarily if required by circumstance. As the need arose, the Regular Army could draft men from the local militias (each community had one or more companies) and the Seven Years' War was one of those occasions.

All through the summer of 1759 the British force had kept the larger French army pent up in the citadel of Quebec, located on a high plateau above the St. Lawrence River. An improbable cliff ascent brought British forces up onto the plain and the French forces under General Montcalm ventured out to confront them, though they would have

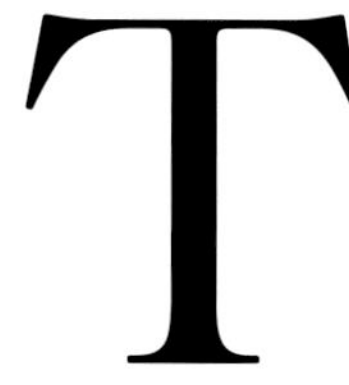

AMERICA SEPTENTRIONALIS
(PRECEDING PAGES)

G. de L'Isle
Amsterdam, about 1700
Engraving on paper, hand-colored
Height: 18⅛"; Width: 23⅞"
Gift of the Stratford Foundation.
1991.8

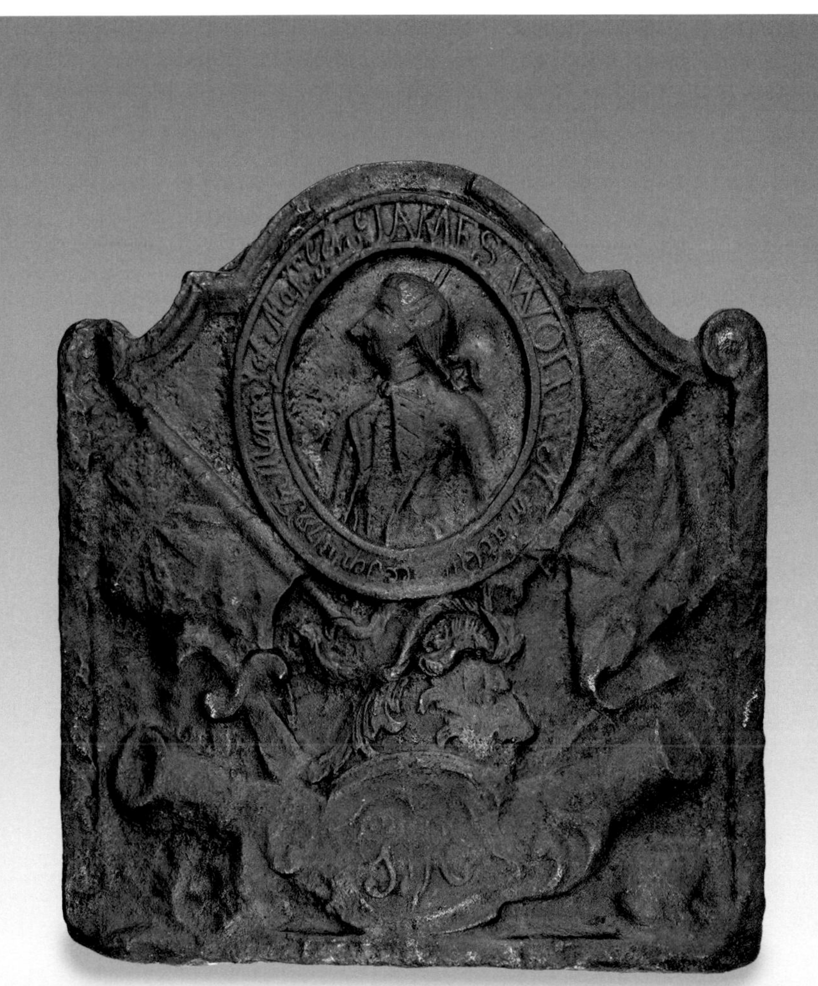

Attributed to Joseph Webb
(1734–1787)
Boston, Massachusetts, 1760–1770
Iron
Height: 26⅞"; Width: 23¾"
Gift of Mr. Russell Hawes Kettell.
H1664

A fireback is a cast iron plate used to protect the bricks in a fireplace. This example was produced, probably in Boston, not long after the conquest of Canada. The oval portrait of James Wolfe that decorates the fireback is derived from a mezzotint by Richard Houston after a portrait by J.S.C. Schaak, which itself was based on a drawing by Wolfe's aide-de-camp, Captain Hervey Smyth. The oval surround is inscribed *"In Memory of Majr Genl James Wolfe Slain at Quebec Sept 13 1759"* and the rest of the space on the fireback is filled with paired flags and cannon and a plumed helmet resting on an escutcheon with the initials *"GR"* for *Georgius Rex*. Joseph Webb's trade card, engraved by Paul Revere, depicts a similar fireback with a variant portrait of James Wolfe, also derived from Houston.

been better advised to stay within the citadel. In the brief fighting that ensued the hero of the day, Major General James Wolfe, was killed at the very moment of victory [no. 1]. General Montcalm was mortally wounded, and the city of Quebec was captured. When the news reached England over a month later, Wolfe became a household name synonymous with heroism. Quebec was indeed the key to French Canada. Not long after Wolfe's singular accomplishment Montreal fell, and when the global Seven Years' War ended with the Treaty of Paris in 1763, Canada was claimed by Great Britain.

After the fall of Quebec, the commercial relationship between England and the English colonies began to change. From that moment when France abandoned a claim to Canada, Thomas Hutchinson would later write, there was *"a higher sense of the grandeur and importance of the colonies."* As Lieutenant Governor, Chief Justice, and Governor of Massachusetts during the political turmoil of the 1760s and 1770s and author of *The History of the Colony of Massachusetts-Bay*, Hutchinson had a good deal of insight into the matter. England and England's colonies seemed to look on Canada, void of the French, with a wild regard.

Wars tend to be conducted on credit, and Great Britain had run up a considerable debt during the Seven Years' War, more than £100 million, a sum difficult to calculate in modern terms because it is so great. One contemporary estimate calculated that it was equivalent to a train of wagons filled with silver that was 203 miles long. Servicing this debt was the responsibility of Parliament, the British legislature. Parliament consists of the lower House of Commons and the upper House of Lords, plus the Crown, the reigning King or Queen. It is the House of Commons that makes laws for financial matters, like war debt. Parliament also had to make provision for the ongoing expenses of the colonies, including an army of as many as ten thousand soldiers stationed in Canada.

Even before the Treaty of Paris was signed in 1763 Parliament began modifying the century-old mercantile laws that governed trade between Great Britain and the colonies. These laws were intended to prevent commercial conflicts in and among the colonies from damaging the overall state of the empire. The theory underlying the mercantile laws was that the colonies, which extended the dominion and the commerce of Britain, would produce raw products and send them to England for credit with which to buy finished goods to take back to sell in the American market. The colonies were not supposed to trade dircctly with any foreign country; everything was to be carried between British ports by British ships.

New England's colonies did not have a staple crop like Virginia's tobacco to trade directly with English merchants for credits to buy finished goods. The principal elements of the New England trade included lumber from the extensive forests then being cleared for agriculture, and fish from the northern fisheries around Newfoundland that were so rich they had been attracting European fishermen for a thousand years. Much of the lumber and the lesser-quality dried cod, sometimes called Jamaica fish, was shipped to the Caribbean islands. Some of the better-quality dried fish, sometimes called Madeira fish, was sent to the island of Madeira in exchange for wine and fruit. The driving wheel of New England's trade, however, was sugar. The Caribbean islands colonized by both France and England produced sugar almost exclusively, which is why they needed to import lumber and food. Much of the profit of sugar stemmed from the industry's exploitation of enslaved labor in its production. One disastrous outcome of an earlier European global dynastic conflict, the War of the Spanish Succession that concluded in 1712, was Spain's assigning of the *Assiento* to England as part of the treaty. The *Assiento* was permission to engage in the African slave trade, and for the rest of the century the British economy was entangled with slavery. British merchants and traders in New England carried sugar in the form of molasses from the Caribbean islands north to be distilled into rum, which was then shipped to West Africa and exchanged for people who were enslaved and shipped to the islands to work in the sugar fields.

The enforcement of the intricate and precise rules pertaining to colonial trade had been allowed to relax for decades before Parliament began to tighten them. New England's merchants had gotten used to circumventing many of the laws governing trade, such as the prohibition on direct trade with foreign countries. The stated purpose of one of the new restrictions, the 1764 Sugar Act, was to raise a revenue to offset the expense of colonial administration and its effect was to increase the cost of doing business. For the next decade New Englanders complained consistently about the effect of laws such as the Sugar Act on trade, but more and more came to complain about the purpose as well. The duties imposed by the earlier mercantile acts were only meant to offset the cost of enforcement, that is, to pay for collectors and inspectors and so following. Duties imposed to raise a revenue were an unwelcome innovation.

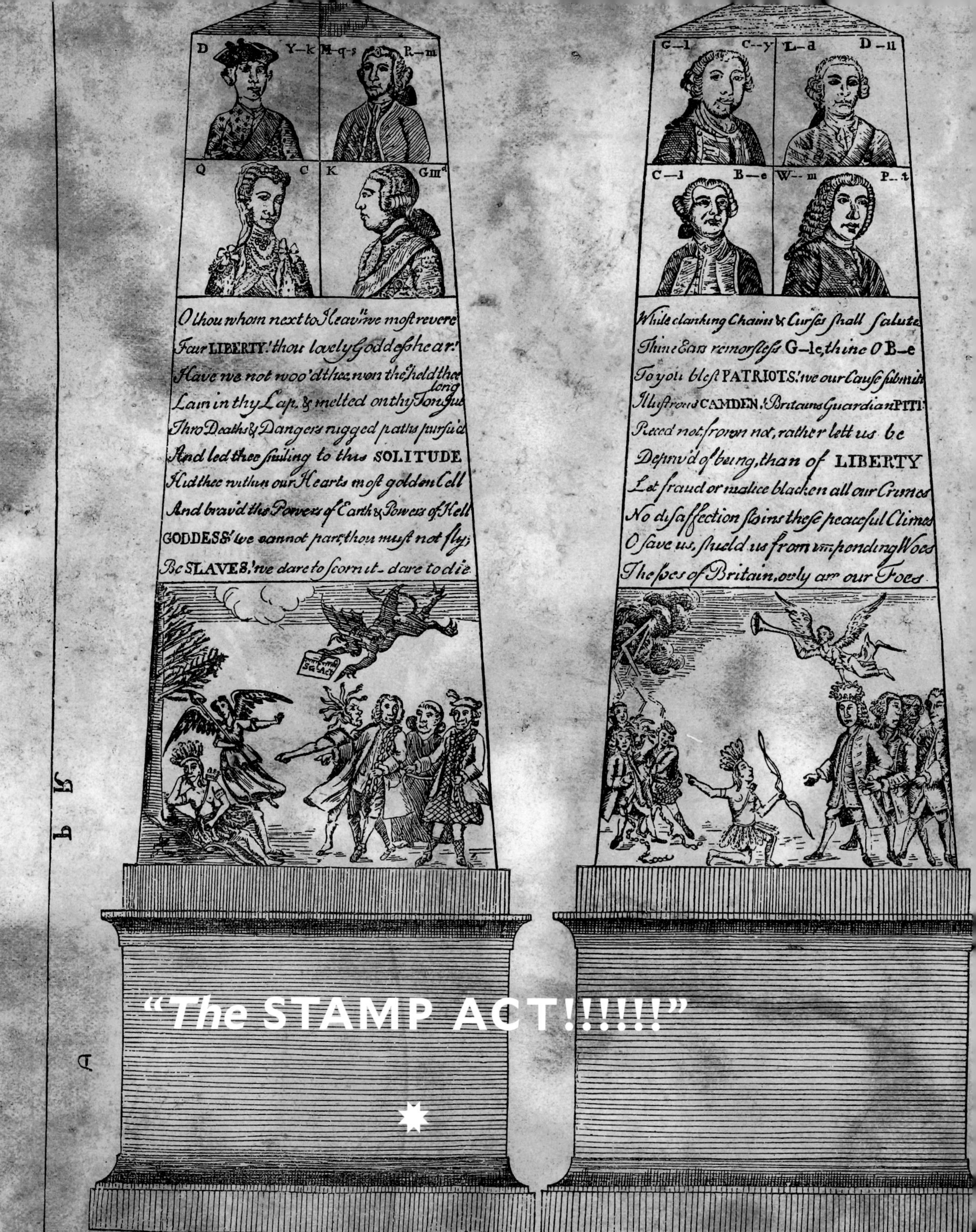

D—Y—k
M—q—s R—m
Q
C—K G III d

O thou whom next to Heav'nve most revere
Fair LIBERTY! thou lovely Goddess hear!
Have we not woo'd thee, won thee held thee long
Lain in thy Lap. & melted on thy Tongue
Thro Deaths & Dangers rugged paths pursu'd
And led thee smiling to this SOLITUDE
Hid thee within our Hearts most golden Cell
And brav'd the Powers of Earth & Powers of Hell
GODDESS! we cannot part, thou must not fly;
Be SLAVES! we dare to scorn it — dare to die.

G—l
C—y
L—d
D—ll
C—l
B—e
W—m P—t

While clanking Chains & Curses shall salute
Thine Ears remorsless G—le, thine O B—e
To you bless PATRIOTS! we our Cause submit
Illustrous CAMDEN! Britains Guardian PITT
Receed not, frown not, rather lett us be
Depriv'd of being, than of LIBERTY
Let fraud or malice blacken all our Crimes
No disaffection stains these peaceful Climes
O save us, shield us from impending Woes
The foes of Britain, only are our Foes

The STAMP ACT!!!!!!

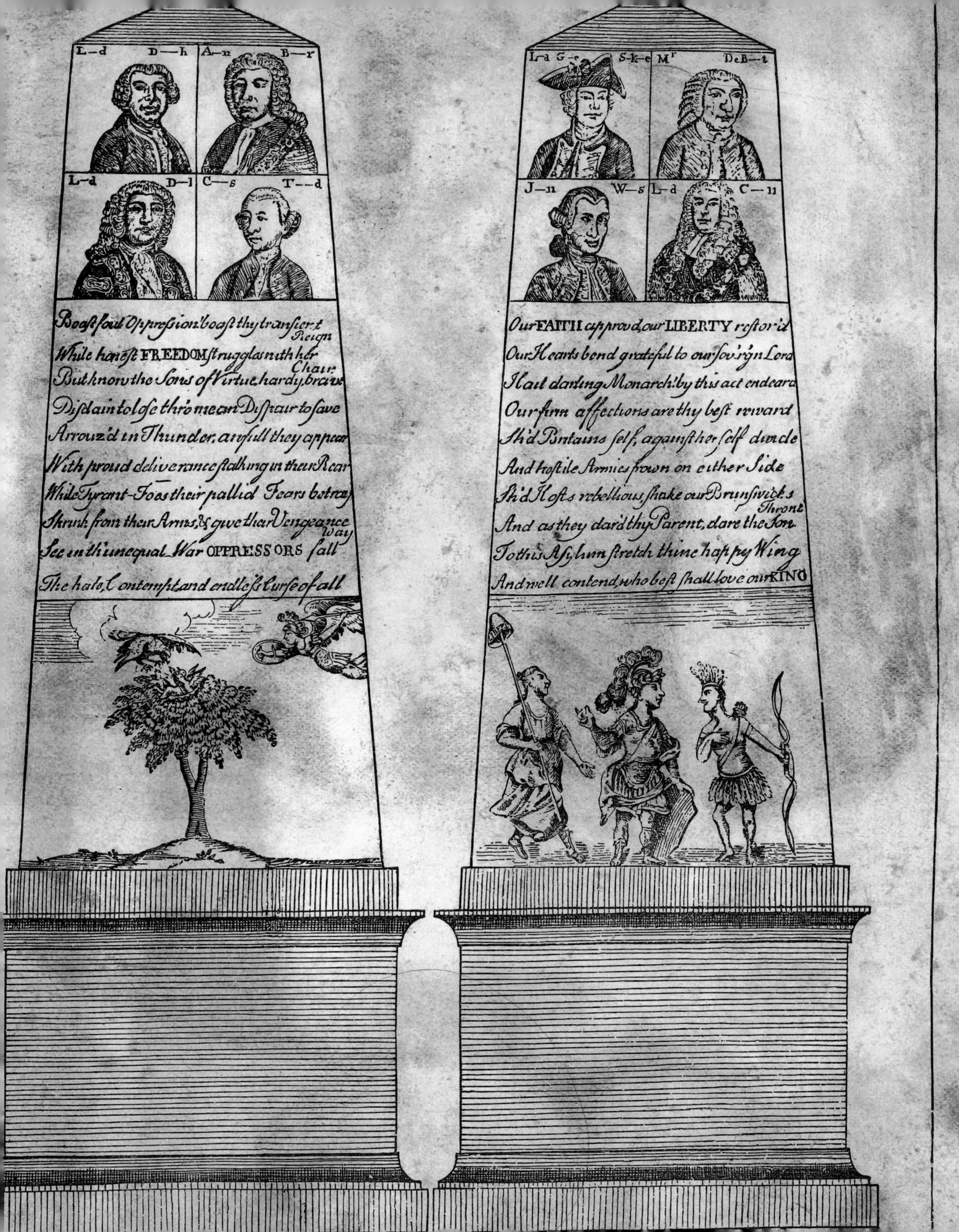

L—d D—h   A—n B—r
L—d D—l   C—s T—d

Boast foul Oppression! boast thy transient
                                    Reign
While honest FREEDOM struggles with her
                                    Chair:
But know the Sons of Virtue, hardy, brave
Disdain to lose thro' mean Despair to save
Arrouz'd in Thunder, awfull they appear
With proud deliverance stalking in their Rear
While Tyrant-Foes their pallid Fears betray
Shrunk from their Arms, & give their Vengeance
                                    Way
See in th' unequal War OPPRESSORS fall
The hate, Contempt and endless Curse of all

L—a G—e   S—k—e   M—r   De B—t
J—n   W—s   L—d   C—n

Our FAITH approv'd, our LIBERTY restor'd
Our Hearts bend grateful to our sov'rign Lord
Hail darling Monarch! by this act endear'd
Our firm affections are thy best reward
Sh'd Britains self, against her self divide
And hostile Armies frown on either Side
Sh'd Hosts rebellious, shake our Brunswick's
                                    Throne
And as they dar'd thy Parent, dare the Son
To this Asylum stretch thine happy Wing
And well contend, who best shall love our KING

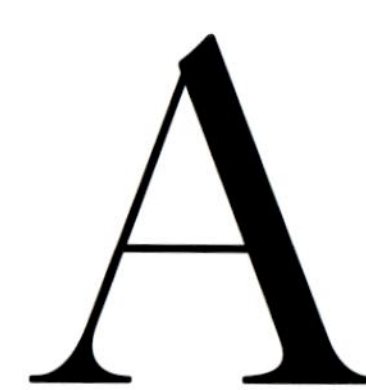

A T THE END OF JANUARY 1765, the Boston newspapers began covering the story of a scheme in Parliament for imposing a general stamp duty in North America. As spring approached, amid the advertisements for garden seeds, the text of petitions from the Virginia legislative assembly (known as the House of Burgesses) to the King, the House of Lords, and the House of Commons stated their principal objection to the proposal: It was fundamental to the British constitution that the people were not subject to any tax not laid on them by themselves or their representatives, and the colonies could not be represented in Parliament. Although the Virginia petitions failed to prevent the passage of the Stamp Act of 1765 as intended, the argument never went away.

The tax was applied principally to transactions by requiring that the paper or parchment recording them bear a stamp that the participants paid for. Noncriminal court documents like wills and probate inventories, deeds, customs documents like bills of lading, bills of sale, contracts — all required the payment of the added tax [no. 2]. Newspapers and pamphlets were also required to be printed on stamped paper [no. 3].

Toward the end of May 1765, one Boston paper fairly screamed the news: *"The STAMP ACT !!!!!! is to take Place in the Colonies on the First Day of November next."* In June the Massachusetts legislature sent a letter to the assemblies of the other North American colonies proposing a congress to be held in New York in October 1765. The suggestion for the Stamp Act Congress came from lawyer James Otis, Jr., a representative for Boston in the House of Representatives, the lower house of the Massachusetts legislature, which was called the General Assembly or General Court. Otis had, in a pamphlet published the year before, made arguments like those of the Virginia House of Burgesses: taxes could be imposed only with the consent of the taxed, either personally or through a representative, and the colonists had no representatives in Parliament. Otis also made the point that taxes should be imposed by

According to the Stamp Act a survey of a piece of land not exceeding 100 acres in size required a six-penny embossed stamp like this one. The *"B"* in the upper left of the stamp indicates the die that produced it. The inked stamp that occurs to the left of the embossed stamp indicates a separate charge for the cost of the paper, in this case nine pence per quire (twenty-four sheets). One ancillary complaint about the Stamp Act was that the official paper was more expensive than other papers of the same quality. The inscription *"Quebec fc"* (French Canada) indicates that this stamp was on a Canadian deed.

2. SIX-PENNY REVENUE STAMP

England, 1765
Embossed and printed paper
Height: 1¹¹⁄₁₆″; Width: 2¹³⁄₁₆″
Gift of the Board of Governors in honor of Désirée Caldwell. 2007.5.1

those who were themselves subject to the tax, and the members of the House of Commons were not liable to any tax imposed on the colonies.

The Stamp Act of 1765 empowered commissioners in Great Britain to appoint officers in America to manage the stamps and the income they generated. The post of stamp distributor should have been prestigious and lucrative, but most of those appointed were coerced into resigning before the Stamp Act officially took effect. Andrew Oliver (1706–1774), secretary of the Province of Massachusetts Bay, was appointed stamp-master for the province but never assumed the duties. Early in the morning of August 14, 1765, an effigy of Oliver appeared hanging from a venerable tree familiar to all near the docks in Boston. The scene became a day-long pageant with a crowd of men and women continually gathering. That night the effigy was paraded through the principal streets of Boston and finally burned. The brick structure Andrew Oliver had just constructed to serve as a stamp office was destroyed. The next day Oliver publicly resigned the post of stamp-master.

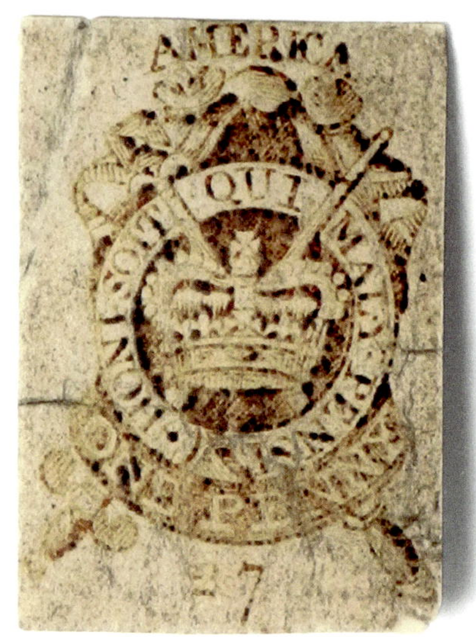

3. ONE-PENNY REVENUE STAMP

England, 1765
Embossed and printed paper
Height: 1⁷⁄₁₆"; Width: 1"
Gift of the Board of Governors in
honor of Désirée Caldwell. 2007.5.2

Printed in ink rather than embossed, a one-penny stamp was required on any newspaper or pamphlet larger than a half-sheet but not exceeding one sheet. The numeral *27* at the bottom is the die number. The penny tax would double the cost of a newspaper.

The credit for the carefully orchestrated pageant is given to the Loyal Nine, a group made up principally of Boston mechanics, that is, people employed in some craft rather than in trade. This core group soon expanded and took the name Sons of Liberty. The tree where Oliver's effigy hung, which after August 14 was known as "Liberty-Tree," became the rally point for many of the public protests that Boston would come to experience. Twelve days after the Oliver affair, on August 26, a nighttime crowd surrounded, sacked, and nearly destroyed the home of Lieutenant Governor Thomas Hutchinson. August 14 came to be celebrated annually by the Sons of Liberty, but they carefully distanced themselves from the events of August 26.

The stamps arrived in Boston Harbor on September 30, but were stored at Castle William, the island fortress that guarded Boston Harbor, and were never distributed. Eventually, the stamps were shipped back to England. November 1, 1765, the day the Stamp Act was to begin, was ushered in with the tolling of bells and with ships' flags in the harbor flying at half-staff. The events in Boston were paralleled in the other colonies, with stamp officers coerced violently into resigning and Sons of Liberty groups forming, their memberships proudly stated to include the most prominent individuals in their respective communities. Within six months of the name taking hold, Sons of Liberty groups were active all over the colonies and began to organize among themselves. In February 1766 the Sons of Liberty in Portsmouth, New Hampshire, received a letter from the Sons of Liberty of New York, Connecticut, and Boston recommending that Portsmouth join with them. The following month, the Sons of Liberty in Providence, Rhode Island, appointed a committee to correspond with other Sons of Liberty groups. The rhetoric of these communications could be fierce; the Sons of Liberty in Wallingford, Connecticut, vowed that they would oppose the Stamp Act *"to the last Extremity, even to Take the Field,"* that is, to march to war.

For each community in the American colonies, refusing to use the stamps meant that their courts could not legally conduct business and the produce of commerce could not legally move in and out of their ports. The disruption in trade, estimated in the hundreds of thousands of pounds, made the Stamp Act unpopular on both sides of the Atlantic. In the words of its eventual repeal, the act was *"greatly detrimental to the Commercial Interest of Great Britain."* At the end of February between two thousand and three thousand people assembled at the Liberty-Tree in Boston to see a staged pageant that involved the ritual burning of a piece of stamped paper. Similar scenes were enacted across the colonies.

Boston newspapers had begun speculating about a repeal of the Stamp Act by January 1766, and by the middle of April enough rumors had arrived to make it seem certain. Early in April the Boston town meeting voted to fix a time for the general rejoicing when the expected news arrived. An editorial in the April 14 *Boston-Gazette* notes that when (not if) the *"general Illumination"* takes place it would be hazardous to have candles in some shops stocking flammable material, and their windows should be exempt from *"Resentment."* In England it was a common practice of the "mobility," as mobs were termed, to resentfully break the windows of any house not illuminated in sympathy with whatever cause the mob supported. This was a moment of regular public protest in England's capital, London, a city whose population of 750,000 was nearly twice that of the whole Massachusetts Bay Colony. The same Boston papers that carried news of the Stamp Act reported on the violent protests of thousands of London weavers who in protesting the importation of fine French silks broke windows with abandon. Protesters in Boston followed the same practice on a smaller scale. In planning for the celebration of the anticipated Stamp Act repeal, Boston's town meeting requested *"that the Inhabitants be desired for the present to restrain their Children and Servants from going abroad on Evenings."*

King George III and Parliament agreed to the repeal on March 18, 1766. Their decision reached North America two months later. When on May 16 the *"Glorious News"* of the repeal of the Stamp Act arrived in Boston on a ship belonging to John Hancock, preparations were already completed for an elaborate celebration. The obelisk, the centerpiece of the celebration, was a pageant project of the Sons of Liberty.

May 19, 1766 was the date the Boston town meeting set for the celebration. That morning, *"By the generosity of some Gentlemen"* all debtors were freed from Boston's jail. The obelisk, designed by Paul Revere (whose engraving of the design was already for sale), was erected on Boston Common [no. 4]. Big enough to contain 280 lamps it had a horizontal box of fireworks fixed at the top. *"Multitudes of Gentlemen and Ladies"* continually passed from one illuminated house to the other

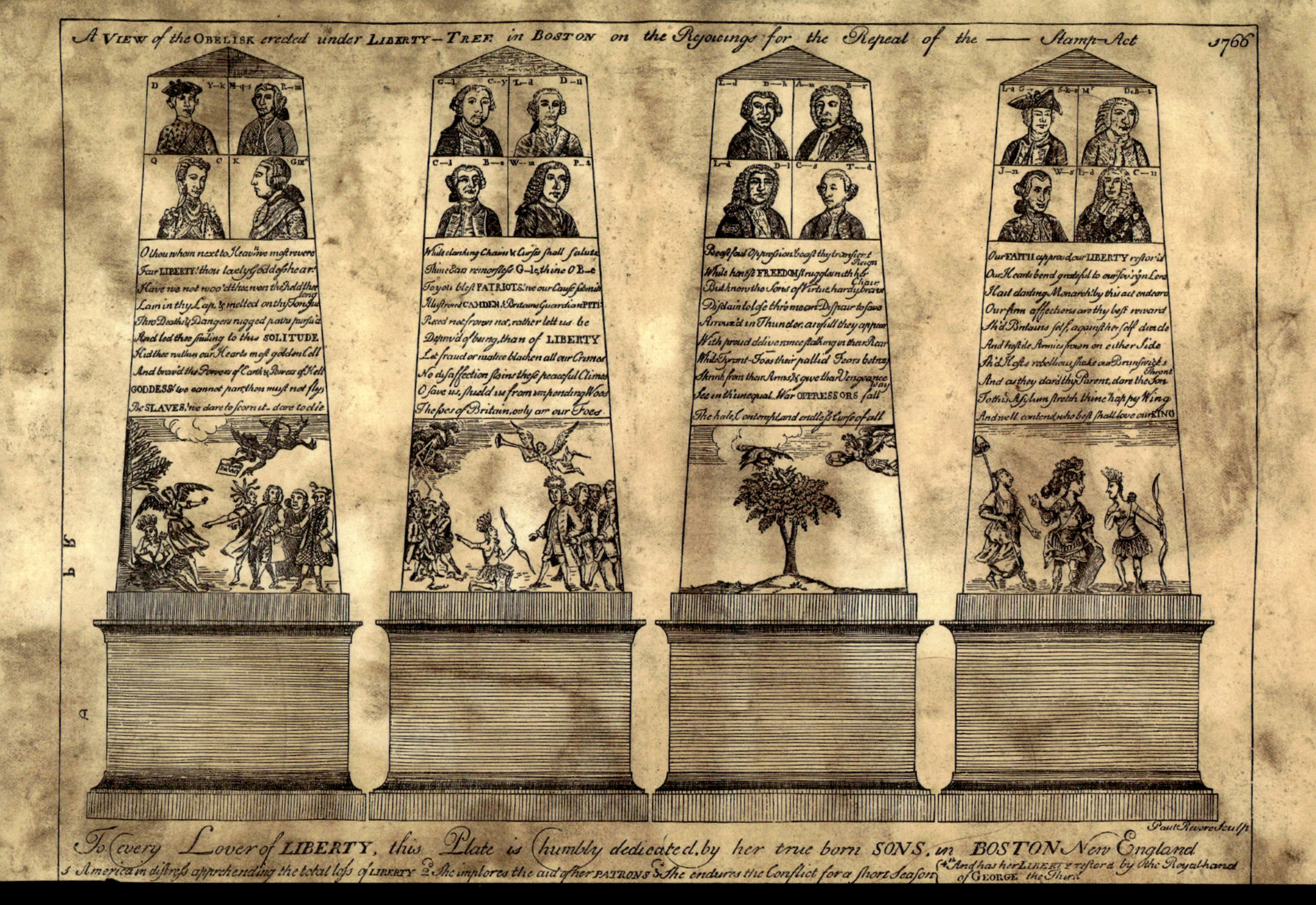

4. A VIEW OF THE OBELISK

Facsimile after Paul Revere's
engraving of 1766
R.D. Child and A.O. Crane
Boston, Massachusetts, about 1881
Engraving on paper
Height: 9⅝"; Width: 14¹⁵⁄₁₆"
Gift of Mr. Russell Hawes Kettell. Pi174

around Boston Common; John Hancock set up a barrel of 126 gallons of Madeira wine for all to enjoy. Liberty-Tree was illuminated with forty-five lanterns in keeping with a general fondness for numerology at these public pageants. The numeral 45 indicates the forty-fifth issue of *North Briton* magazine, which because it was deemed libelous to King George III, made its editor John Wilkes a fugitive and, as a committed supporter of the sanctity of the freedom of speech, an international symbol of social liberty. The 280 lamps in the obelisk reflect the majority vote in the British House of Commons in favor of repeal (the number was actually 276) and the number of lanterns on Liberty-Tree was increased on the next night to 105, the differential between the "ayes" and "nays" of the repeal vote. At 11 p.m. the horizontal wheel at the top of the obelisk was set off and the event concluded, though not entirely without incident. At about 2 a.m. the obelisk caught fire, apparently from the lamps not being extinguished, and was destroyed.

Boston reveled in the result of the Stamp Act protest. On the anniversary of Andrew Oliver's forced resignation as a stamp-master, the Sons of Liberty drank fourteen toasts, the fourteenth being *"May the noble Design and happy Effect of the FOURTEENTH OF AUGUST One Thosand seven Hundred and Sixty-five never be forgotten."* Among the other toasts was a detestation of the events of August 26, the destruction of Thomas Hutchinson's house. However, the repeal of the Stamp Act came with a poisoned pill. A resolve that passed unanimously both the House of Commons and House of Lords just prior to the repeal vote stated that Parliament *"have always had the undoubted Right to Tax the colonies."* In the words of the Declaratory Act of 1766, Parliament had the right to legislate for America *"in all cases whatsoever."* Less than a year after reporting on the joyous celebration of May 19, 1765, the Boston newspapers reported rumor of a new plan for taxing America. By the end of August the Revenue Act of 1767, one of the new Townshend Acts introducing more taxes and regulations, was published in the Boston newspapers. The Revenue Act imposed duties on tea, glass, paper, and painters' colors imported into America, the revenue to go toward paying for the administration and defense of the American colonies.

Calls for an American response in the form of a trade embargo began immediately and continued through the fall. At the beginning of November, a Boston town meeting with James Otis as moderator

The said colonies and plantations in America have been, are, and of right ought to be, subordinate unto, and dependent upon the imperial crown and parliament of Great Britain in parliament assembled, had, hath, and of right ought to have, full power and authority to make laws and statutes of sufficient force and validity to Bind the colonies and people of America, subjects of the crown of Great Britain, in all cases whatsoever.

— THE DECLARATORY ACT, 1766

produced a subscription form pledging not to purchase a long list of imported items. Within weeks Boston's example had been emulated by towns in Rhode Island, Connecticut, New York, New Jersey, and Pennsylvania, as well as the towns of Plymouth, Sandwich, Truro, Lexington, Boston, and Grafton in Massachusetts, and Portsmouth, New Hampshire.

Just at this time the letters signed "A Pennsylvania Farmer," who was later revealed to be John Dickinson of Philadelphia, began to appear serialized in the *Boston-Gazette*. In the tenth of those letters, Dickinson maintained that the colonies formed one political body, and the united actions of their assemblies should help make a resistance to the Townshend Acts as successful as the resistance to the Stamp Act. By the time that letter was published in Boston, the Massachusetts House of Representatives had already begun the process Dickinson advocated. On February 11, 1768, the House of Representatives sent a letter to the representatives of the other colonies' legislative assemblies on the American continent. Addressing the matter of taxes imposed on America by Parliament, the letter asserts that it is an *"essential unalterable right in nature"* that what has been honestly acquired cannot be taken away constitutionally without consent. Parliament's imposition of a tax infringed that natural right because the colonists were not and could not be represented there. The purpose of the letter was to get the various assemblies to harmonize in their responses to the Revenue Act. The circular letter began to receive positive responses from the other colonies, but after the usual delay of thirty to fifty days each way to cross the ocean a decidedly negative response came from the newly established Secretary of State for American Affairs, Lord Hillsborough. Hillsborough ordered Massachusetts Bay governor Francis Bernard to order the Massachusetts House of Representatives to rescind the circular letter, which represented an *"unwarrantable Combination"* of the colonial assemblies. The representatives refused by a margin of 92 to 17 (soon to be prominently memorialized in a silver bowl made by Paul Revere for the Sons of Liberty, today in the collection of the Museum of Fine Arts Boston), and Governor Bernard dissolved the assembly. That meant they were not just adjourned to another day, but also there would have to be a new election before the Massachusetts House of Representatives could meet again.

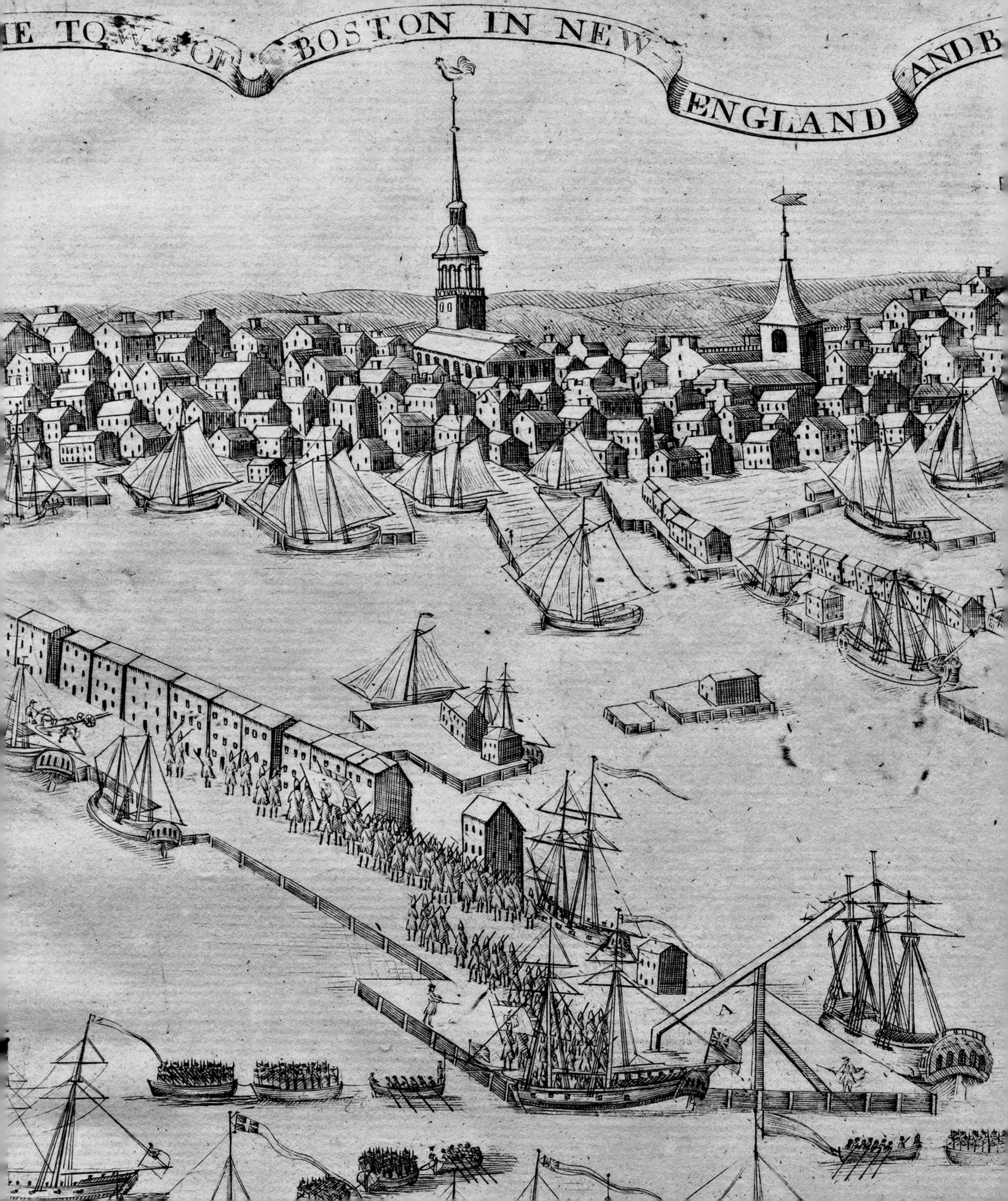
E TOWN OF BOSTON IN NEW-
ENGLAND AND B
A

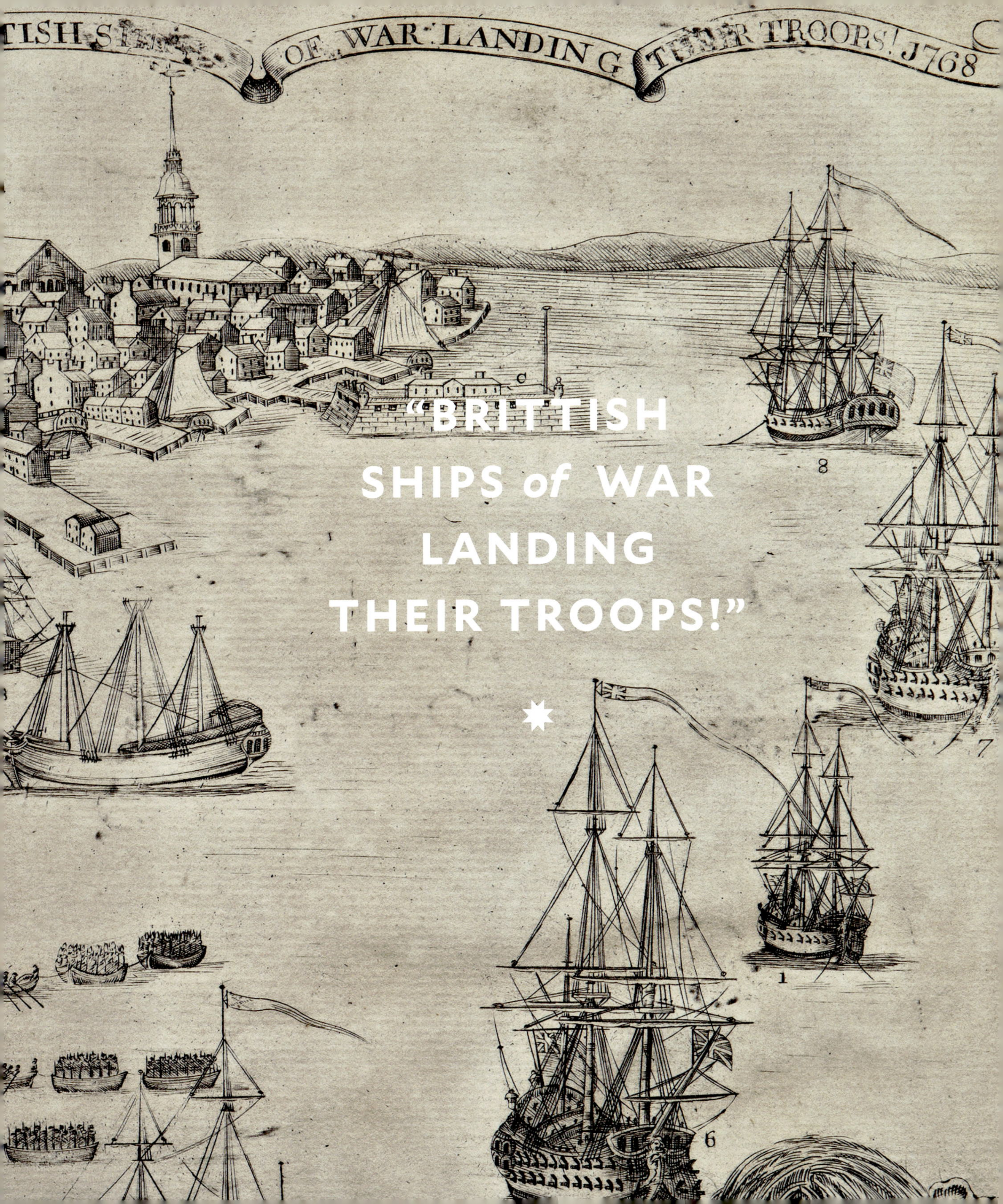

"BRITTISH SHIPS *of* WAR LANDING THEIR TROOPS!"

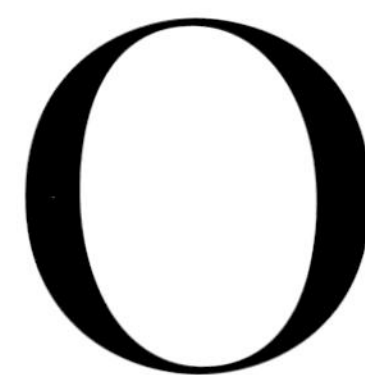

O N JUNE 10, 1768, about two weeks before the dissolution of the House, a group of officers and sailors from the fifty-gun H.M.S. *Rodney*, which lay in Boston Harbor, seized the sloop *Liberty*, which belonged to John Hancock. There was a suspicion that Hancock had smuggled some wine from Madeira, and though charged the merchant was later acquitted. That night, however, a crowd gathered, some Board of Customs officials were abused, and a vessel belonging to one of them was dragged through the streets of Boston and burned on the Common. The customs officials in Boston, feeling unsafe, fled first to the *Rodney* and then to Castle William. That incident, together with a milder example of unrest on the anniversary of the repeal of the Stamp Act (an evening concluded *"without riot or RUMPUS"* according to the *Boston-Gazette* and later dismissed as *"the hallooing of children"*) led Hillsborough to order several regiments of British soldiers to Boston.

A Boston town meeting beginning on September 12, 1768 proceeded on the assumption that three regiments were on the way to Boston, two of them to be quartered in the town and one of them at Castle William, though Governor Bernard would not confirm the fact. Citing *"the first Principle in Civil Society, founded in Nature and Reason"* that *no* law (not just laws concerning property as had been earlier cited) could be binding on the individual without consent, the town meeting did something without precedent. Since Governor Bernard claimed to be unable to summon the General Court, the town chose members of a "Committee in Convention" that would meet with similar committees from the other Massachusetts Bay towns to consult on measures necessary for the peace and safety of the province. The town then voted that the Boston selectmen write to the selectmen of the other towns in the province proposing a convention to be held at Faneuil Hall, Boston's large indoor marketplace, on September 22. In another vote the town cited the 1689 Bill of Rights provision *"That the Subjects, being Protestants, may have Arms for their Defence,"* deeming that it was founded in *"Nature, Reason, and sound Policy."* The same vote also made note of provincial laws that every householder should always be provided with a *"Firelock-Musket, Accoutrements and Ammunition,"* vaguely citing apprehension of an approaching war with France as an excuse for mentioning it. The intention was later denied, and the recommendations of the Convention when it did meet were quite mild, but it was not lost on the House of Lords in England that the Convention of September 22 usurped the duties of government. Nor was it lost on Governor Bernard who refused to accept the petition forwarded from the Convention because it would legitimate the undertaking, which was illegitimate because calling an assembly of the people by private persons violated the Crown's constitutional authority.

On September 28, 1768, the 14th and the 29th Regiments arrived in Boston Harbor from Halifax, Nova Scotia. The *Boston Evening Post* reported that *"the Ships of War came up and ranged themselves on the North East Side of the Metropolis, as if intended for a formal Siege."* Several sources note that the ships had springs on their cables, which is a device that in a siege allows a vessel to swivel without having to use sails or wind, permitting them to aim their guns wherever they would. The image was terrifying: *"14 ships of war, with springs on their cables, and their broad sides to the town!"* This is the scene that Paul Revere illustrated nearly two years later when some of the consequences of having soldiers in the town were better known [no. 5].

Christian Remick, a sailor turned painter, painted a watercolor view of Boston Common that depicts the open space Boston normally used to pasture a few cattle with a military encampment imposed on it [no. 6]. At about noon on Saturday, October 1, 1768, *"the 14th Regiment landed at the Long Wharf, and having formed, marched with Drums beating, Fifes playing, and Colors flying."* The soldiers of the 29th Regiment also landed and marched to the Common. The 14th Regiment was allowed to use Faneuil Hall as a barracks, but *"The 29th, having brought their Field Equipage with them, are encamped on the Common, with the Artillery."* Remick's view depicts the tents of the 29th Regiment set up with stacks of arms in front of them. Two companies drilling with drums beating are being watched by a fashionable couple and the ubiquitous pack of boys that these colorful scenes reliably attracted. The backdrop for this scene is the impressive stone house built by merchant Thomas Hancock. Over the door is a lozenge-shaped hatchment of the arms of Hancock, a sign of mourning for Thomas who had died four years earlier. The house belonged to John Hancock, the nephew of Thomas: in front of it John had set up the barrel of Madeira wine for the celebration of the repeal of the Stamp Act. It was also in this area that the

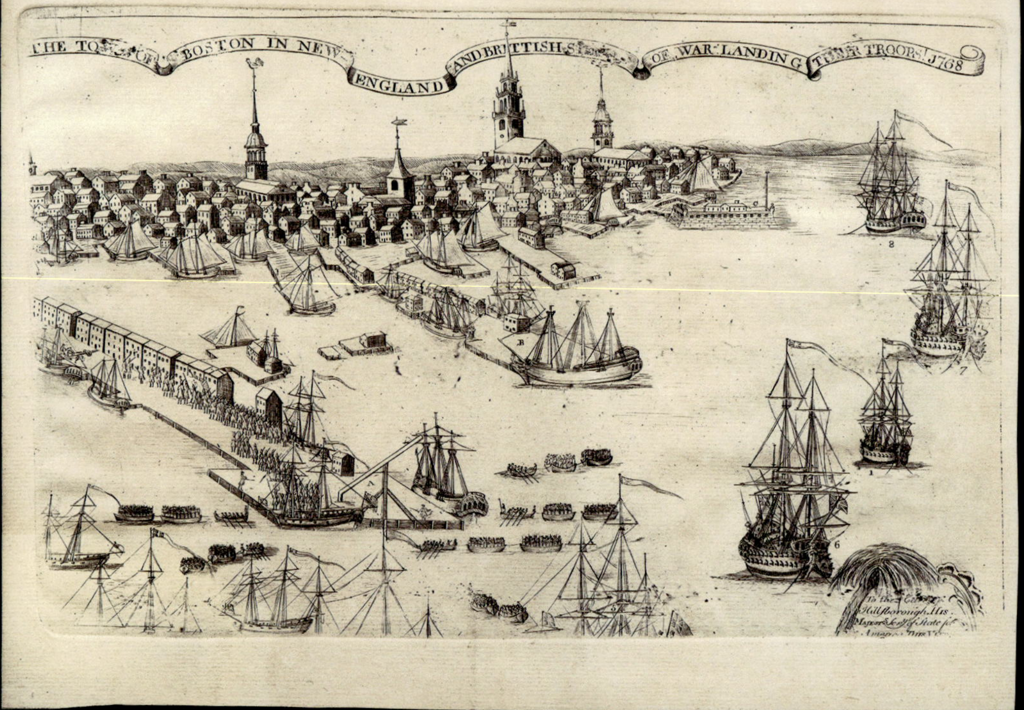

THE TOWN OF BOSTON IN NEW ENGLAND AND BRITTISH SHIPS OF WAR LANDING THEIR TROOPS! 1768

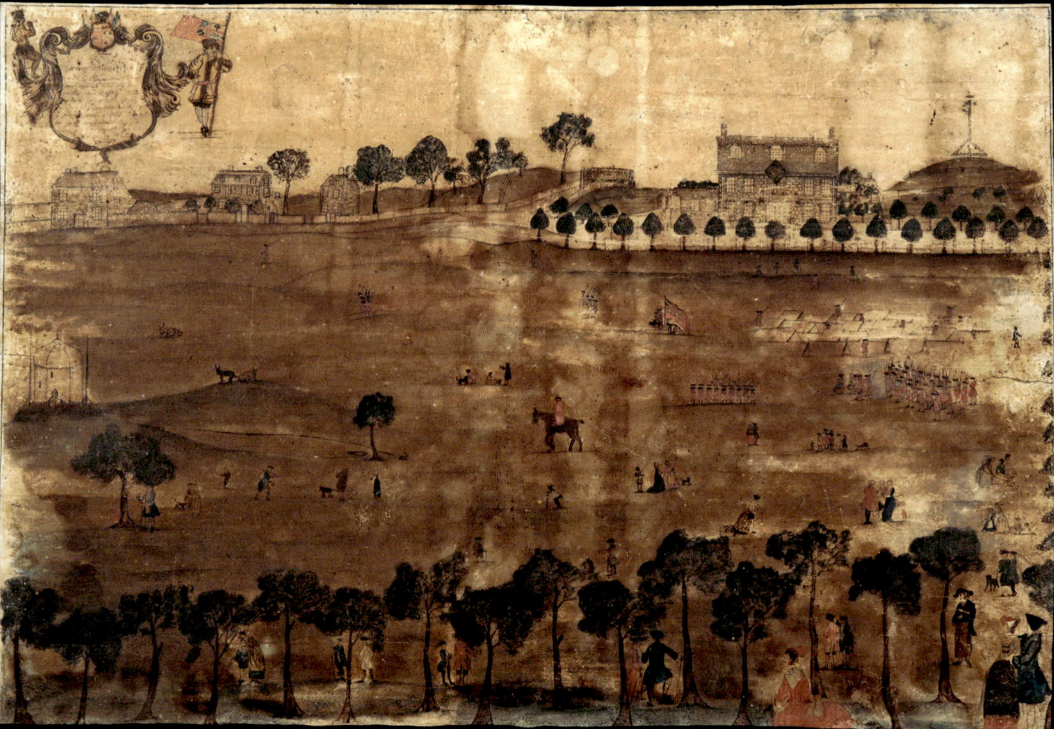

5. A VIEW OF PART OF
THE TOWN OF BOSTON

Paul Revere (1734–1818)
Boston, Massachusetts, 1770
Impression taken from the original
plate about 1850
Engraving on paper
Height: 9¹¹⁄₁₆"; Width: 12¹¹⁄₁₆"
Gift of Cummings E. Davis. Pi406

Paul Revere offered impressions of this print for sale in April 1770. The design is apparently the work of painter Christian Remick *"lately from Spain,"* who advertised in 1769 *"an accurate View of the Blockade of Boston, with the landing of the British Troops on the first of October 1768."* Revere in 1775 would cut the plate for this engraving down in order to engrave currency on the other side, which is why the plate survived in the Massachusetts State Archives. At that time the inscription at the bottom, noting springs to the cables on the war ships, was cut off.

Tolman 1911, 528: **"ENGRAVING BY PAUL REVERE, 'The Town of Boston in New England, and British Ships of War landing their Troops, 1768.' Reprinted about 1850 from the original plate, then and now in the possession of the Commonwealth."**

— From George Tolman, editor, *Catalogue of a Portion of the Collection of The Concord Antiquarian Society* (Concord, MA: The Society, 1911), page 528. Hereafter, Tolman 1911 will refer to excerpts from this catalogue.

6. *PROSPECTIVE VIEW OF*
PART OF THE COMMONS

Christian Remick (b. 1726)
Boston, Massachusetts, 1770
Watercolor on paper
Height: 20³⁄₁₆"; Width: 28¾"
Gift of Mr. John Brown, Jr. Pi409

The colophon in the upper left includes the dedicatory inscription *"To / John Hancock Esqr / This Prospective View of / part of the Commons & the / encampment of the 29th Re- / giment & Field Pieces &c / as taken from the grove on / Ye first of October 1768 / is most humbly dedicated by his / most Faithfull Servant / Christian Remick."*

Tolman 1911, 102: **"ENGRAVING, ENCAMPMENT OF BRITISH TROOPS ON BOSTON COMMON, 1768 from original water color by Christian Remick, now in the possession of the Concord Antiquarian Society. Engraved by Sydney Smith; published by Charles e Goodspeed. No. 70 of only 100 copies printed."**

private boat belonging to a customs official was burned on the night of June 10, the event that helped trigger the arrival of the British troops.

On the far right is the beacon that gave Beacon Hill its name [detail 1]. The frame at the bottom, referred to as a skillet, was meant to hold one or more barrels of pine tar that would be ignited and raised up in an emergency as a signal to the surrounding towns. An empty barrel was placed on the skillet as a threat just before the troops arrived, Thomas Hutchinson recounted in *The History of the Colony of Massachusetts-Bay*. Despite Boston newspapers asserting, *"Not the least attempt has been made or even contemplated to oppose the landing of the King's Troops,"* something seems to have been contemplated; an account of the event from a Virginia newspaper mentions beacon signals and notes ominously *"that it was said at least 40,000 men, well armed, and properly officered, could be got together in a few days."*

There are three references to the presence of Black people in Boston in the Remick view. One of the drummers beating time for the drilling 29th is Black, as were the other drummers as well as the fifers in that regiment. Regimental drummers were responsible for administering punishments, which were brutal. A newspaper account records a regimental drummer administering 100 lashes, and another reports on "one of the negro drummers, who received 100 lashes" for playing drum at a nonmilitary concert on the Common. The frequent public punishments, including executions for desertion, were a common cause for complaint from the inhabitants of Boston. Toward the right edge of the Remick view is a group of three figures, perhaps a family group, including a woman with a wheelbarrow, a man, and a boy [detail 2]. They might be free people, but another figure walking behind two women is almost certainly an enslaved servant. An estimated ten percent of the population of Boston was Black at mid-century and although that percentage had declined somewhat by the end of the 1760s there were over a thousand Black residents in a town of nearly fifteen thousand. As many as nine out of ten of those Black residents were enslaved.

The pages of the Boston newspapers in the 1760s were regularly dotted with offers to sell people. The advertisements sometimes include details of the individual being sold, like the *"Two NEGRO MEN, that understand the Cooper's Business,"* as well as a boy *"who has worked at the Cooper's trade,"* a thirty-six-year-old man who understands the sawing business and would be suitable for a cabinetmaker,

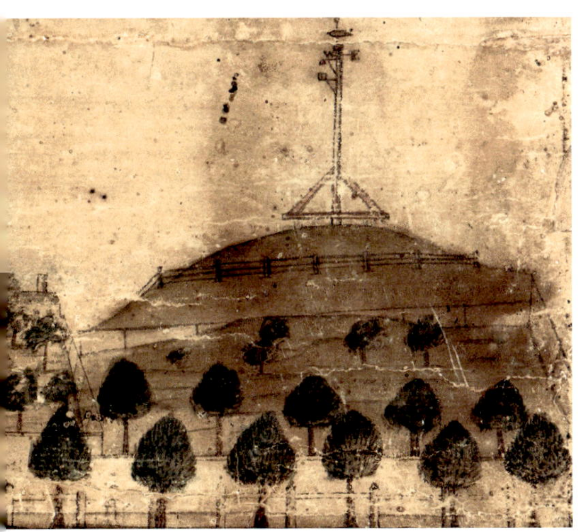

Detail 1: *Prospective View of Part of the Commons*

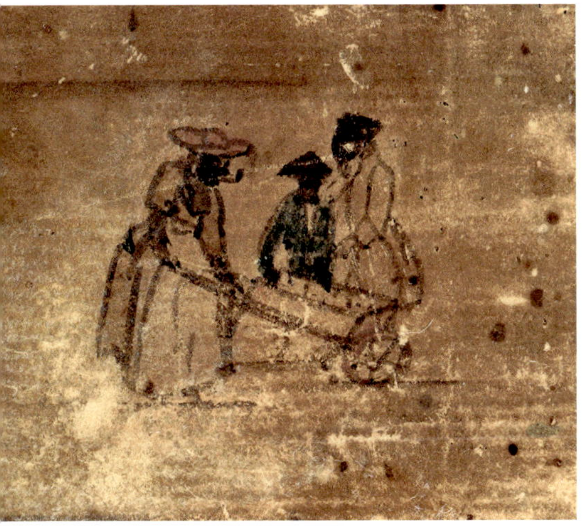

Detail 2: *Prospective View of Part of the Commons*

and a sixteen-year-old who speaks English and French and can sort, cut, and spin tobacco. More often there is little detail but the advertisements are frequent, with as many as four separate offers to sell children appearing on one page and five offers to sell men appearing on another. The notices can be breathtakingly casual: *"At private sale Two pipes of Sterling Madeira, a Negro Man 40 years of age, a Boy of 14, and two Girls about 12 years of Age, a second–hand chaise…"* People could be simply commodities in Boston, with a price; £280 in one instance. The situation was too obvious to ignore entirely but it did not feature regularly in the political discourse. James Otis, Jr. had raised the issue in 1764, and in 1767 Nathaniel Appleton's *Considerations on Slavery* received favorable attention. In March 1767 a bill to ban the slave trade in Massachusetts was introduced into the House of Representatives, but two weeks later the bill had *"miscarried."* Later that year Worcester's town meeting instructed its representative to try again to obtain a law to end slavery in Massachusetts.

There are occasional references to the hypocrisy of slaveholders blaming Parliament for attempting to enslave America. In 1902 Concord Antiquarian Society secretary George Tolman delivered an address to the membership titled "John Jack, the Slave, and Daniel Bliss, the Tory." The address, later published, tells the story of a Concord lawyer, Daniel Bliss, who wrote an epitaph in 1773 for the grave marker of John Jack, *"a native of Africa."* The epitaph says of John Jack: *"Tho' born in a land of slavery, He was born free. Tho' he lived in a land of liberty, he lived a slave."* The pointed irony, penned by the only person in Concord whose property was seized for political reasons during the American Revolution, was noticed by a British officer who saw it in Concord's hillside burying ground. The officer quoted the epitaph in a letter home that found its way into the London newspapers and from there was broadly reprinted. The unease Boston could feel about the imposition of slavery on others could sometimes be expressed as fear. A report of an officer of another of the newly arrived regiments (the 59th) attempting to foment a slave uprising led the Boston selectmen to advise the town watch to *"take up all Negroes… abroad at an unseasonable Hour."*

The regiments stationed in Boston were a relatively quiet presence for much of 1769 apart from frequent complaints of military music on the Sabbath and of sentries confronting inhabitants with the challenge *"Who comes there?"* Boston's commercial conflict, however, became increasingly violent. Boston's organized merchants and traders had voted in August not to import anything (with a few exceptions) from England from January 1, 1769 to January 1, 1770. They also appointed a committee to correspond with the merchants of the other colonies and began receiving positive responses to their communications. Even before the trade embargo began there were newspaper rumors of the impending repeal of the Revenue Act of 1767.

Sisters Ame and Elizabeth Cuming, who were born and raised in Concord, had been advertising English imports, particularly milli-nery goods, from their shop on Cornhill in Boston since the beginning of 1766. Although they were direct importers of British goods into Boston, they did not subscribe to the pledge to cease imports until the Revenue Act was repealed. In April 1769, with the embargo some months in operation, the Cuming sisters (the name was often spelled Cumings in the public press) undertook a new venture. On the same page as an announcement in the *Boston-Gazette* that the Merchants and Traders of Boston had appointed a committee of seven to exam-ine shipping manifests in order to identify those who were importing contrary to the agreement, the sisters' announcement appeared: *"Ame & Elizabeth Cumings Hereby inform the PUBLICK, THAT on the first of May next, they intend to open their School for instructing young Ladies in Embroidery, Coat of Arms, Dresden, Catcut, and all Sorts of colour'd Work, at their House in Cornhill, opposite to the Old Brick Meeting. Where they have to sell, a great Variety of GOODS suitable to the Season."*

Despite the ongoing turmoil in Boston, Mary Jones of Weston elected to attend the Cuming sisters' fashionable school. The only daughter of Elisha Jones, one of the largest landowners in Weston, Mary at the age of twenty-one was completing the sort of education expected of the children of the elite. Attending the Cuming school must have been a profoundly unsettling experience for the students, however, as Mary's final project, an embroidered coat of arms, suggests [no. 7; see also no. 49]. The Boston Merchants and Traders association had grown increasingly hardline about strict adherence to the nonimportation agreement and Ame and Elizabeth Cuming were eventually singled out for their noncompliance.

In October 1769, Elizabeth Cuming witnessed at close quarters two of the most violent incidents that Boston had experienced in the five years since the protest over the Stamp Act began. The first involved Boston newspaper editor John Mein, who had for some time been examining the manifests that detailed what incoming vessels were importing, and to whom. Mein published the findings, which tended to

Mary Jones (1748–1830)
Boston, Massachusetts, about 1770
Silk embroidery on a silk satin ground
Height: 21⁵⁄₁₆"; Width: 21¼"
Gift of Cummings E. Davis. T900

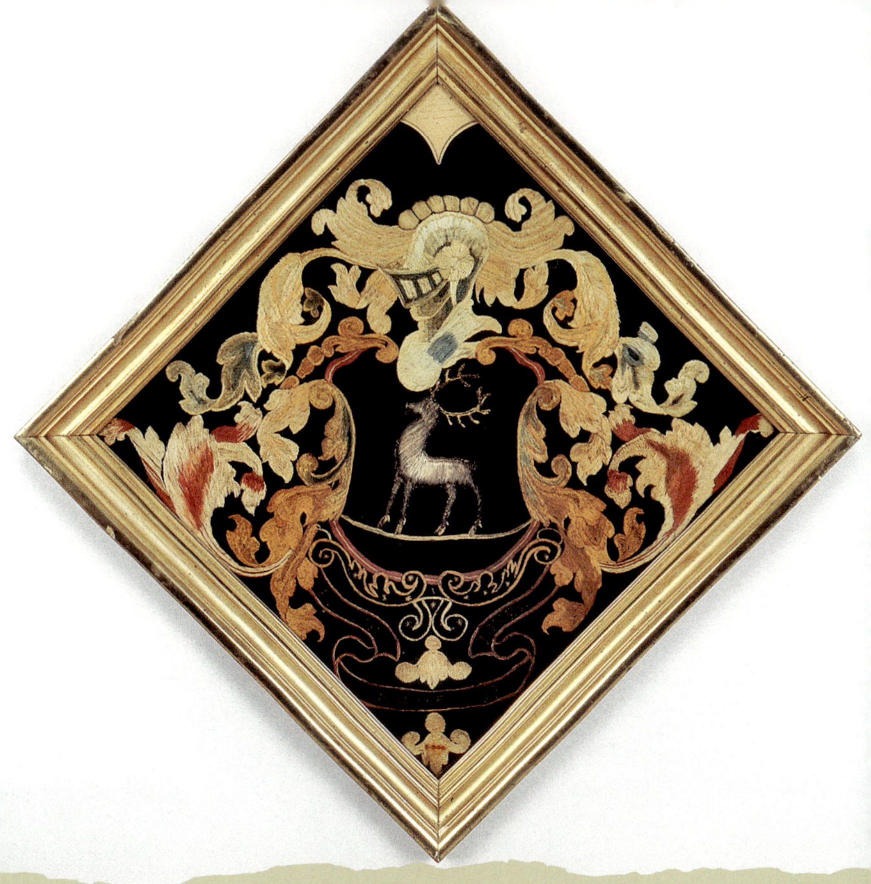

The elaborate embroidered coat of arms Mary Jones worked in the Cuming school is an example of what would typically be the last piece of needlework a student would produce in a regular course of study. The scrolled mantling that surrounds the emblazoned shield is of a pattern convincingly associated with painter / stainer John Gore and the pattern seems to have migrated from one school to another in Boston for decades. More than twenty needlework coats of arms based on the Gore pattern survive. The arms are those assumed by Mary's father Elisha, who in addition to being a large landowner was a colonel in the local militia, and an outspoken defender of the Royal Government.

It is difficult to imagine how a school of young women could continue to operate with events like those Elizabeth Cuming described transpiring just outside the window. Mary Jones does not appear to have completed the needlework for her final project. There are passages left unworked that in other related examples were filled in, such as the banner that bears the inscription *"By the Name of Jones."* Creases in the silk ground indicate that at one point the piece was folded into a five-inch square. The appearance it gives is that when Ame and Elizabeth Cuming closed their school amid the turmoil of Boston in 1769 or early 1770, Mary Jones folded the beautiful, unfinished needlework and went back home to Weston.

Tolman 1911, 534: "EMBROIDERY, The Arms of Jones of Monmouthshire, assumed by Col. Jones, of Weston, Henry Thoreau's mother's maternal grandfather. The blazon is – Sa. A Stag ar. Armed and unguled or., and the embroidery was done by Mrs. Jones."

erode confidence in the embargo within Massachusetts and across the colonies because they revealed proscribed items sent to signers of the nonimportation subscription.

On the night of October 28, Mein was assaulted in the street by a crowd of twenty people and forced to take shelter. Elizabeth Cuming wrote about the nighttime experience to a friend and patron, Elizabeth Murray:

> We was alarmed with a violent Skreeming Kill him Kill him, I fleu to the Windue & to my grate surprize saw Mr. Meen [John Mein] at the head of a larg Crowd of those who Call themselves Gintelmen, but in reality they ware no other thin Murderers for their designe was certinly on his life.

John Mein also believed assassination was the design of the pursuers, some and perhaps all of whom Mein knew. Brandishing a pistol, Mein escaped but the intimidation succeeded, and it was not long before the publisher left Boston.

The second violent event took place on the same night, when a much larger crowd attacked a Board of Customs informant named George Gailer, a mariner. Informants were paid for information they gave to customs officials on vessels for whose cargoes the proper duties had not been paid. Informants were among the army of small office holders attached to the Board of Customs service administering the Revenue Act that were seen as a threat as great as that posed by a standing army. Customs officials were the almost exclusive target of the violence of tarring and feathering, the most personal and dangerous of the methods of public shaming that the American protesters employed.

Elizabeth Cuming understandably confused the attack on Gailer with the attack on Mein. Gailer had informed customs officials about some undocumented wine aboard a ship that had docked in Boston. One or more of the interlocking committees taking an active interest in the resistance to the Revenue Act seem to have found out because the affair, although chaotic to the distressed observer, was carefully choreographed into a nighttime pageant Elizabeth also observed and related to Elizabeth Murray.

Such nighttime spectacles involving crowds of three or more had been illegal in Boston since 1753, as the Boston newspapers were requested to remind their readers two days later.

A larg Mob of ful a thousand Man & boys aranged themselves befor our Dorr & on a Kart a Man was Exibited as we thought in a Gore of Blod; & poor meen we was shure was the sufrer but we was happyly mistaken it was an informer they had caught the moment Meen found Shalter, & instintly posted him on a kart tard him all over the town then fathered him all under our windo thin carid him threu the town obliging him to carry the lantren in his hand & calling to all the inhabitince to put Candles in their Windoes.

— Elizabeth Cuming

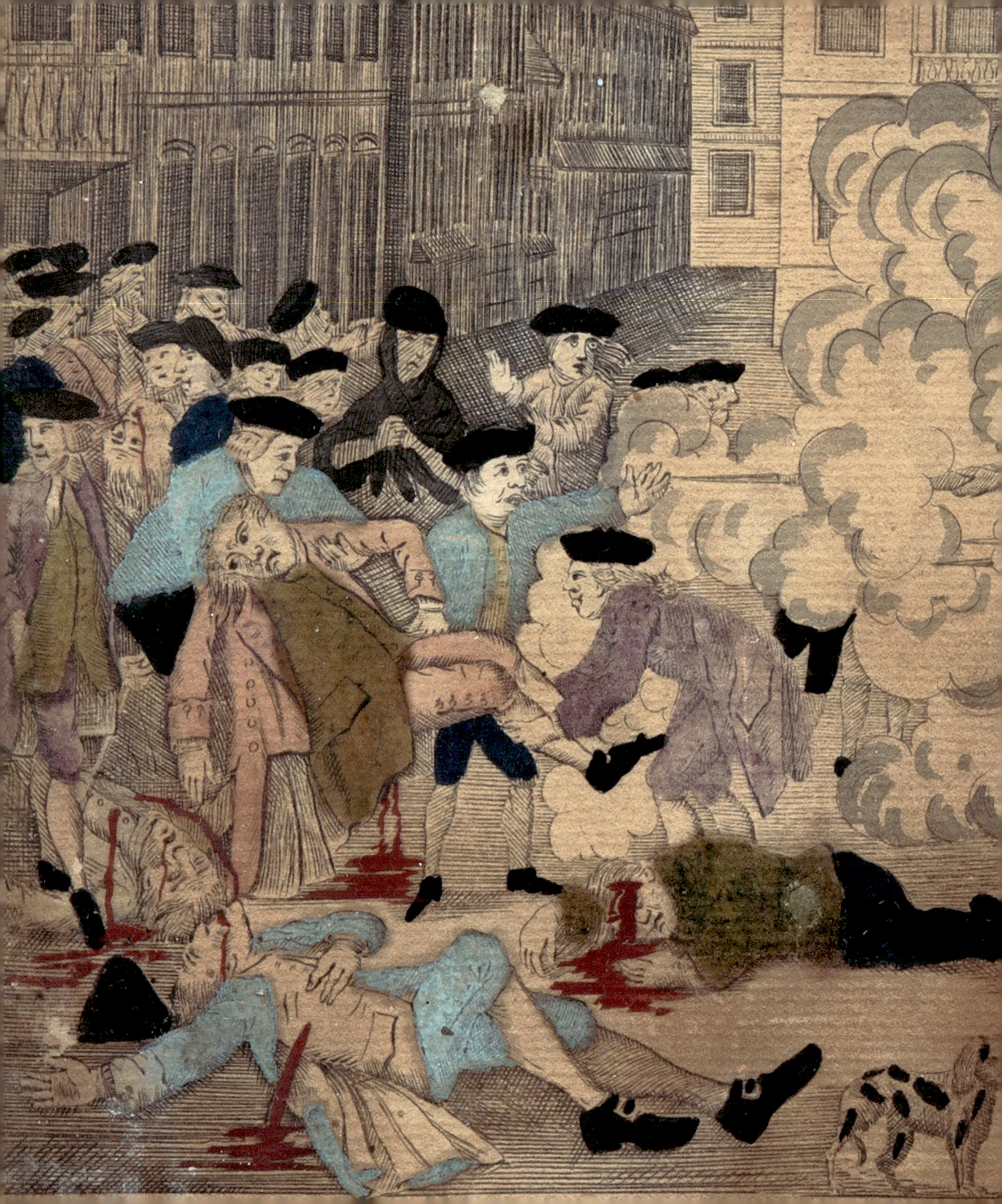

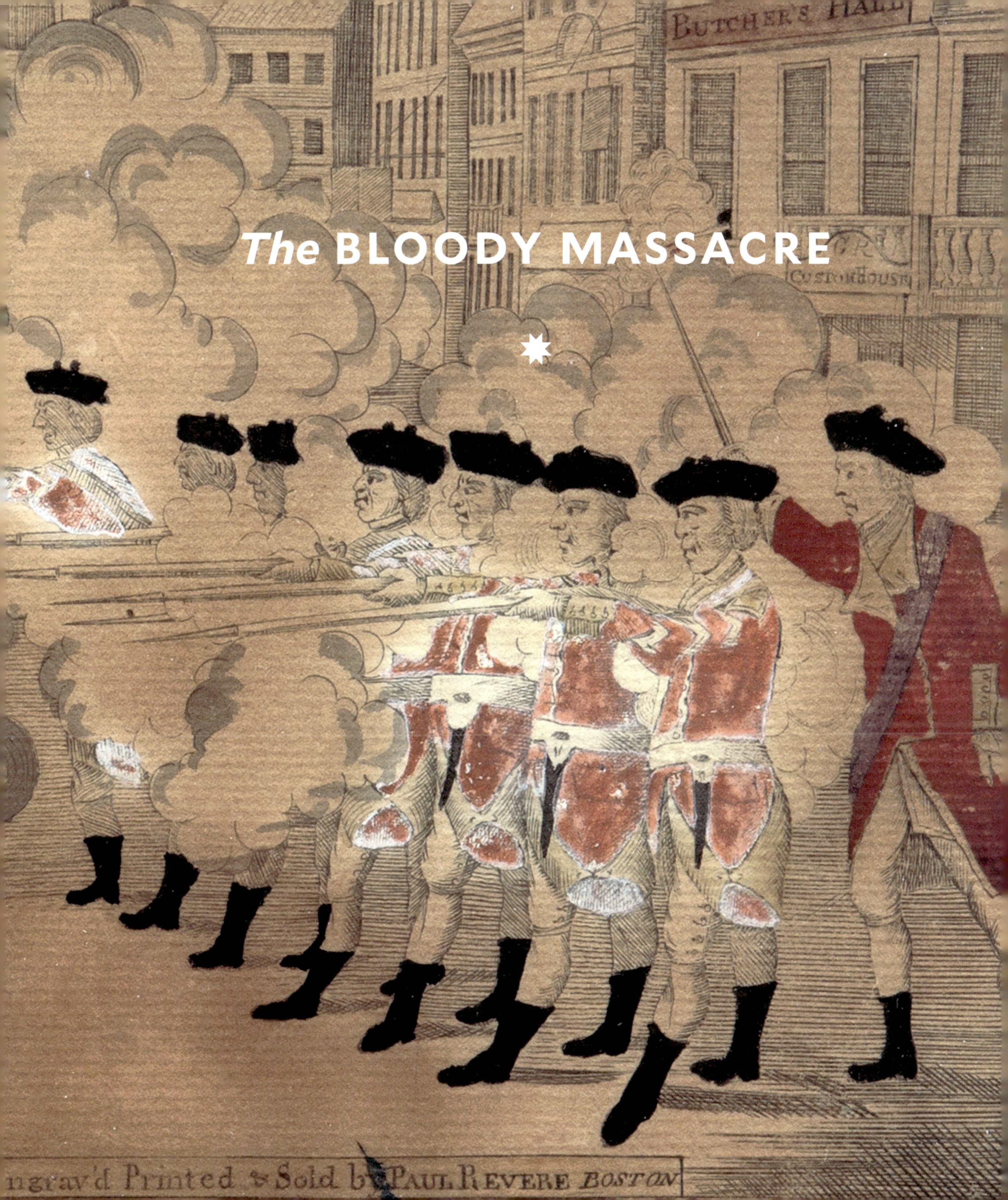

BUTCHER'S HALL
CUSTOMHOUSE
The BLOODY MASSACRE
ngrav'd Printed & Sold by PAUL REVERE BOSTON

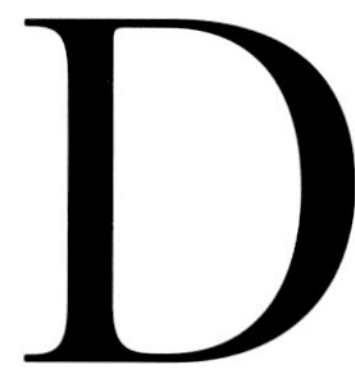

ESPITE INCREASING RUMORS in the press that the Revenue Act of 1767 would be repealed, the Boston Merchants and Traders kept up their efforts at enforcing the nonimportation pact. The names of the few holdouts among the Boston merchants, including two sons of Lieutenant Governor Thomas Hutchinson and eventually Ame and Elizabeth Cuming, were published in the papers weekly.

Noncompliant merchants and their customers were physically intimidated as well. *"It is said some Boys have besmeared the Sign Board of his Honor's* [Lieutenant Governor Hutchinson's] *two Children,"* a Boston newspaper reported, meaning that the trade sign of merchants Thomas Jr. and Elisha Hutchinson had been coated with the contents of a privy. Another shop was surrounded by boys and its customers intimidated while nonimporting merchants watched. Boys were granted ready access to the streets of Boston day or night and they seemed always to turn out when something happened. Black servants, although enslaved, seemed to have a similar access to the streets of nighttime Boston. In 1766, in planning the celebration of the repeal of the Stamp Act, the Boston town meeting had requested *"that the Inhabitants be desired for the present to restrain their Children and Servants from going abroad on Evenings."* Similar notices went out with respect to the November 5 anniversary of the foiling of the Gunpowder Plot (the 1605 attempt to blow up the Houses of Parliament), which was traditionally celebrated boisterously in the streets of Boston. This generally accepted freedom tended to put boys on the front line of any excitement.

A piece of street theater in February 1770 revealed how risky the front line could be. On the morning of February 22 *"A Number of Boys had been diverting themselves with the Exhibition of a Piece of Pageantry"* which was directed at the shop of Theophilus Lillie, one of the importers whose name was printed weekly in the newspaper. A neighbor, Ebenezer Richardson, got involved. Richardson was widely known to be an informer for the Board of Customs commissioners, like George

Gailer, and the boys gathered nearer to the Richardson house. A skirmish involving thrown stones began, and Richardson fired into the crowd. Eleven-year-old Christopher Seider was hit and soon died. Physician Joseph Warren, who attended the wounded boy and later conducted the autopsy, removed eleven pieces of swan shot, an irregularly shaped form of lead shot, from the wound. The right hand of the young victim was pierced by the shot, which suggests the awful possibility that Christopher Seider saw the discharge coming (flintlocks take some time to complete the firing process) and raised a hand in an automatic, futile, gesture of defense. Notice of the funeral referred to the victim as *"this little Hero and first Martyr to the noble Cause"* and mentions poignantly that Seider was carrying a piece of literature extolling General James Wolfe, the British hero of the conquest of Quebec. At the funeral of Christopher Seider, which was reported in the *Boston-Gazette* on March 5, 1770, *"The little Corpse was set down under the Tree of Liberty, from whence the Procession began. About Five Hundred School Boys preceded; and a very numerous Train of Citizens followed."* The estimate was that there were two thousand people in the procession, a tremendous number for a town of only 15,000. Ebenezer Richardson was tried for murder and convicted, though the conviction was later overturned.

On the night of the funeral, a small crowd began taunting a British Army sentry posted at the Customs House on the square in front of the State House. Disputes between inhabitants and soldiers were frequent, enough so that the newspapers apologized for not being able to report on all of them. On this occasion, when church bells began to ring, the usual sign of a fire, more and more people began arriving in the square. The sentry was reinforced by other soldiers and an officer of the 29th Regiment, Captain Thomas Preston, and the soldiers loaded their muskets. In the midst of taunts and thrown projectiles from the crowd, one of the soldiers was knocked down by a chunk of ice and immediately rose and fired, killing Crispus Attucks, a laborer who had been enslaved by the Brown family of Framingham. More of the soldiers then fired, though not in unison. In addition to Crispus Attucks, Samuel Gray, Samuel Maverick, and James Caldwell were killed and Patrick Carr was mortally wounded, dying two weeks later.

Three weeks after the soldiers of the 29th Regiment fired on the crowd in front of the State House the Boston publishers Edes and Gill advertised *"A Print, containing a Representation of the horrid Massacre in King-Street."* Paul Revere apparently saved some time in the publication process by appropriating the design from engraver Henry Pelham to Pelham's annoyance. *The Bloody Massacre* engraving was offered for sale already framed and hand-colored, ready to hang in the parlor and proclaim the owner's political orientation [no. 8]. *The Bloody Massacre* came out quickly enough to influence public opinion about the event before the trial of the officer and soldiers involved began. Eight soldiers and Captain Preston were committed to jail for the shooting that night, though it took the rest of the year for their trials to be completed. Some of the delays were deliberately engineered by Lieutenant Governor Thomas Hutchinson (Governor Francis Bernard had been recalled to England the previous June) in the service of tempering the local emotions, which were agitated. A letter from Salem that appeared in the Boston papers two weeks after the incident boasted that *"if a proper signal should be given, not less than Fifteen Hundred Men from this town and Marblehead, would turn out, at a Minute's Warning."*

Paul Revere's account book includes a charge dated March 28, 1770, to publishers Edes and Gill for *"Printing two hundred Impressions of Massacre."* One of those impressions belonged originally to Emerson Cogswell (1743–1808), a hatter who had been in Concord at least since 1774 and is listed in the Concord minute company of Captain David Brown. Concord town records include payment for Cogswell's service on April 19, 1775, and Cogswell also served in Rhode Island in 1778. The print, which survives with its original frame and hand coloring and has a watermark "W" in the paper, may have hung in the Wright Tavern at some point, as Cogswell lived there.

The Bloody Massacre was not entered formally as evidence at any of the trials but the effect of the image on public perception of the event was addressed. *"The prints exhibited in our houses have added wings to fancy"* lawyer Josiah Quincy, Jr. cautioned in defense of six of the soldiers, *"and in the fervor of our zeal, reason is in hazard of being lost."* Quincy's critique was justified. In the print, the figure of Captain Prescott raises a sword as if giving the order to fire, which the trial determined did not happen. The soldiers also fire in unison, an act also refuted in the trial. The Customs House, despised seat of the Board of Customs commissioners, has been relabeled "Butcher's Hall" and a musket fires from the window as a few witnesses alleged happened on March 5, though the testimony was dismissed during the trial. The scenario also looks disturbingly like a reference to the shooting of Christopher Seider by customs informant Ebenezer Richardson. The dog deliberately placed in the middle of the foreground (what dog would stand still amid that chaos?) closely resembles a King Charles spaniel. As such it might be read as a Jacobite symbol pointing toward the Scottish uprising of 1745, though no contemporary observers seem to have taken note of it. Captain Preston was acquitted as were six of the eight soldiers; two other soldiers were convicted of manslaughter but avoided the death penalty.

Four of the victims were buried on March 8 in coffins identified by silver plates engraved by Paul Revere. The newspaper account of the funeral termed it a *"melancholy demonstration of the destructive Consequences of quartering Troops among Citizens in a Time of Peace."* The funeral procession was estimated to consist of more people than had ever been together on the American continent at the same time. By the time of the funeral the soldiers of the 29th Regiment were already out of Boston, removed to Castle William, and the soldiers of the 14th were on the way there. The removal of the soldiers had been negotiated on March 6 between the Lieutenant Governor, the overall commander of the troops, and a Boston town meeting said to consist of four thousand freeholders and inhabitants, all of whom participated in the voting. Toward the end of May 1770, the 29th departed for New Jersey.

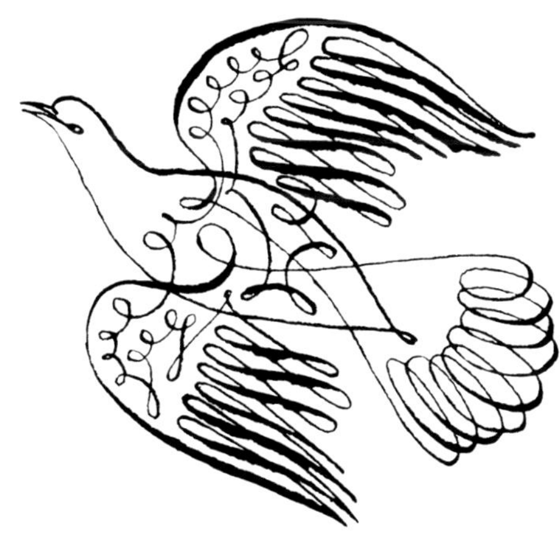

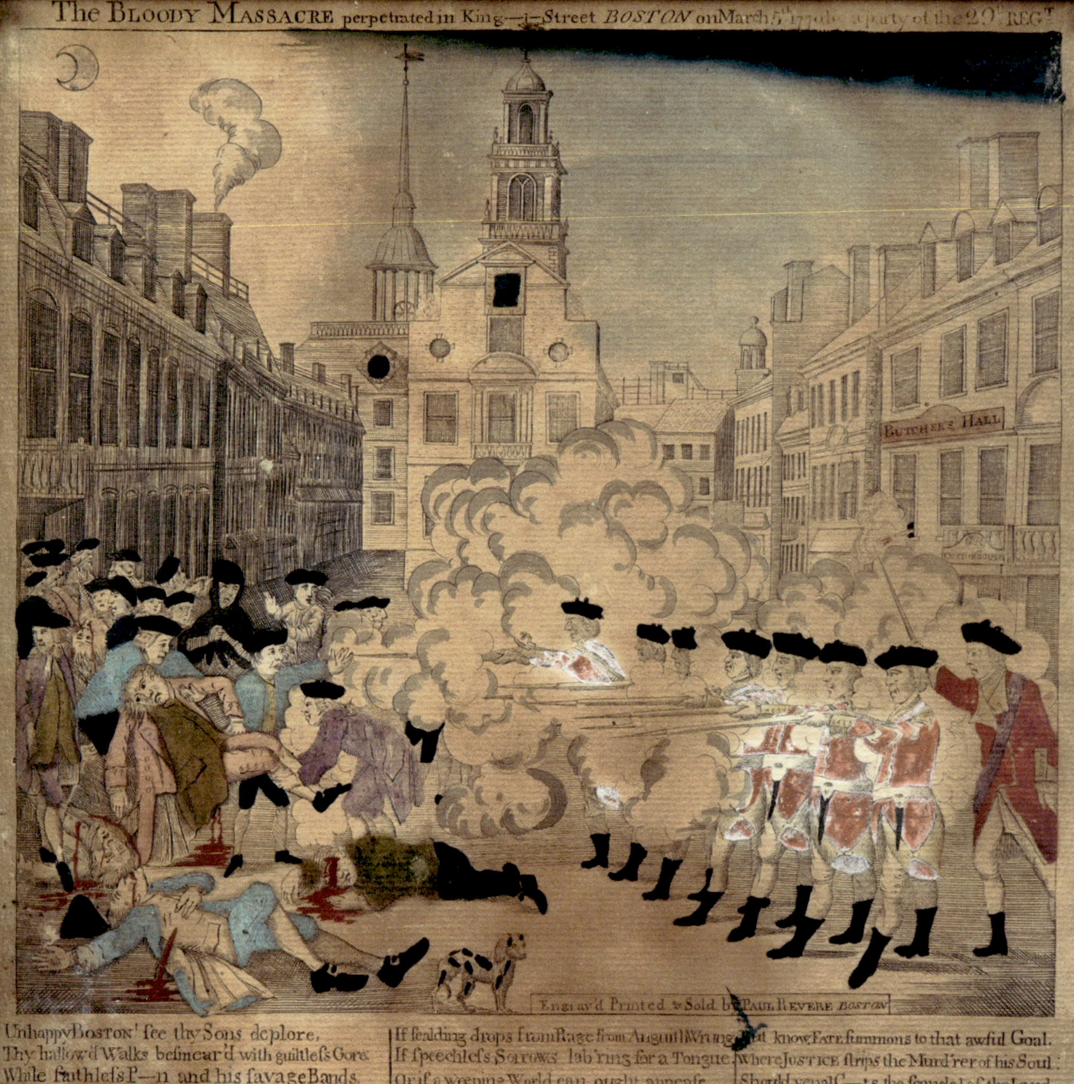

Unhappy BOSTON! see thy Sons deplore,
Thy hallow'd Walks besmear'd with guiltless Gore:
While faithless P—n and his savage Bands,
With murd'rous Rancour stretch their bloody Hands;
Like fierce Barbarians grinning o'er their Prey,
Approve the Carnage and enjoy the Day.

If scalding drops from Rage from Anguish Wrung
If speechless Sorrows lab'ring for a Tongue.
Or if a weeping World can ought appease
The plaintive Ghosts of Victims such as these;
The Patriot's copious Tears for each are shed,
A glorious Tribute which embalms the Dead.

But know, FATE summons to that awful Goal.
Where JUSTICE strips the Murd'rer of his Soul:
Should venal C—ts the scandal of the Land,
Snatch the relentless Villain from her Hand,
Keen Execrations on this Plate inscrib'd,
Shall reach a JUDGE who never can be brib'd.

The unhappy Sufferers were Messrs. SAML. GRAY, SAML. MAVERICK, JAMS. CALDWELL, CRISPUS ATTUCKS & PATK. CARR
Killed. Six wounded; two of them (CHRISTR. MONK & JOHN CLARK) Mortally

8. *THE BLOODY MASSACRE*

Paul Revere, Jr. (1734–1818)
Boston, Massachusetts, 1770
Engraving on paper, hand-colored
Height: 12¼"; Width: 11⁵⁄₁₆"
Gift of Margaret Urquhart, The
Robert T. and Ruby N. Priddy Fund
of Communities Foundation of
Texas, and anonymous donor.
2002.13

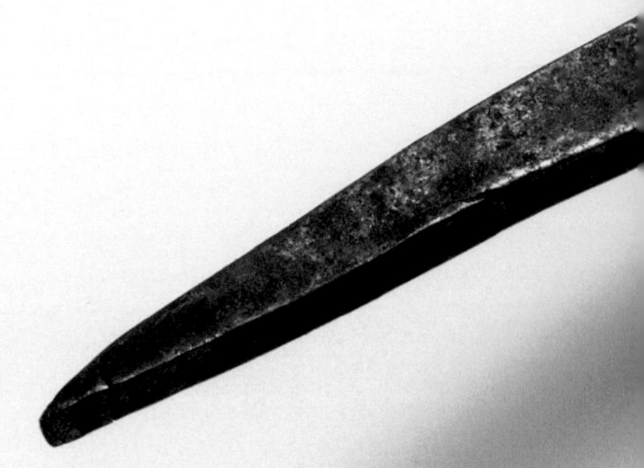

The TEA ACT

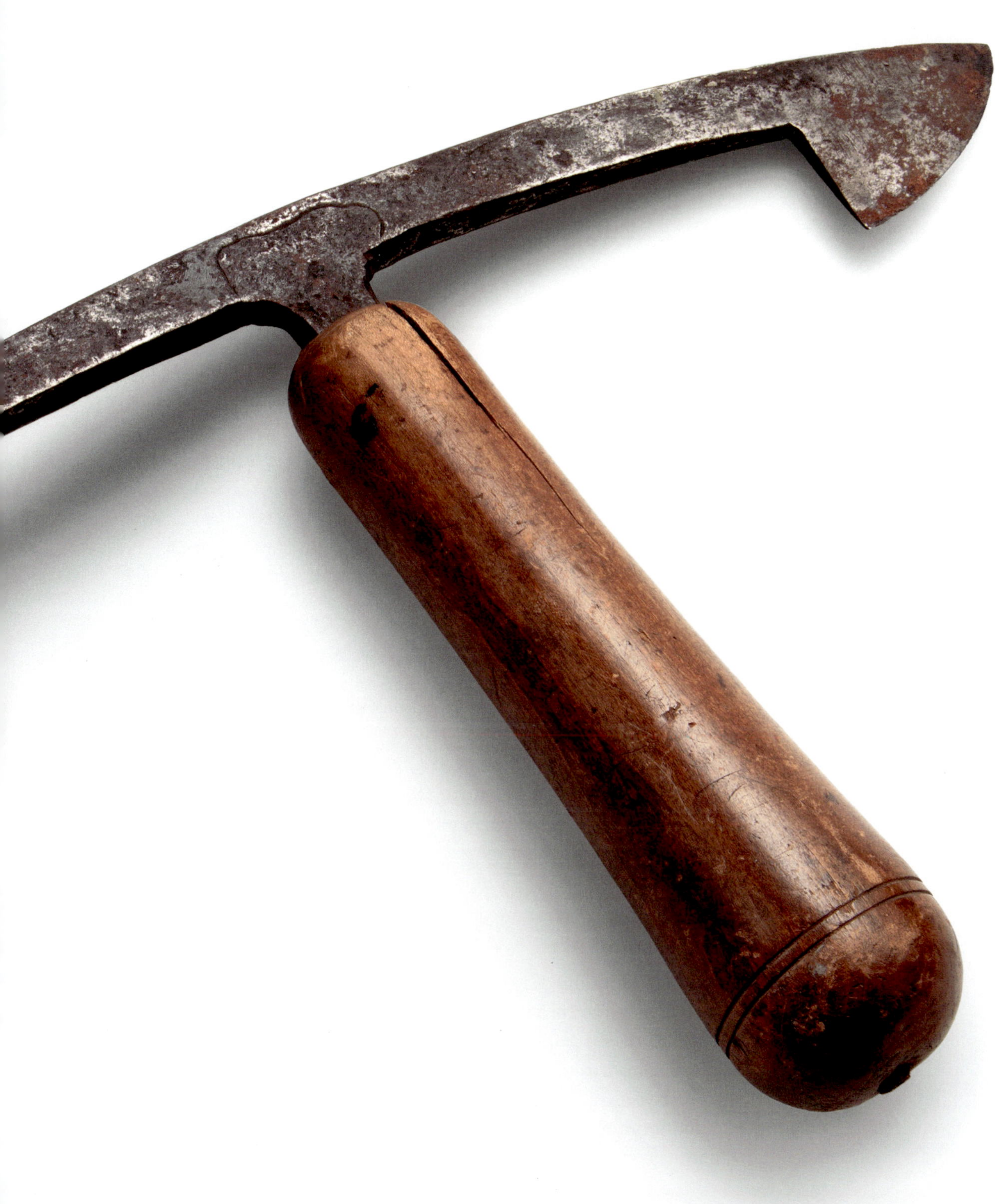

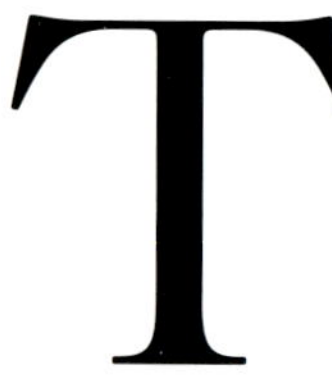HESE TERRIBLE SCENES were followed by a period of relative peace that lasted for three years. After the repeal of the Townshend Revenue Act in April 1770 on the grounds that it was "uncommercial," commerce between Massachusetts Bay and England returned to seemingly normal levels. The repeal, however, came with a hitch. The duties on paper, glass, and painters' colors were all removed, but the three-pence tax on tea was retained as an assertion of Parliament's right to legislate for America in all cases whatsoever.

Another act of Parliament ended the peace. With the Tea Act of 1773 Parliament tried to strengthen the finances of the British East India Company by allowing them to sell their tea directly in the colonies, rather than through merchants in England as previously; it was not as evidently a revenue measure as the Townshend Acts had been. Merchants in the port towns of all the colonies were, by the provisions of the act, chosen to broker the East India tea. Two merchants chosen for Boston were the two sons of Governor Thomas Hutchinson whose trade sign had been defaced by local boys in 1769.

The objections to the Tea Act expressed in all the colonies were much the same as those raised in objection to the Stamp Act of 1765: that Parliament, despite their Declaratory Act, did not have the right to take the property of anyone without their consent, and the colonies had no representatives in Parliament that could grant that consent.

In Boston the merchants to whom the first shipment of East India tea was consigned were forced to flee to the safety of Castle William just as the tax stamp distributors had been in 1765. Three ships loaded with tea arrived in Boston; one other was grounded by a storm on Cape Cod. Resolutions passed by the Boston town meeting—which during this crisis sometimes had thousands of attendees, many of them not actually qualified to vote—called for the ships not to be unloaded. By law the ships had to be unloaded and the duties on the cargo paid within twenty days of the arrival of the ship in port. Governor Thomas Hutchinson again employed delay as a tactic, being determined not to

9. EBENEZER SWAN'S TWIVEL
(PRECEDING PAGES)

England and America,
eighteenth century
Steel, maple
Height: 7$\frac{3}{16}$"; Width: 10$\frac{15}{16}$"
Gift of Cummings E. Davis. H2055

Tolman 1911, 409: "CHAIRMAKER'S TOOL. Used in making 'rush-bottoms.' Gershom Swan, 1770. Said by Mr. C.E. Davis to have been used for breaking open tea chests in the celebrated 'Boston Tea Party.'"

allow the ships to leave without paying the duties. Eventually the time ran out.

On the twentieth day after the first of the ships arrived, another Boston town meeting, this one held at Old South Meeting House because it was so large, broke up and *"they left what they call their lawful Assembly in Dr Sewalls Meeting house [Old South] & reassembled at Griffins Wharffe"* where *"three of the Vessels having on board 340 chests of tea lay & in about two hours the whole of it was hoisted out and thrown into the dock the chests being first opened."* Some of those who destroyed the tea had painted faces and disguised clothing in direct contradiction to the 1753 act governing nighttime pageants in Boston. The chests were each about twenty inches square and made of half-inch wood. One of the men who broke them up used a twivel (sometimes spelled twybyl or twibil) to do the job, a tool normally used to cut rough mortises in pieces of wood when fashioning temporary structures like the portable sections of fence called sheep hurdles. An ink inscription on the handle of the tool [no. 9] written by Cummings Davis reads *"1765 / Ebenezer Swan."* Ebenezer Swan was the great-great-grandfather of Cummings Davis; it was the son of Ebenezer, Gershom, who used the tool to break open tea chests.

Parliament responded quickly to the destruction of the tea. Despite the three months consumed in sending communication back and forth across the Atlantic Ocean, by the middle of May 1774, Bostonians could read the provisions of the Boston Port Act in the newspaper. After June 1 no goods could be landed anywhere on the shore of Boston Harbor. Because commerce could not safely be carried on there, the act declared, the busiest port in New England would remain closed until the tea, later valued between £12,000 and £14,000 by Thomas Hutchinson, had been paid for. Also in the middle of May General Thomas Gage arrived in Boston as the new Governor and Commander in Chief of Massachusetts Bay Colony, replacing Hutchinson who had been appointed governor in 1771. Former governor Hutchinson left Boston for England on the same day that the port closed, which was the same day that the General Court, the Massachusetts provincial legislature, was ordered to convene in Salem.

The General Court session of July 1774 did not proceed amicably. The representatives, the popularly elected members of the lower house of the legislature, chose the members of the Council, the upper house, as they had done under the provisions of the Massachusetts Bay

Charter since 1691, and General Gage rejected most of the choices. The first resolutions generated by the General Court took the form of complaints from the representatives about the necessity of travelling twenty miles from Boston to meet. When on July 17 a committee formed to consider what actions to take with respect to the Boston Port Act recommended that there be a congress of all the American colonies in Philadelphia on the first of September and put this proposal to a vote to the whole assembly, meeting behind locked doors, General Gage dissolved the General Court. Dissolving rather than adjourning it meant that a new election of representatives would have to take place before the court met again.

The elements of the Massachusetts Government Act, the second action taken by Parliament in response to the destruction of the tea, were public knowledge by the middle of July 1774. The act revoked part of the Massachusetts Bay Royal Charter of 1691 and restructured several features of Massachusetts governance. The members of the Council were after August 1 to be Royal appointments and no longer elected by the lower house; jurors were to be selected by sheriffs and no longer elected in town meeting, and the sheriffs were to be chosen by the Governor without the consent of the Council, as was the Chief Justice. Another provision addressed town meetings. *"Whereas,"* in the words of the Massachusetts Government Act, *"a great abuse has been made of the power of calling such meetings"* and the participants had *"been misled to treat upon matters of the most general concern, and to pass many dangerous and unwarrantable resolves,"* they were no longer to be convened by the town selectmen or by petition of voters, apart from an annual meeting, without the permission of the Governor.

Years earlier British government officials had denounced the 1765 Stamp Act Congress, which was first proposed at a Boston town meeting, as an *"unwarrantable Combination."* Warrantable or not, combinations and associations in and among the American colonies had proliferated over the next decade. By the spring of 1766 the Sons of Liberty groups that arranged many of the public demonstrations protesting the revenue stamps had formed their own combination, unifying groups from Massachusetts, Connecticut, New Hampshire, Rhode Island, and New York through correspondence. The Boston merchants and traders who had been meeting together to consider the effect on trade of Parliamentary legislation in 1768 formed a committee to communicate with other organizations of merchants, in other towns and in other colonies, which helped sustain the nonimportation agreement that was aimed at the repeal of the Townshend Revenue Act. The Boston town meeting in 1772 formed a committee to correspond with the other towns in the province about matters they considered to be in their mutual interest but to which they could not get the government to attend. These committees of correspondence began to multiply within Massachusetts and beyond and assumed an increasingly formal role in public affairs over the next two years. Worcester, for example, in 1774 hosted a convention of representatives of committees of correspondence from each town in Worcester County, demonstrating that the combinations were themselves capable of forming combinations.

In July 1774, the Boston newspapers reported that *all* the newspapers in the colonies were filled with the same news: meetings and resolutions in towns and counties complaining of oppression, calling for a general colonial congress, recommending a cessation of trade with Great Britain, and soliciting contributions for the relief of the poor of Boston suffering through the closure of the port. The Virginia, Connecticut, and Maryland assemblies had each recommended a "grand continental congress" a few weeks before the Massachusetts legislature voted for one, with the Maryland assembly asserting that *"Boston is now suffering in the common cause of America."*

Legislative assemblies in all the thirteen colonies but Georgia began choosing delegates to the congress slated to convene in Philadelphia on September 5, 1774. Before that body met, however, General Gage undertook a strategic operation that triggered an astonishing reaction, one that reached beyond the borders of Massachusetts. In order to limit the military resources available to the Provincial militia, on September 1, 1774 General Gage sent an early morning expedition to seize the gunpowder stored in the powder house in Charlestown. The raid was successful in that the powder, 250 half barrels of it, was removed to Castle William, but a nearly disastrous consequence followed. Report of the clandestine raid quickly spread across Middlesex County, according to the report in the September 5 *Boston Evening Post*. On the evening of September 1, the paper noted, people *"began to collect in large bodies with their arms, provisions, and ammunition."* The next morning *"some thousands of them had advanced to Cambridge"* armed only with sticks as they had left their firearms behind. The Cambridge Committee of Correspondence saw the crowd and sent express riders to Charlestown and Boston with this news, *"and their respective committees proceeded to Cambridge without delay."* The committees witnessed the forced resignation of Lieutenant Governor Thomas Oliver from the royally appointed Council, though Oliver was permitted to insert in the statement *"My House at Cambridge being surrounded by about four Thousand people, in compliance with their commands I sign my Name. THOMAS OLIVER."*

An incident unrelated to the staged resignations of appointed councilors provided a brief distraction for part of the crowd assembled in Cambridge. Benjamin Hallowell, a customs commissioner, happened to pass through Cambridge in a chaise and was chased out of town. Israel Putnam of Connecticut believed that the Hallowell story merged with the account of the seizure of gunpowder and what Putnam heard was that on September 2 *"men of war and troops, began to fire upon the people last night at Boston."* Putnam, who over the course of the Revolutionary War would rise to the rank of brigadier general, passed on the alarm that Boston was *"laid in ashes by the fire of ships of war";* the nightmare scenario that the sight of the fleet surrounding Boston with springs to their cables had conjured in the minds of anxious Bostonians in October 1768 had reportedly come to pass.

The alarm was spread from community to community by express riders carrying written messages requesting that assistance be immediately sent to Boston. Within a few days the news had reached New York and Philadelphia. Estimates in the Boston newspapers of the number who responded to the alarm before discovering it was false ran to an implausibly high forty thousand.

As the elected delegates to the Continental Convention began heading for Philadelphia, counties in Massachusetts began holding conventions in response to the writs issued for an election of representatives to a General Court to be convened in Salem on October 5, 1774. Just as town meetings had been reproved for doing in the Massachusetts Government Act, these conventions treated upon matters of the most general concern. Among the resolves of the Middlesex County Convention held in Concord at the end of August, which were published in the Boston newspapers, was the exhortation *"We must NOW exert ourselves"* or the efforts of the past ten years would be frustrated. Addressing the matter of governance philosophically, as these committees and conventions more and more tended to do, the Middlesex

County Convention cited the need for equilibrium in legislative bodies, a balance disturbed by the provisions of the Massachusetts Government Act, and — referring to the restraint on town meetings in the same act — asserted that every people have a right to meet together. By a vote of 146 to 4 the Middlesex County Convention proposed a new combination when they recommended that each town send delegates *"to attend a Provincial Meeting to be holden at Concord on the second Tuesday of October next."* The Essex County Convention on September 6 endorsed the Middlesex County Convention's call for a provincial meeting and further proposed that the representatives chosen in the upcoming election *"will properly form such Provincial Congress."*

A convention of the towns of Suffolk County, which included Boston, also met during the first week of September 1774. The resolves of the convention — the Suffolk Resolves — stated that the province had no obligation to obey the late acts of Parliament, declared the appointed Council illegitimate, and advised tax collectors to retain revenues, essentially sweeping away the government of General Thomas Gage. In its place the Suffolk Resolves advocated a provincial congress to be held in Concord as the conventions for Middlesex County and Essex County did and pledged *"all due respect and submission"* to the Continental Congress then deliberating in Philadelphia. The resolves also dealt with the organization of the provincial militia, advising officers to resign the commissions [nos. 10 and 11] they held from the Governor and for towns to elect militia officers, and advising that the militia train in the *"art of war"* at least once a week but to *"act merely in the defensive."*

The last of the resolves detailed how Suffolk County should respond if *"hostilities should commence."* A member of the committee of correspondence or a selectman *"shall dispatch couriers with written messages to the select men, or committees of correspondence, of the several towns in the vicinity, with a written account of such matter who shall despatch others to committees more remote."* The expense of the couriers was to be defrayed by the county. The seizing of the gunpowder in Charlestown elicited almost exactly this response, with the committees of correspondence getting involved, express riders carrying written messages, and the spread of the alarm to more remote areas. Courier Paul Revere carried the text of the Suffolk Resolves to the Continental Congress members in Philadelphia who endorsed them with their first official resolution. The secure transmission of written communication is an aspect of

FRANCIS BERNARD, Efq;
Captain General and Governor in Chief, in and
over His Majesty's Province of the *Massachusetts-
Bay* in *New-England,* and *Vice-Admiral of the same*

To *Nathan Barrett Gent.* Greeting.

By Virtue of the Power and Authority in and by His Majesty's Royal Commission to Me granted to be Captain General, &c over this His Majesty's Province of the *Massachusetts Bay* aforesaid I do by these Presents (reposing especial Trust and Confidence in your Loyalty, Courage and good Conduct) constitute and appoint You the said *Nathan Barret* ———— to be Ensign of the *third military company of Foot in Concord whereof Thomas Davis is Captain and in the third Regiment of militia in the County of Middlesex whereof Elisha Jones Esqr is Colonel*

You are therefore carefully and diligently to discharge the Duty of an *Ensign* in leading, ordering and exercising said *Company* ———— in Arms both inferior Officers and Soldiers and to keep them in good Order and Discipline and they are hereby commanded to obey you as their *Ensign* ———— and you are your self to observe and follow such Orders and Instructions, as you shall from time to time receive from your Captain or other your Superior Officer according to military Rules and discipline, pursuant to the trust reposed in you

Given under my Hand and Seal at Arms at BOSTON, the *26th* Day of *march* ———— In the *Sixth* ———— Year of the Reign of His Majesty King GEORGE the THIRD, Annoq; Domini, 1 7 66

By His Excellency's
Command,

Jn.o Cotton D Secry

May 5. 1766
Ensign Nathan Barret Repeated and Subscribed the Test or Declaration and Took the Several Oaths by Law required to be Taken in order to Qualify him for the Execution of the Trust reposed in him by this Comn.

Before Charles Prescott *Thos Jones*

appointed to administer the same

THOMAS HUTCHINSON, Esquire;
Captain-General and Governor in Chief, in and
over His Majesty's Province of *Massachusetts-Bay*
and Vice-Admiral of the same.

To *Eleazer Brooks Gent.* **Greeting.**

By Virtue of the Power and Authority in and by His Majesty's Royal Commission to Me granted to be Captain-General, &c. over His Majesty's Province of *Massachusetts-Bay* aforesaid, I Do by these Presents (reposing especial Trust and Confidence in your Loyalty, Courage and good Conduct) constitute and appoint you the said *Eleazer Brooks* to be *Captain of a military Company of Foot in the Town of Lincoln, in the Regiment of militia in the County of Middlesex whereof Elisha Jones Esqr is Colonel*

You are therefore carefully and diligently to discharge the Duty of a *Captain* in leading, ordering and exercising the said *Company* in Arms, both Officers and Soldiers, and to keep them in good Order and Discipline, and they are hereby commanded to obey you as their *Captain* and you are yourself to observe and follow such Orders and Instructions as you shall from time to time receive from *your Colonel* or other your superior Officer, according to Military Rules and Discipline, pursuant to the Trust reposed in you.

Given under my Hand and Seal at Arms at BOSTON, the *11th* Day of *July* in the *13th* Year of the Reign of His Majesty King GEORGE the THIRD, Annoque Domini, 177 3

By His Excellency's
Command

Jn.o Cotton D Secry

Novr 10th 1773 Sworn

10. COMMISSION OF NATHAN BARRETT TO BE CAPTAIN

Engraved by Nathaniel Hurd
(1730–1777)
Engraving and manuscript on paper
Boston, Massachusetts, 1766
Height: 17¼"; Width: 13⁷⁄₁₆"
Gift of Carolyn C. Baldwin. 2000.84

11. COMMISSION OF ELEAZER BROOKS TO BE CAPTAIN

Engraved by Nathaniel Hurd
(1730–1777)
Engraving and manuscript on paper
Boston, Massachusetts, 1773
Height: 27³⁄₁₆"; Width: 22³⁄₁₆"
Gift of Wade Rubinstein, Edward G. Tiedemann, and Chip and Margaret Ziering. 2023.13.1

In 1773 Massachusetts governor Thomas Hutchinson *"made a general settlement of the militia through the province, being only careful to give commissions to such persons as were well affected to government, as far as he could inform himself."* Boston silversmith Nathaniel Hurd engraved the plate used to print the new commissions. The plate is signed *"Nathl Hurd Sc."* on the body of the dove beneath the elaborate initial *"B"*; *"Sc"* refers to sculpsit, which means engraved.

The governor, in hindsight, may not have been that well informed. Nathan Barrett (1735–1791) and Eleazer Brooks (1727–1806) were both commissioned captains in the reorganized militia and both resigned their commissions just over a year later. The eleventh of the Suffolk Resolves in September 1774, the resolves that the Continental Congress endorsed, had recommended that all commissions for militia officers be taken away and that each town elect officers, either those who held the resigned commissions or others in their place if they happened to be *"well effected to government."* Barrett and Brooks both resigned their commissions from the Governor, both were elected officers, both were at the North Bridge on April 19, 1775, and both rose in the Provincial militia ranks, with Nathan Barrett ultimately becoming a colonel and Eleazer Brooks a brigadier general.

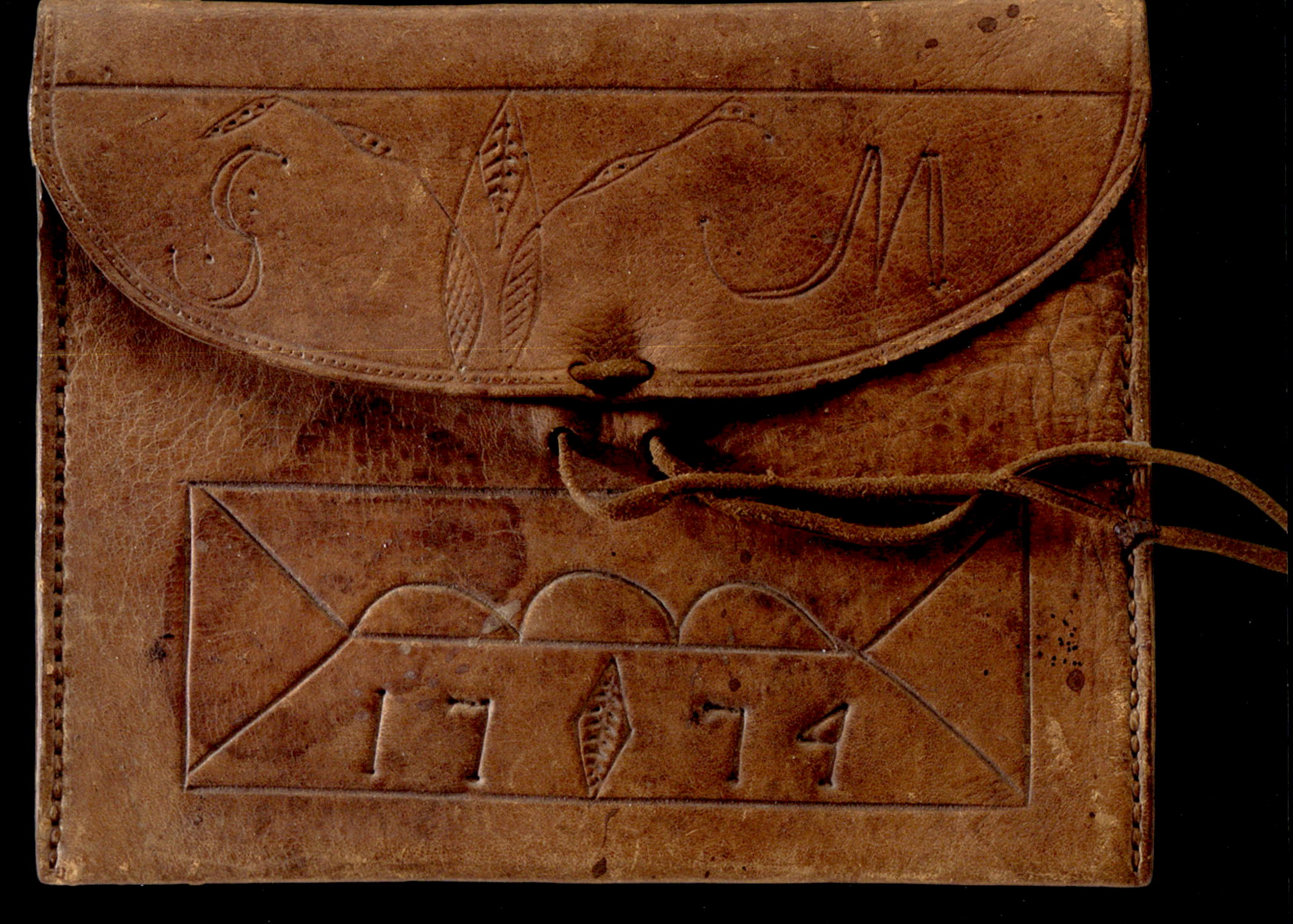

12. DISPATCH CASE

Concord, Massachusetts, 1774
Leather
Height: 6″; Width: 8⅟₁₆″
Gift of Cummings E. Davis. A2075.1

military organization as critical as it is constant. Dispatch cases with a closure secured by leather ties could be relied on to safely carry orders from one place to another.

Paul Revere may have used a case much like the one opposite [no. 12] to carry messages for the Provincial Congress. On the flap of this case the embossed letters "SM" flank a stylized ear of corn; the body is embossed with the date "1774." The initials are those of Silas Mann (1745–1782) of Concord. Mann was a member of David Brown's minute company and was paid for service on April 19. Later in 1775 Mann was an ensign in Abishai Brown's company. Ensigns are responsible for transmitting orders from officers to soldiers, a role for which the dispatch case would have been useful. The case is neatly made by a competent leather worker. Given where and when the case was used, one candidate for maker might be saddler Reuben Brown who produced cartridge boxes and other supplies for the Massachusetts Bay Colony, some of which were discovered and burned on April 19.

The Boston town meeting assembled on September 26, 1774 advised their elected representatives that the General Court would likely be dissolved by Governor Thomas Gage, in which case they were to join with other representatives in a provincial congress. This was the same recommendation that the Essex County Convention had made three weeks earlier. Two days after the Boston town meeting, on September 28, Governor Gage excused representatives from attending at Salem because of *"the extraordinary Resolves which have been passed in many of the Counties"* as well as the instructions given by town meetings to their representatives.

Despite having been discharged by the Governor an estimated ninety representatives met at the Salem courthouse on October 5 [no. 13]. They waited a day for the Governor and Council and when they did not appear the representatives chose John Hancock chair and Benjamin Lincoln clerk of the meeting and voted to *"Resolve themselves into a Provincial Congress."* The new Provincial Congress was the ultimate combination for Massachusetts Bay. *"The people, by their own authority, formed a legislative body,"* Thomas Hutchinson later wrote. The Revolution, the great turn from a monarchy to a republic, was already over well before April 19, 1775, the day the Revolutionary War began.

The resolves of the representatives democratically elected by the towns pertained to the entire province, and the Provincial Congress acknowledged neither the authority of the Royal Governor nor of Parliament to govern their affairs.

13. PORTRAIT OF ELEAZER BROOKS

Attributed to Benjamin Blyth
(1746–1811)
Salem, Massachusetts, 1774
Pastel on paper
Height: 23⁷⁄₁₆"; Width: 20⅛"
Gift of George and Lisa Foote, Candace
Brooks Carr, and anonymous donor.
2005.1

One representative present at that epochal October 5 meeting in the Salem courthouse was Eleazer Brooks (1727–1806) of Lincoln. Brooks served on the committee of correspondence for Lincoln (a town once part of Concord) and drafted the town's response to the destruction of the tea in Boston Harbor in December 1773. In the 1774 election Lincoln chose Brooks to be a representative to the General Court. Eleazer Brooks seems to have improved the occasion of the establishment of an independent provincial government by commissioning a portrait. It was drawn by Benjamin Blyth (1746–1811) who advertised the *"Performance of Limning in Crayons"* (painting pastel portraits) in the *Salem Gazette* in 1769. As a contemporary depiction of a member of the first Provincial Congress who also had a distinguished career of military service throughout the Revolutionary War, the Eleazer Brooks portrait has few comparatives. John Singleton Copley had painted the portraits of others who were present, including John Hancock and Samuel Adams, and Benjamin Blyth had painted a pastel portrait of John Adams five years before, but the Brooks portrait issues from the very time and place that the Provincial Congress formed. Brooks was perhaps wearing the same orange coat when the Congress voted to adjourn to Concord.

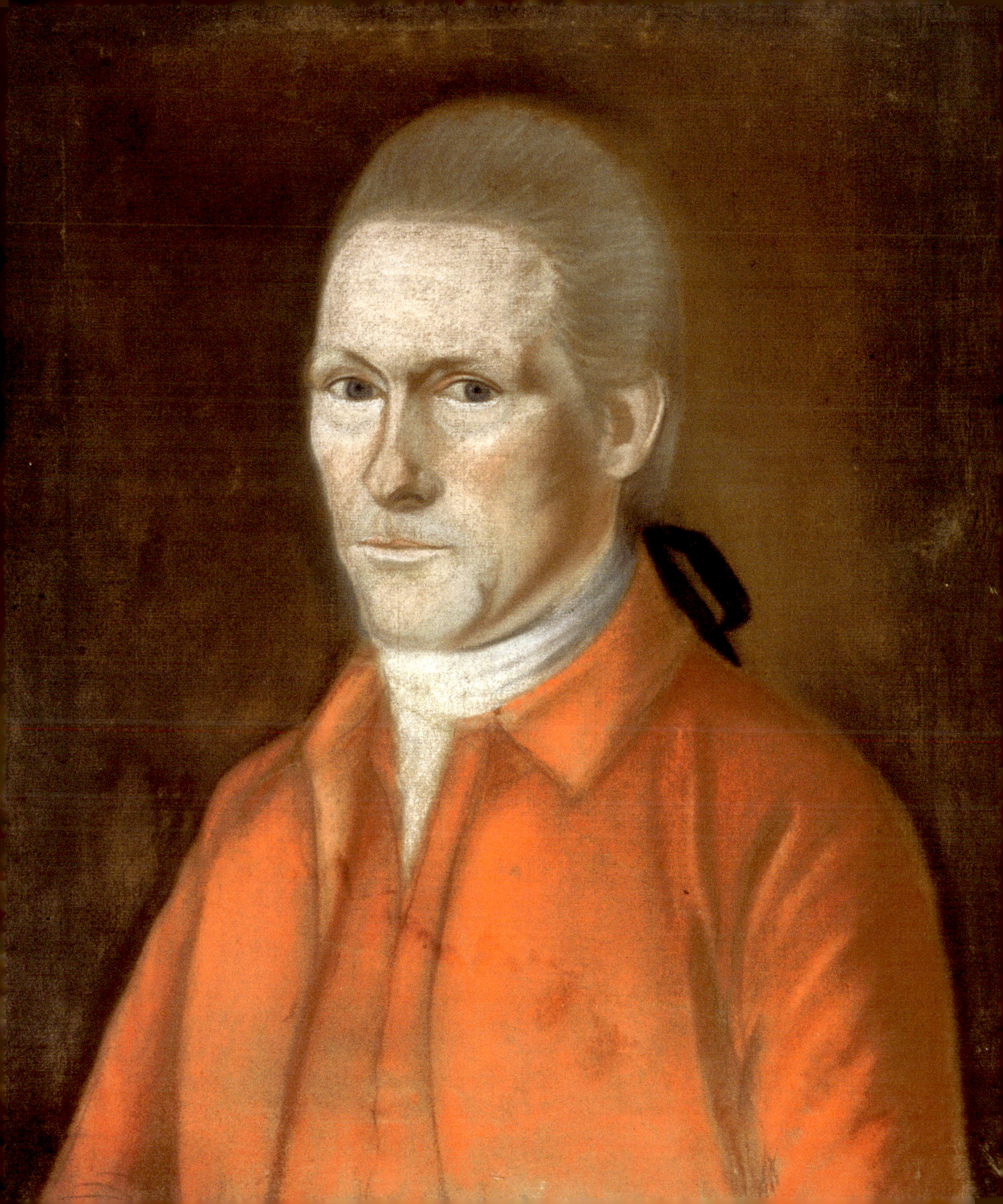

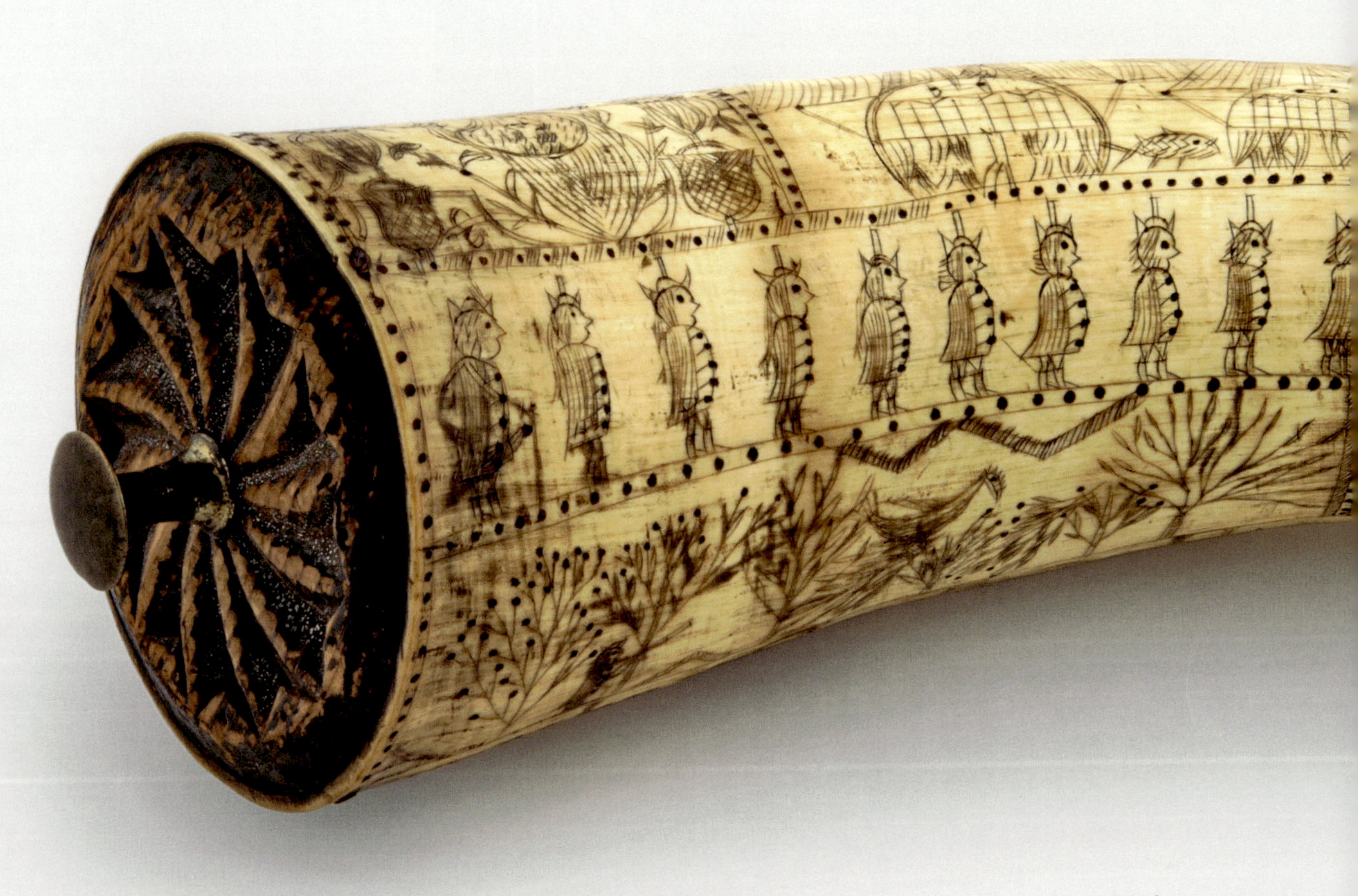

The MASSACHUSETTS ARMY

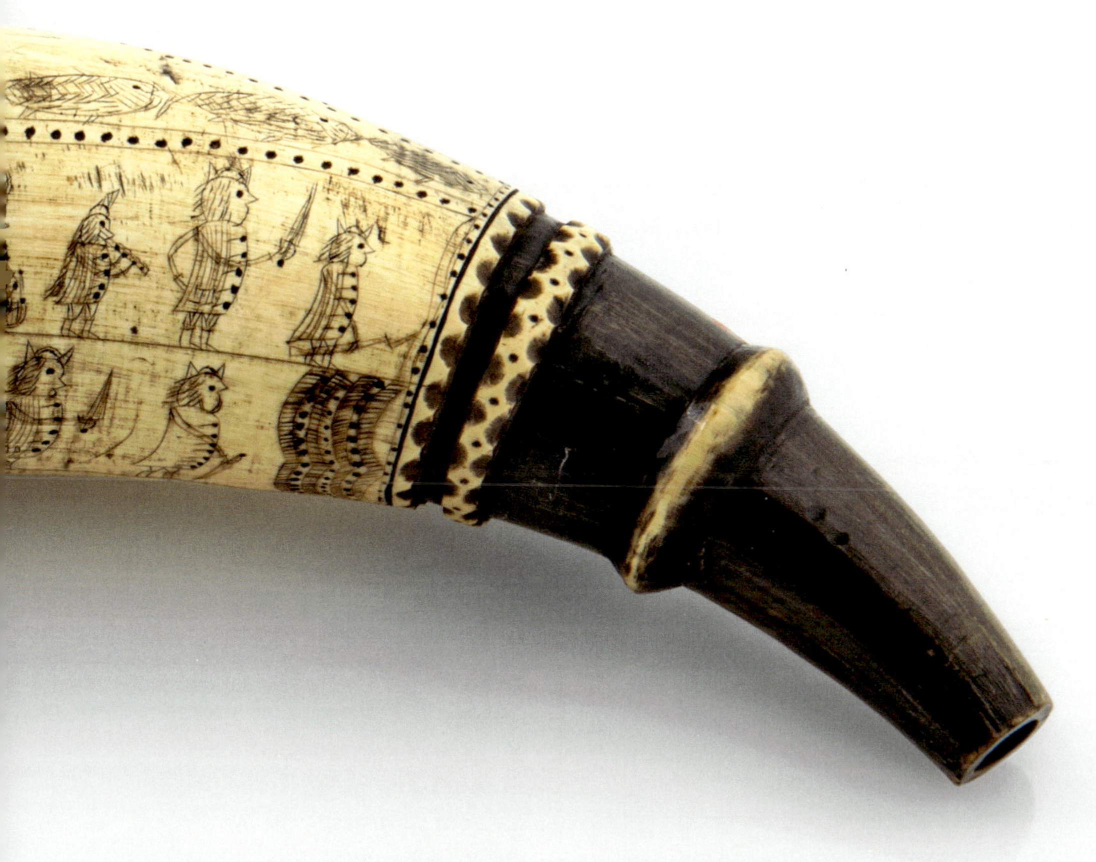

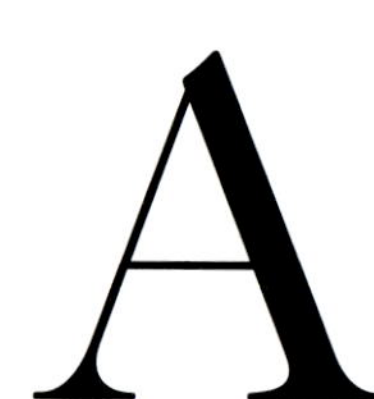

GREAT DEAL OF THE ACTIVITY of the new Provincial Congress was directed to putting Massachusetts on a firm military foundation. These actions were quickly denounced by Governor Gage as *"a new and unconstitutional regulation of the militia."* Within three weeks of forming, the Provincial Congress had ordered a committee *"to consider what is necessary to be now done for the defence and safety of the province."* When that committee reported three days later, another committee was ordered to consider *"the most proper time for this province to provide a stock of powder, ordnance [cannon], and ordnance stores."* The next day, October 24, 1774, that committee announced they would *"attend on Congress in a few minutes. The committee came in accordingly, and reported, as their opinion, that* now *was the proper time for the province to procure a stock of powder, ordnance, and ordnance stores."* Brief as they are, the minutes of the Provincial Congress convey a powerful sense of urgency.

The Continental Congress meeting in Philadelphia, in response to the Suffolk Resolves, sent a letter to the Boston Committee of Correspondence advising that they *"persevere in the Line they are now conducting themselves, on the Defensive."* The Continental Congress had also stated ominously in a letter to General Gage *"that the Town of Boston and province of Massachusetts-Bay are considered by all America as suffering in the common Cause."*

Two days later the Provincial Congress took measures its members believed to be *"perfectly consistent with such resolves of the Continental Congress as have been communicated to us."* The first of the measures was the establishment of a Committee of Safety whose business it was to observe persons who attempt *"the destruction, invasion, detriment or annoyance of this province"*; this committee was given the power *"to alarm, muster and cause to be assembled with the utmost expedition, and completely armed, accoutred, and supplied"* as much of the militia as they deemed necessary for the emergency. Another resolution made provision for paying the officers and soldiers in that event. A second committee, which came to be called the Committee of Supplies, was also established. This committee was charged with provisioning the militia, if assembled, and, with £20,000 in taxes (equivalent to a century of wages for a laborer) that had been withheld from the provincial treasury, to purchase arms and ammunition *"to be deposited in such secure places as the said committee of safety shall direct."*

At the first recorded meeting of the Committee of Safety held in Cambridge on November 2, 1774 with Provincial Congress president John Hancock as chair, the committee recommended to the Committee of Supplies to *"as soon as may be"* procure 1,000 barrels of pork and flour along with hundreds of bushels of dried peas and barrels of rice and deposit them in Worcester and Concord. On November 8 the Committee of Safety in a joint meeting advised the Committee of Supplies *"to procure all the arms and ammunition they can"* from neighboring provinces and *"engage to pay for the same."* In December the Committee of Safety voted *"that the committee of supplies endeavor to procure"* 2,000 spades, 150 iron shovels, 150 pick-axes, 1,000 six-quart iron pots, 200 bill hooks (for cutting brush), and 1,000 wooden mess bowls, along with some ordnance supplies.

These efforts to gather provisions and arms took a great leap forward on February 21, 1775, when it was *"Voted, unanimously, by the committee of safety, that the committee of supplies purchase all kind of warlike stores, sufficient for an army of fifteen thousand to take the field."* At that time, General Gage had fewer than four thousand troops stationed in Boston. The Provincial Congress wanted an overwhelming advantage in numbers of soldiers, nearly four to one, and were evidently confident they could achieve it.

The responsibility for receiving and distributing these supplies fell principally to James Barrett and Jonas Heywood, both of Concord. A partial list of the supplies in their care includes musket balls and cartridges, cartridge paper, tents, iron spades [nos. 14 and 15], wood axes, billhooks, sets of harness for horses, candles, medicine chests, wooden spoons [no. 16], oatmeal, canteens, wooden dishes, gunpowder, butter, beef, salted fish, wine, raisins, salt, and rice.

In the early months of 1775, tons of warlike supplies were in constant motion all across Massachusetts, not just in Concord. Their movements were carefully recorded with written receipts. Hundreds of receipts (many of them in the American Antiquarian Society collection) document the actions taken by James Barrett and Jonas Heywood in assembling the mountain of supplies stored at Concord. Although the supporters of government would sometimes refer to what the

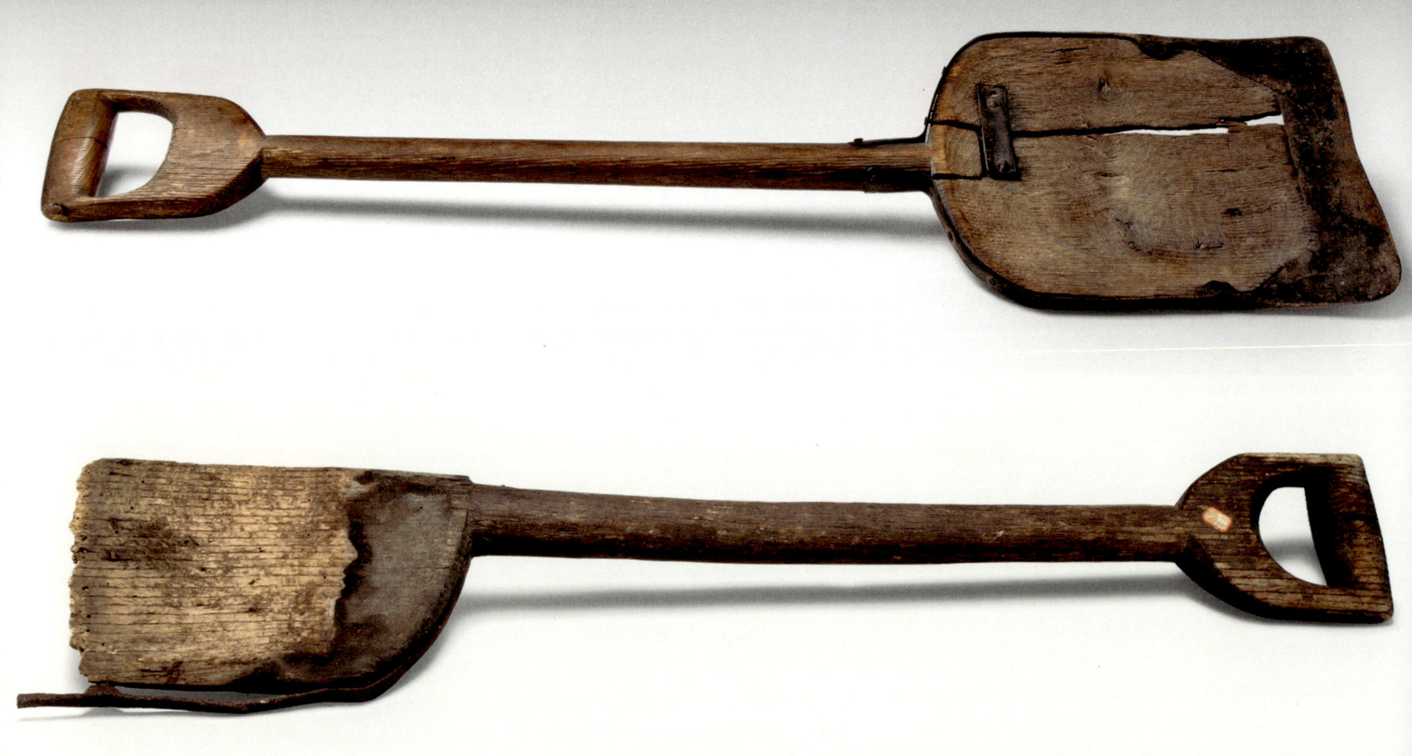

14–15. IRON SPADES

England, 1770–1774
Oak, iron
Above: Height: 39⅛"; Width: 9⁷⁄₁₆"
Gift of Cummings E. Davis. H2030
Below: Height: 35³⁄₁₆"; Width: 6⁹⁄₁₆"
Concord Museum Collection. H1802

Another surviving item that was probably among the supplies stored in Concord is a shovel of the type that the Committee of Supplies referred to as an *"iron spade."* To make these, the working edge of an oak spade is reinforced with an iron shoe of a distinctive shape resembling a pair of drawn curtains. Boston hardware merchant Harbottle Dorr advertised *"English Spades, or Shovels"* in 1775, which may be a reference to this form.

The iron parts from spades of this type sometimes turn up in an archaeological context at former military forts and encampments, but intact examples are vanishingly rare. This example was given to the Concord Museum by the Middlesex County Agricultural Society in the nineteenth century. A partial example of an iron spade with no recorded history is also in the Concord Museum collection [no. 15, below]. For two examples of such a rare form of military entrenching tool to be recovered in one small town is remarkable and suggests that they were among the stored supplies.

Tolman 1911, 421:
"FARMER'S SHOVEL of pre-Revolutionary times; from Middlesex County Agricultural Society."

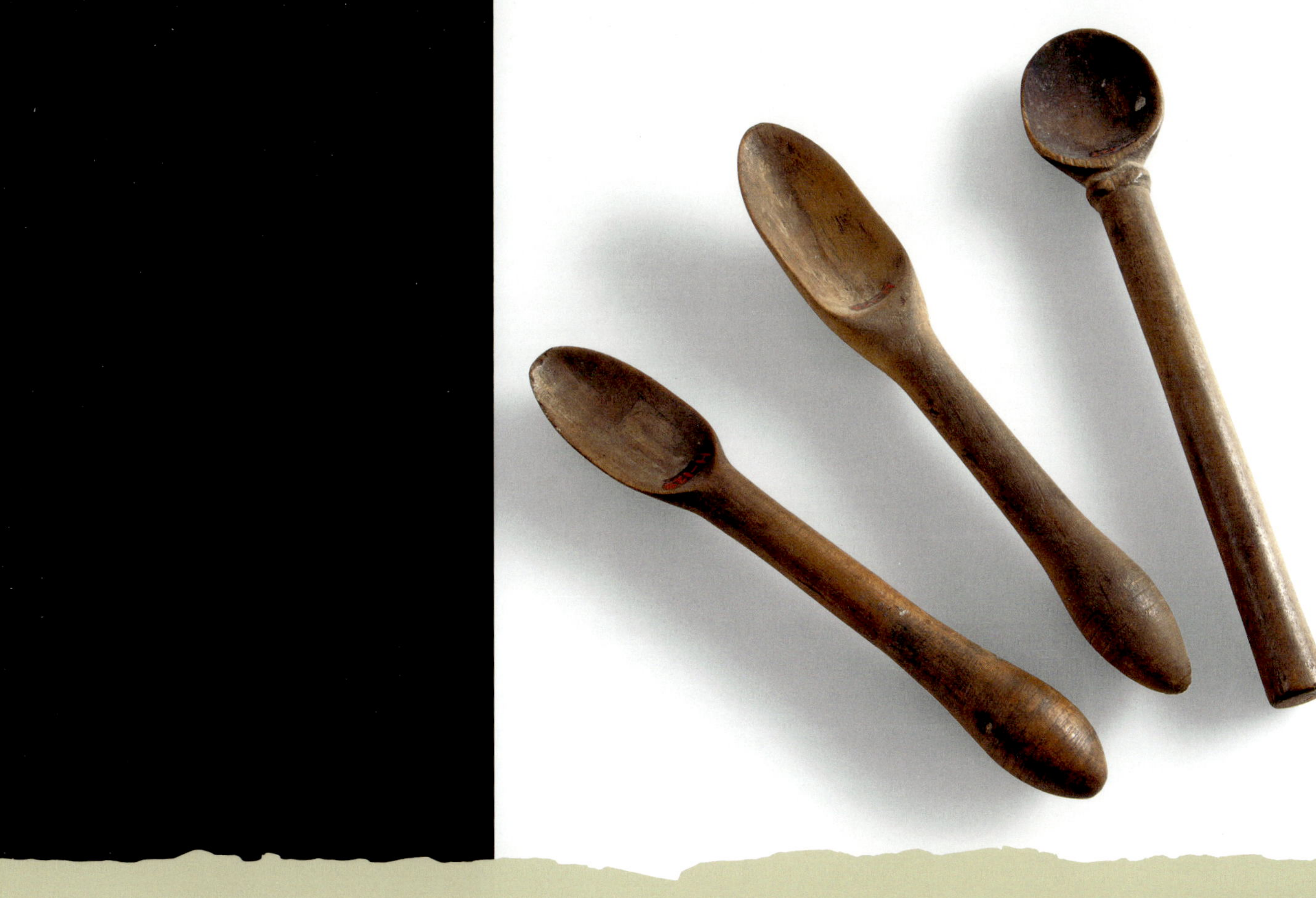

16. SPOONS

Probably Hingham, Massachusetts, 1774–1775
Cherry
Length of Longest: 9¹¹⁄₁₆″;
Width of Longest: 2″
Gift of Cummings E. Davis. H127, H128, H129

Three surviving wooden spoons are probably representative of the barrels full of spoons stored in Concord. Two of them were made by turning a billet (a squared stick) of cherry into a dumbbell shape on a lathe and then hollowing one end, a very economical process suited to mass production. The source for the spoons is not recorded but it might have been the town of Hingham in Suffolk County. Woodworkers in Hingham produced 15,000 wooden canteens for the Committee of Supplies; those canteens were stored in Concord. The three spoons were used by members of the company of Captain Abishai Brown of Concord.

Tolman 1911, 296–298: "THREE WOODEN SPOONS, used by soldiers of Capt. Abishai Brown's company in camp at Cambridge in 1775."

Provincial Congress was doing as anarchy, the little pieces of paper
beg to differ: they are the markers of an effective bureaucracy at work.

A receipt from Hampshire County [no. 17] is in many ways typical of
the records kept of the transfers of military supplies. It states: *"Jan.y
23d. 1775. / Received of Oliver Partridge Esqr Thirty three Cartridge Boxes /
belonging to the Province of the Massachusetts Bay for which / I promise to be
accountable to the said Olr Partridge when / thereto required as Witness my
hand Israel Chapin."* Oliver Partridge (1712–1792) of Hatfield was from
one of the most politically and economically prominent Connecticut
River Valley colonial families. Although he was a delegate to the 1765
Stamp Act Congress, Partridge was unwilling to endorse forcible resistance to Royal government a decade later.

There may be another dimension to this particular receipt, how-
ever. In 1774 Oliver Partridge was suspected of colluding with Israel
Williams, also of Hatfield, to raise the local militia in defense of the
Royal government, not in opposition. Circumstances related to that
episode may have led to the transfer of military supplies, enough
cartridge boxes for half a company of militia, recorded in this receipt.
Israel Chapin (1740–1795), who signed the receipt, was captain of a
Hatfield militia company.

While pursuing this effort to arm and equip a potential army, the
Provincial Congress made provision to assess the readiness of the
actual soldiery of the Massachusetts Bay province: the militia. On
February 14, 1775, in order that they may *"be made fully acquainted with
the number and military equipments of the militia and minute men in this
province, as also the town stock of ammunition in each town and district,"*
the Congress recommended to each commanding officer of the

17. HAMPSHIRE COUNTY RECEIPT

Hatfield, Massachusetts, 1775
Manuscript on paper
Height: 2¹³⁄₁₆"; Width: 8"
Gift of the Cummings Davis Society.
2009.8

regiments of minutemen and each colonel of the militia in the province that they review their companies and *"take an exact state of their numbers and equipment."*

On February 25, 1775, in compliance with the Provincial Congress recommendation, the order for the muster of one of the militia companies in Concord went out. Two copies of the same order, for some reason never separated or delivered, were issued by Nathan Barrett, captain of Concord's third company of foot soldiers. The orders were addressed to the two corporals in Barrett's company, John Barrett, Jr. and Samuel Heald, Jr. [no. 18] The orders stated:

> You are hereby Required to warn and give notice to all the Training Soldiers within your Squadron to appear at the usual place of Parade in Concord on Monday the Thirteenth day of March next with arms and Ammunition According to law. Also to warn and give notice to all the alarm men to appear at the same time and place with their arms and Ammunition according to law. Hereof fail not and make do Return of your doings herein.

The "Training Soldiers" mentioned in the orders were the minute companies, the quarter of the militia meant to be ready "on the shortest notice" and the usual place of parade was the Common in the center of Concord. The alarm men comprised the balance of the militia, including men over the usual age of enlistment. It would have been the responsibility of the clerk of the company to write these orders out, one for each commissioned officer. Whatever accident kept these two orders from being delivered also fortuitously preserved them; no other example of an order for this muster is known.

Four days before Nathan Barrett's muster order was issued, minister Samuel Webster from Temple, New Hampshire, travelled twenty miles south to preach in Groton, Massachusetts, *"At the Desire of the Officers of the Companies of Minute Men in that Town."* In the sermon, published soon after in Boston, Webster's scriptural reference was the Old Testament story of Rabshekah and Hezekiah from the second book of Kings, an exhortation to trust in God in the face of military aggression. Webster then turned the lesson to the present circumstance and reviewed the provincial complaints levelled against the operation of the Boston Port Act, including: *"Troops, to the amount of thousands, stationed in the Capital of this Province; the general of the army appointed Governor of the Province … a naval force in our principal Harbours; batteries erected at the entrance of our Capital."* This list of grievances echoes

By Nathan Barrett.

To Corpl. John Barrett jur.

You are hereby Requird to warn and give notice to
all the Training Soldiers within your Squadron to appear
at the usual place of Parade in Concord on Monday, the
Thirteenth day of March Next with arms and Ammunition
Acording to Law. also to warn and give Notice to all the Alarm
Men to appear at the same time and place with their Arms and
Amunition Acording to law. hereof fail not and make due
Return of your doings herein

Concord February 25th 1774/5

To Corpl. Samuel Hield jur.

You are hereby Requird to warn and give notice to all the
Training Soldiers within your Squadron to appear at the asual
place of Parade in Concord on Monday the Thirteenth day of
March Next with Arms and Amunition Acording to Law
Also to warn and give Notice to all the Alarm men in s.d Squadron
to appear at the same time and place with their arms & Amunition
Acording to law. hereof fail not and make due Return of your
doings herein —

Concord February 25th 1774/5

You are hereby Required to warn and give notice to all the Training Soldiers within your Squadron to appear at the usual place of Parade in Concord on Monday the Thirteenth day of March next with arms and Ammunition According to law. Also to warn and give notice to all the alarm men to appear at the same time and place with their arms and Ammunition according to law. Hereof fail not and make due Return of your doings herein.

— **Nathan Barrett muster**

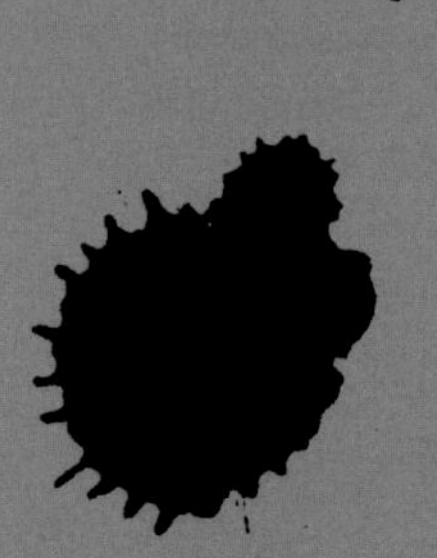

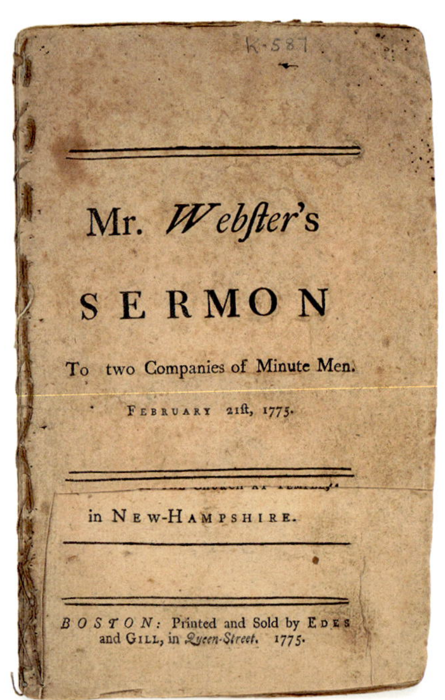

those included in the resolves of seemingly every committee and town meeting, right up to the Provincial Congress. Webster then got to the heart of what the minutemen were mustering for: *"If just Heaven should call us to the field; we know not yet all the enemies we shall have to encounter. We are told — they will be, mostly or all, regular troops."* [no. 19]

At Concord's muster on March 13, 1775, minister William Emerson (1743–1776) addressed the militia and minute companies in similar terms. A reference to Rabshekah in Emerson's sermon suggests a possible familiarity with Webster's. Emerson assured the gathering that *"Our Military Preparation here for our own Defense is not only excusable but Justified in the Eyes of the impartial World."* He added a significant caution: *"Let me drop this one Word: — Let every single Step taken in this most intricate affair, be upon the Defensive. God Forbid that we should give our Enemies the Opportunity of saying justly that we have brought a civil War upon ourselves, by the smallest offensive Action."* Addressing the militia, Emerson conveyed in a phrase what the audience already knew to be the purpose of the muster: *"Gentlemen: in all Probability you will be called to real Service."*

In an episode that may have influenced William Emerson's sermon a free Black man named Thomas Nichols was arrested in Natick in January 1775 and charged with *"being concerned in enticing divers Servants to desert their Masters, causing the Minds of said Servants to be inimical"* and for *"endeavouring to form an unlawful combination against their Masters."* The term "servant" was often used at that time to indicate someone who was enslaved; Thomas Nichols was charged with inciting enslaved people in Natick to *"desert their Masters,"* that is, to emancipate themselves, and to conspire collectively against their enslavers. Arrested and charged with Nichols was William Benson, a free Black man from Framingham.

In his March 13 sermon to the assembled minute and militia companies of Concord, minister William Emerson listed some reasons that could justify the current state of alarm, which included the statement that *"our servants have been flattered with Freedom if they would imbrue their Hands in the Blood of their Masters."* Emerson was reporting that local enslaved people — *"our servants"* — had been promised freedom if they would murder their enslavers. Fears of organized resistance from the enslaved were endemic among the enslavers, but Emerson may have been referring specifically to the incident involving Thomas Nichols. Although the story of Nichols's arrest had not been printed in the local

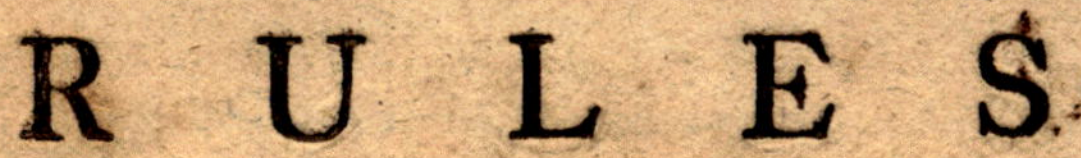

R U L E S

AND

REGULATIONS

FOR THE

MASSACHUSETTS
A R M Y.

PUBLISHED BY ORDER.

S A L E M:

Printed by Samuel and Ebenezer Hall.

1775.

Rules and Regulations for the Massachusetts Army was ordered to be prepared by the Provincial Congress on April 5, 1775. One edition was published in Salem by brothers Samuel and Ebenezer Hall on May 3; another edition was printed in Boston by Edes and Gill on July 14. There were no subsequent editions. This copy once belonged to the legendary collector and historian William Guthman. It is inscribed *"Capt. Abijah Wyman's Martial Book — given Him by Coll.* [Colonel] *Prescott, June 1775."* Abijah Wyman (1745–1804) of Ashby was captain of one of the companies in the regiment of minutemen commanded by William Prescott (1726–1795) of Groton. In June of 1775 Prescott's regiment was in Cambridge; it was Colonel Prescott who was given the responsibility to create the fortifications in Charlestown the day before the Battle of Bunker Hill.

papers, Emerson may have heard about the incident at home. William Benson, arrested with Thomas Nichols, was the brother of Francis Benson, a man who was enslaved in William Emerson's household.

Because the ordinary operations of the courts in Massachusetts had been interrupted by the protest over the Massachusetts Government Act, Nichols and Benson were released in February. The difficulties faced by Thomas Nichols over this affair were not yet at an end.

On February 9, 1775, just prior to the general muster of the militias and minutemen of Massachusetts, the Provincial Congress ordered that Nathan Cushing of Scituate, Colonel Joseph Cushing of Hanover, and Colonel Joseph Palmer of Braintree form a committee to prepare rules and regulations *"for the officers and men of the constitutional army which may be raised in this province."* The term "constitutional army" seems chosen as a direct response to Governor Gage's condemnation of the Provincial Congress's *"new and unconstitutional regulation of the militia."* The very next day, February 10, *"may be"* became *"shall,"* with the Congress making provision for committee action *"until the constitutional army shall take the field."* The Rules and Regulations Committee reported on March 27. For ten days the Provincial Congress considered and amended the text. On April 1 during these deliberations the Congress referred to the *"constitutional army"* as the *"provincial army,"* and four days later it was the *"Massachusetts Army."* [no. 20]

The preamble to the adopted *Rules and Regulations for the Massachusetts Army*, in part echoing the Suffolk Resolves, rehearsed some of the current grievances of the Massachusetts Bay Colony much as minister Samuel Webster did, including a standing army in the colonies in time of peace and a naval fleet in Boston Harbor, Parliament's insistence on its *"Right to make Laws binding upon us in all Cases whatsoever"* (the language of the Declaratory Act of 1766), and *"the large Reinforcement of Troops expected."* The preamble goes on to state the need for any such rules: *"Whereas the great Law of Self-Preservation may suddenly require our raising and keeping an Army of Observation and Defence, in order to prevent or repel any farther attempts to enforce the late cruel and oppressive Acts of the British Parliament,"* in which case *"it will be necessary that the Officers and Soldiers in the same be fully acquainted with their Duty."* Most of the fifty-three articles in the *Rules and Regulations* have to do with what offenses require a court-martial and how the courts-martial will be conducted. The preamble notes carefully that the Massachusetts rules will not call for the *"cruel Punishments as are usually practiced in standing Armies."* The *Rules and Regulations* are *"Signed by Order of the Provincial Congress, John Hancock, President. A true Extract from the Minutes, Benjamin Lincoln, Secretary."*

Late in February 1775, one member of the Provincial Congress wrote a letter to another member that, in expressing a concern about the Committee of Safety, outlines the military chain of command in place at that moment within Massachusetts and across the colonies. *"I have been most seriously contemplating the commission and most important trust of our committee of safety, and especially that branch of it which relates to their mustering the minute men and others of the militia, when they shall judge that the late acts of parliament … are attempted to be carried into execution by force,"* Joseph Hawley wrote to Thomas Cushing. Assembling the militia had been part of the charge for the Committee of Safety since its creation four months previously. The problem, as Hawley expressed it, was that the soldiers *"will suppose it is their duty to fight."* They would not question whether it is the proper time to fight but *"will suppose that the continent have devolved the resolution of that question upon this province, and that this province have devolved it on the committee of safety, and that the committee, by calling them, have decided it."*

"Thus," Hawley concluded, *"hostilities will be commenced; which we must suppose, will, thenceforward, continue, and be most vigorously pushed, until the fate of America be decided."* Joseph Hawley knew, and gave the soldiers of Massachusetts credit for knowing, that the actions they took implicated the entire continent. The somewhat moderate Hawley was concerned not that the response system put in place by the Provincial Congress wouldn't work, but that it would.

Three days after ordering that the *Rules and Regulations* be printed, the Provincial Congress took a momentous step edging Massachusetts a little closer to the commencement of hostilities that Joseph Hawley anticipated. On April 8 Congress resolved to raise and establish the "constitutional," "provincial," "Massachusetts" army that they had been gathering supplies for since the previous October and further voted *"that committees be appointed forthwith to repair to Connectucut, Rhode Island and New Hampshire, to inform them of our resolution, and desire their co-operation, &c."* At the same time Congress contacted the Stockbridge Band in western Massachusetts, now the Stockbridge-Munsee Band of Mohican Indians, with a similar appeal for their support, which was forthcoming.

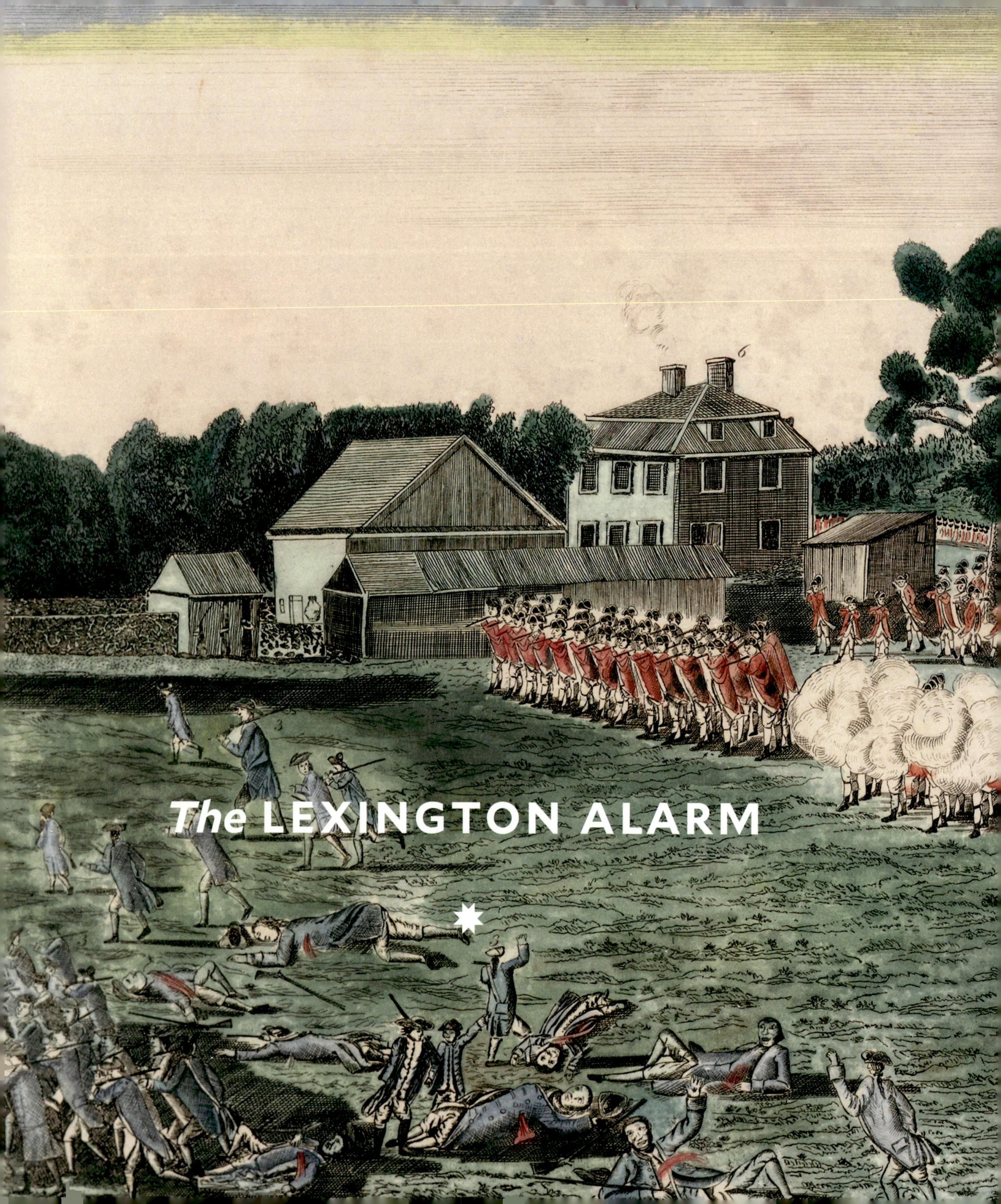

The LEXINGTON ALARM

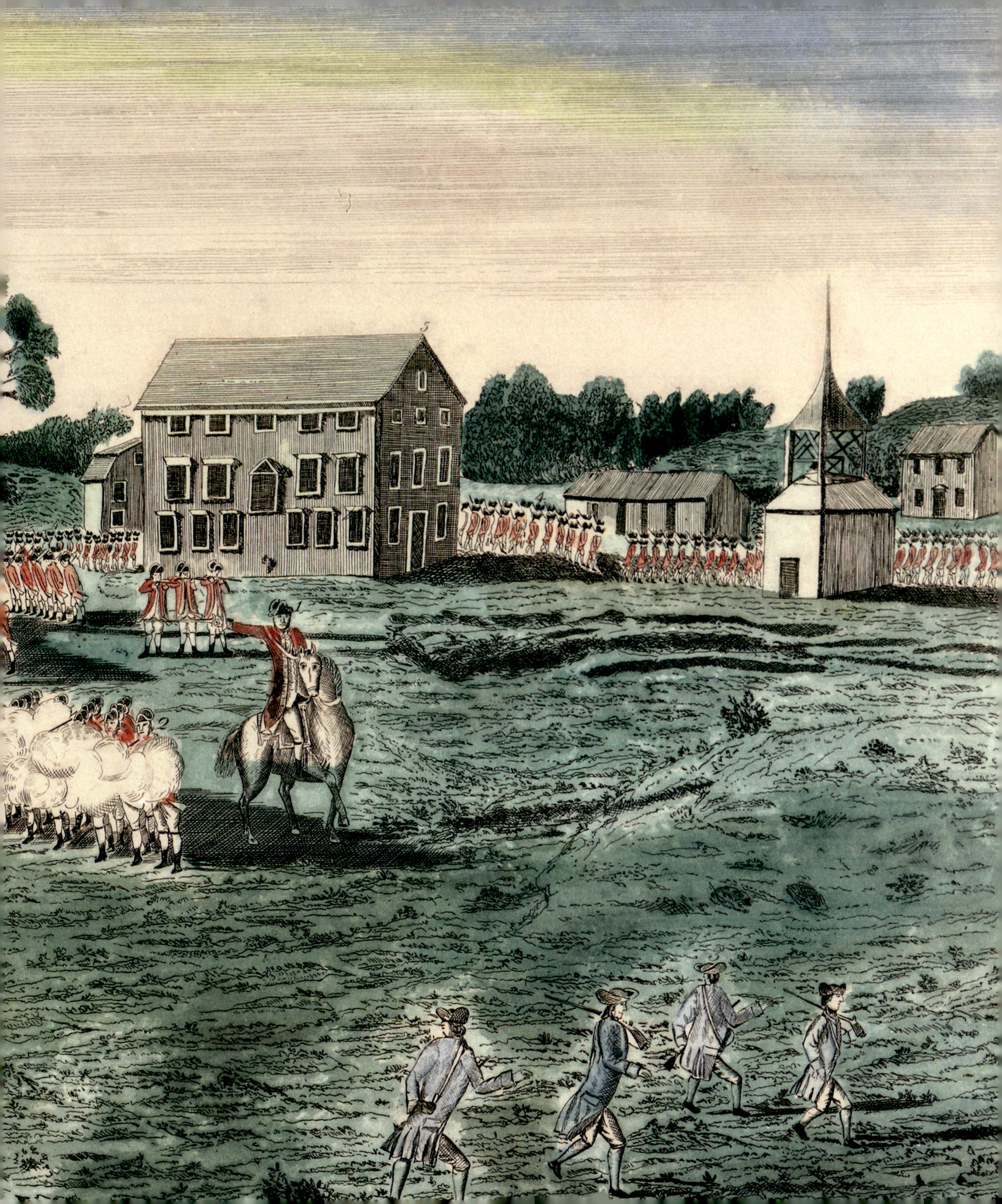

T HE TRIGGER FOR the sequence of events that the perspicacious Joseph Hawley feared would inevitably lead to a general conflict was an alarm system structured like the one that had been recommended in the nineteenth of the Suffolk Resolves, passed by the Suffolk County convention in September 1774 and endorsed by the Continental Congress that same month. The resolve recommended that in the event of an emergency couriers be sent *"with written Messages to the Select Men, or Committees of Correspondence, of the several Towns in the vicinity, with a written Account of such Matter, who shall dispatch others to Committees more remote, until proper and sufficient Assistance be obtained."*

Paul Revere had considerable experience by 1775 as a courier of important messages for the provincial leadership in Massachusetts. It was Revere, for instance, who carried the Suffolk Resolves to the Continental Congress in Philadelphia the previous September, and who had brought news of the 1773 destruction of the tea in Boston Harbor to the same city. Sent by Joseph Warren with a message to Samuel Adams and John Hancock in Lexington on April 16, 1775, Revere stopped in Charlestown on returning and arranged a signal there with a colonel of the local militia. The signal was meant to convey a simple message, which by Revere's account was *"if the British went out by Water, we would shew two Lanthorns in the North Church Steeple, and if by Land, one, as a Signal; for we were apprehensive it would be difficult to Cross the Charles River, or git over Boston neck."* [no. 21] On April 16 it was not a question of *if* the British Regulars would conduct a raid on the military stores that the Committees of Safety and Supplies had been accumulating, but of *when* and by what route they would travel.

Two days later the route the Regulars would take was revealed by the actions of the troops in Boston, and Revere had the information needed to make the lantern signal effective. Revere would later testify:

> I was sent for by Docr. Joseph Warren, of said Boston, on the evening of the 18th of April, about 10 oClock; When he desired me, to go to Lexington, and inform Mr. Samuel Adams, and the

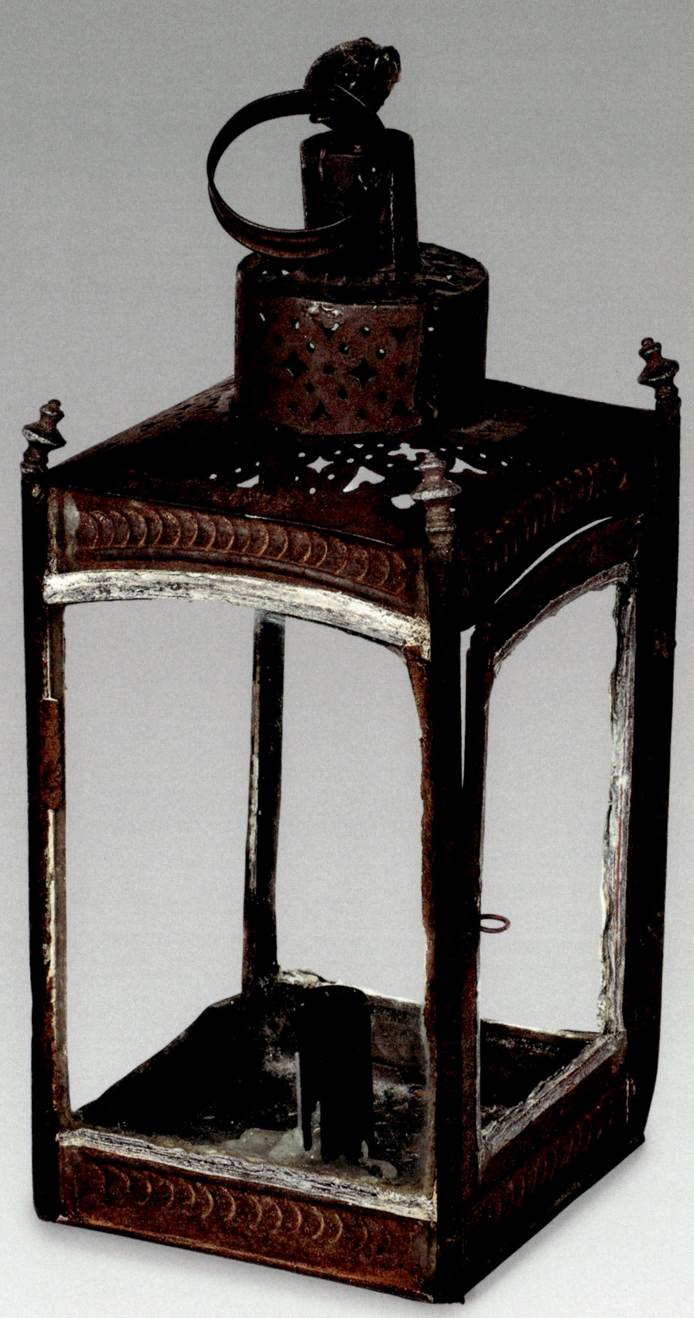

21. LANTERN HUNG AS A SIGNAL FROM THE NORTH CHURCH BELFRY

Boston, 1765–1770
Tinned iron
Height: 13"; Width: 5"; Depth: 5"
Gift of Cummings E. Davis. M400a1

The lantern is built around four slim cylinders of tinned iron that are capped with cast pewter finials, one of them absent. All the other structural elements are soldered to the cylinders. The slightly domed top is pierced decoratively by five or six different punches, as are the two cylinders above it. A wire link joins the crimped suspension ring to the upper cylinder which is open at the top as a vent; a circular disk on the link protects the hand holding the ring. The lantern was once painted overall in a vermillion paint. Three of the four panes of glass are missing; some shards of glass remain in the pool of wax at the bottom. The lead caming that once held the glass on the hinged door bears traces of the vermillion paint and appears to be original.

Tolman 1911, 155: "Lantern, bought in 1782 by Capt. Daniel Brown, of Concord, from the sexton of Christ Church in Boston, and affirmed by the said sexton at that time to have been one of the two lanterns flashed from the belfry of that church by order of Paul Revere, on the evening of the 18th of April, 1775. From Captain Brown's grandson it came into the possession of Mr. C.E. Davis in 1853, with the legend as here given."

Dear Sir,

Having a little leisure, I wish to fullfill my promise, of giving you some facts, and Anecdotes, prior to the Battle of Lexington, which I do not remember to have seen in any history of the American Revolution. . . .

If the British went out by Water, we would shew two Lanthorns in the North Church Steeple, and if by Land, one, as a Signal; for we were apprehensive it would be difficult to Cross the Charles River, or git over Boston neck.

— Paul Revere to Jeremy Belknap, 1798

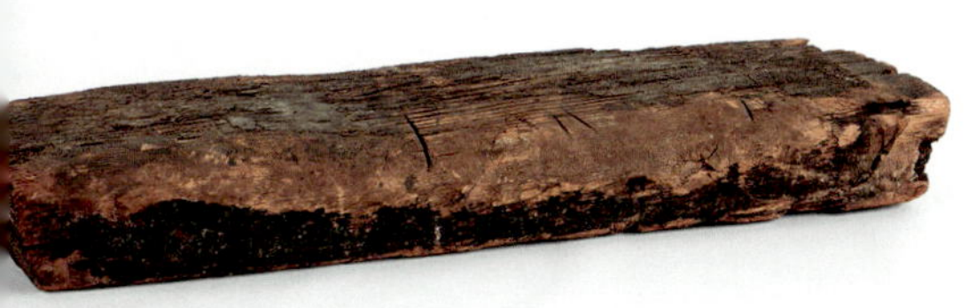

Honl. John Hancock Esqr. that there was a number of Soldiers, composed of Light troops, and Grenadiers, marching to the bottom of the Common, where was a number of Boats to receive them; it was supposed, that they were going to Lexington, by the way of the Cambridge River, to take them, or go to Concord to distroy the Colony Stores.

Paul Revere wrote an account of the alarm ride to Jeremy Belknap, secretary of the Massachusetts Historical Society in 1798. *"I left Dr. Warrens,"* Revere wrote of the lantern signal, *"called upon a friend, and desired him to make the Signals."* The friend climbed the stairs [no. 22] of the belfry and briefly exposed two lighted lanterns.

The lantern signal worked, and against all odds Revere was also able to get out of Boston with the alarm message, though it took rowing under the seventy guns of the H.M.S. *Somerset* in the light of a moon just past full to do it. After setting off from Charlestown on horseback Revere evaded capture by a group of British Regular officers who had been stopping travelers on the Lexington road all evening. Riding at times at a full gallop Revere made it to Lexington not long after midnight.

There was already a guard of ten at Lexington minister Jonas Clarke's home where John Hancock and Samuel Adams were staying, placed there in response to reports of the roaming officers on the road, when shortly after midnight Revere delivered the alarm message from Dr. Warren. Reverend Clarke in a sermon delivered on the first anniversary of the Lexington alarm quoted the message Paul Revere delivered:

> that a large body of the king's troops (supposed to be a brigade of about 12[00], or 1500) were embarked in boats from Boston, and gone over to land on Lechmere's point (so called) in Cambridge: And that it was shrewdly suspected, that they were ordered to seize and destroy the stores, belonging to the colony, then deposited at Concord.

At the Clarke house Paul Revere was joined by William Dawes, another courier sent out by Joseph Warren with the alarm. Dawes had left Boston *"by Land,"* that is, by way of Roxbury Neck. Revere and Dawes continued on their mission to warn Concord of the raid and were joined by Samuel Prescott. A Concord physician, the young Prescott had been visiting his fiancée Lydia Mulliken in Lexington. In Lincoln the three were accosted by the British Regular officers Revere had earlier evaded. Prescott and Dawes managed to escape but Paul Revere was captured. Warned on pain of death not to lie under questioning Revere told the officers, *I had alarmed the country all the way up, that their Boats, were catch'd a ground, and I should have 500 men their soon.* If not an outright lie, the statement was certainly close. And it was effective, for Revere's putative 500 men took on a ghostly reality before dawn. The officers with Revere and several others they had captured rode back toward Lexington. Within sight of the meeting house the officers took Revere's horse and rode off. Freed, Revere returned to the Clarke house where Hancock and Adams remained.

General Thomas Gage's orders to Lieutenant Colonel Francis Smith of the 10th Regiment, dated "Boston, April 18, 1775," read in part:

> Having received intelligence, that a quantity of Ammunition, Provision, Artillery, Tents and small arms, have been collected at Concord, for the Avowed Purpose of raising and supporting a Rebellion against His Majesty, you will March with the Corps of Grenadiers and Light Infantry, put under your command, with the utmost expedition and Secrecy to Concord, where you will seize and destroy all artillery, Ammunition, Provisions, Tents, Small Arms, and all Military Stores whatever. But you will take care that the Soldiers do not plunder the inhabitants or hurt private property.

The *"utmost expedition"* (greatest speed) part of Gage's order quickly went by the board. The 700 soldiers taking part in the raid were, much as Revere had indicated, *"catch'd a ground"* where they had landed near Phip's Farm (Lechmere's Point) in Cambridge after crossing the Charles River from Boston. Logistical delays, including waiting for provisions, kept the men standing idle for three hours. The secrecy part of the order fared no better. The alarm begun by the lantern signal and carried forward by an exponentially increasing number of couriers spread radially away from Boston as rapidly as seven miles an hour. The people of Concord may have heard about the raid from Samuel Prescott before the grenadiers and light infantry even began their fourteen-mile march from Cambridge to Lexington.

Nathaniel Mulliken, Jr. [no. 23], the brother of Lydia Mulliken, attested four days later:

> On the nineteenth of April instant [most recent], about one or two o'clock in the morning, being informed that several

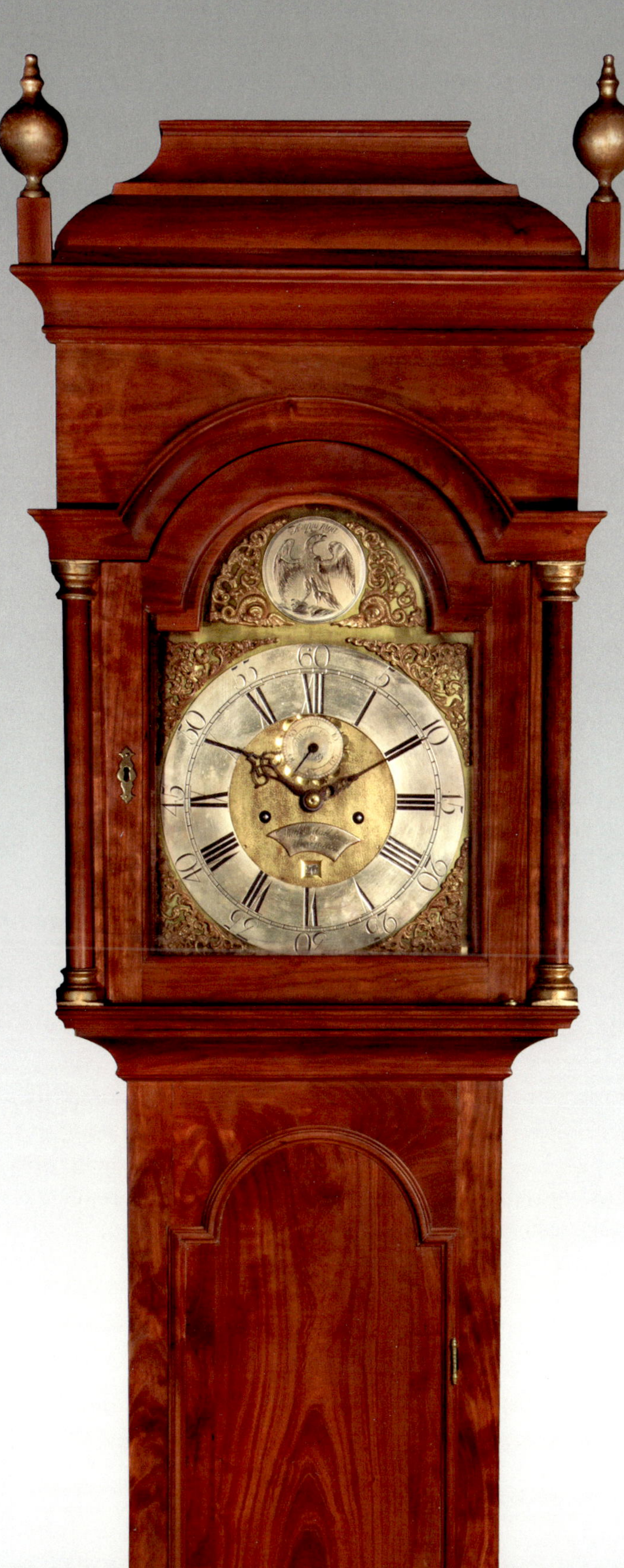

23. EIGHT-DAY CLOCK DIAL AND MOVEMENT

Nathaniel Mulliken (1722–1767)
Probably finished by journeyman
Benjamin Willard (1743–1803)
Lexington, Massachusetts, 1769
Brass, steel, silvered brass
Height of Dial: 16½″; Width of Dial: 12″
Gift of the Decorative Arts Fund with
assistance of Malcolm R. Mahan. F2512

Nathaniel Mulliken, Sr. died in 1767 and the house and shop became the property of Nathaniel's widow Lydia Mulliken. Benjamin Willard of Grafton worked in the shop for several years, turning parts made by Mulliken into finished clocks. Willard may have worked with the assistance of Nathaniel Mulliken, Jr., who was seventeen in 1769 and in 1775 was part of John Parker's company on Lexington Common. Only the movement and composite-sheet brass dial of this clock are original; the case is a recreation made by William Huyett in 2019.

officers of the Regulars had, the evening before, been riding up and down the road, and had detained and insulted the inhabitants passing the same; and also understanding that a body of Regulars were marching from Boston towards Concord, with intent (as it was supposed) to take the stores belonging to the Colony in that Town, we were alarmed; and having met at the place of our Company's parade, were dismissed by our Captain, John Parker, for the present, with orders to be ready to attend at the beat of the drum.

The place of *"our Company's parade"* was Lexington Common, an open green bordered by the meeting house, the separate town belfry, and Buckman's Tavern. With John Parker's order the Lexington militia dissipated, some to nearby homes and some to the tavern, to await the beat of the drum.

At Captain Parker's order drummer William Diamond sounded the promised summons just at sunrise on April 19 and sixty or seventy of the Lexington militia company reassembled on the Common. The column of British Regulars had arrived. The order of the column had been adjusted along the way by Colonel Smith who reported to General Gage, *"I detached six light infantry companies to march with all expedition to seize the two bridges on different roads beyond Concord."*

Major Pitcairn of the British Marines reported: *"When we were advanced within about Two miles of Lexington, Intelligence was received, that about 500 Men in arms were assembled, determined to oppose the Kings Troops, and retard them in their March — On this intelligence, I mounted my Horse, and Galloped up to the Six Light Companies."* Paul Revere's claim that *"I should have 500 men their soon"* had been passed on as fact, and believing it seems to have affected for some British officers the perception of what was transpiring before them. Major Pitcairn reported seeing *"near 200 of the Rebels"* on Lexington Common, nearly four times the number present. Lieutenant Barker of the 4th Regiment, who had also heard the rumor of 500 men in arms assembled, reported seeing two or three hundred on the Common.

Paul Revere's own estimate of the number of Lexington militia gathered on Lexington Common was more modest. Having briefly left Lexington in company with John Hancock and Samuel Adams, Revere

sett off with another man to go back to the Tavern, to enquire the News; when we got there we were told the troops were, within two Miles. We went into the Tavern to git a Trunk of papers, belonging to Col. Hancock, before we left the House, I saw the Ministeral [Regular Army] Troops from the Chamber window. We made haste, and had to pass thro' our Militia, who were on a green behind the Meetinghouse, to the number as I supposed, about 50 or 60, I went thro' them; as I passed I heard the commanding officer speake to his men to this purpose, "Lett the troops pass by, and don't molest them, without they begin first."

The admonition expressed in the Suffolk Resolves and reiterated by the Continental Congress to always act on the defensive was clear to John Parker, who later testified, referring to the light infantry, that *"upon their sudden approach, I immediately ordered our Militia to disperse and not to fire."* Parker's order was followed by the Lexington company as Major Pitcairn's report verifies; the militia *"began to File off towards some stone Walls on our Right Flank,"* much as Connecticut engraver Amos Doolittle would depict in an engraving, and *"the Light Infantry observing this, ran after them."* [no. 24] At this moment Paul Revere was half a gun-shot away with a trunk full of John Hancock's papers. *"When one gun was fired, I heard the report, turned my head, and saw the smoake in front to the Troops, they imeaditly gave a great shout, ran a few paces, and then the whole fired."* Revere later recounted that the first shot *"appeared to be a Pistol."*

The ragged fire on Lexington Common killed eight: seven members of Lexington's militia company and one civilian who had been detained by the officers on the road and then released. Several others were wounded, including Prince Estabrook, one of possibly three or four Black soldiers who mustered at the beat of the drum. The horrific wound suffered by one of the Lexington militia corroborates the testimony of Captain Parker among others that the militia were dispersing when fired upon by the British, as the bullet struck the unfortunate soldier in the back.

The six light infantry companies rejoined the rest of the column, which can be seen in Doolittle's depiction beyond the meeting house on the Concord road, but not before a celebration to which Lexington minister Jonas Clarke was an outraged witness. *"After the militia company was dispersed and the firing ceased,"* said Clarke, in an anniversary sermon, *"the troops drew up and formed, in a body on the common, fired a volley and gave three huzzas, by way of triumph."* The column then, in the words of Colonel Smith, *"marched on to Concord without any further happening."*

The Battle of Lexington. April 19th 1775 Plate I.

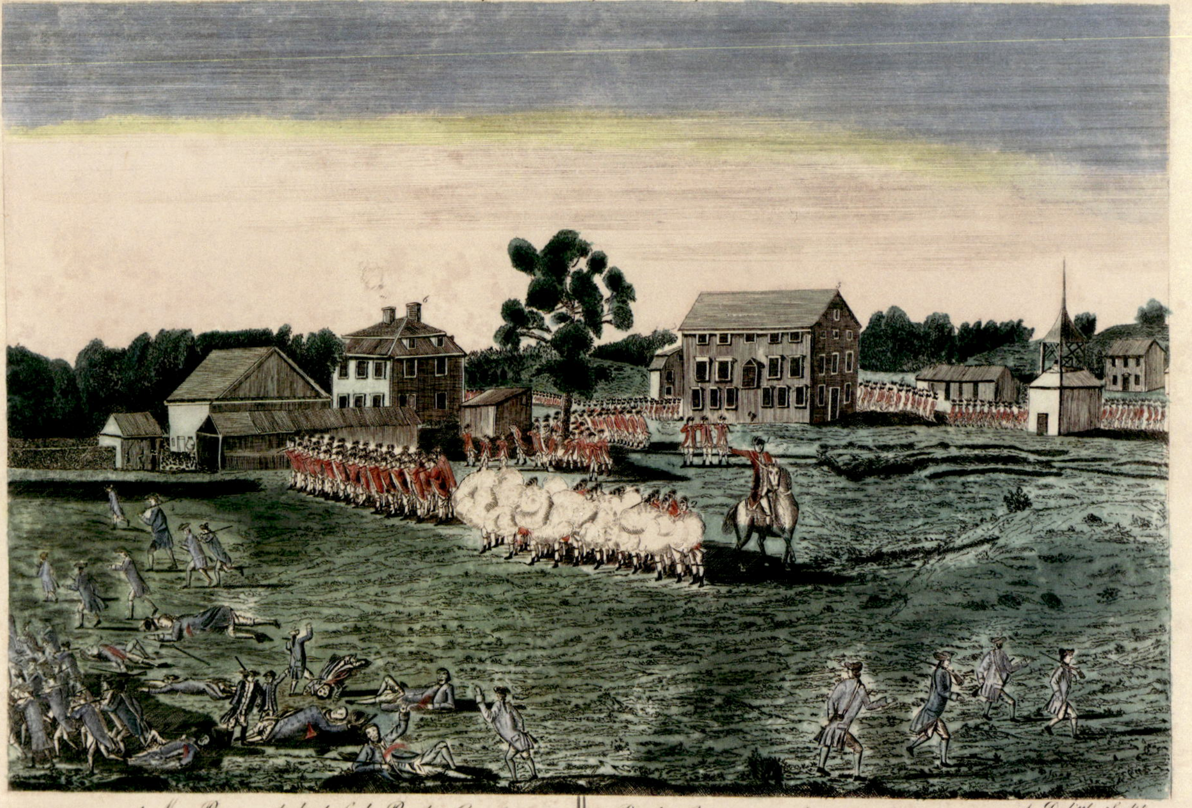

1 Major Pitcairn at the head of the Regular Granadiers
2 The Party, who first fired on the Provincials at Lexington.
3 Part of the Provincial Company of Lexington
4 Regular Companies on the road to Concord.
5 The Metinghouse at Lexington
6 The Public Inn
A. Doolittle. Sculp.

24. *THE BATTLE OF LEXINGTON, APRIL 19TH 1775, PLATE I*

After Amos Doolittle
Engraved by Sidney L. Smith
Boston, Massachusetts, 1903
Engraving on paper, hand-colored
Height: 19³⁄₁₆"; Width: 23¼"
Gift of Charles E. Goodspeed. Pi402

Connecticut engraver and militia-man Amos Doolittle depicted the Lexington fight in an engraving produced a few months after the event. Doolittle's view, faithfully reproduced in 1903, shows the Lexington meeting house to the right of center. To the right of the meeting house is the town belfry, and to the left is the gambrel-roofed Buckman Tavern. Major Pitcairn, the mounted figure, had led the six leading light infantry companies behind the meeting house onto Lexington Common. Much like Paul Revere's *The Bloody Massacre* engraving Amos Doolittle's rendering of the action on Lexington Common suggests more order to the firing than was apparently there. Major Pitcairn with upraised sword seems to issue a command and the central squad seems to fire in unison. However, Lieutenant Gould of the 4th Regiment later testified, *"Our Troops rushed on shouting and huzzaing previous to the firing,"* agreeing with the account of Lieutenant Barker, also of the 4th, who reported *"our Men without any orders rushed in upon them, fired and put 'em to flight."*

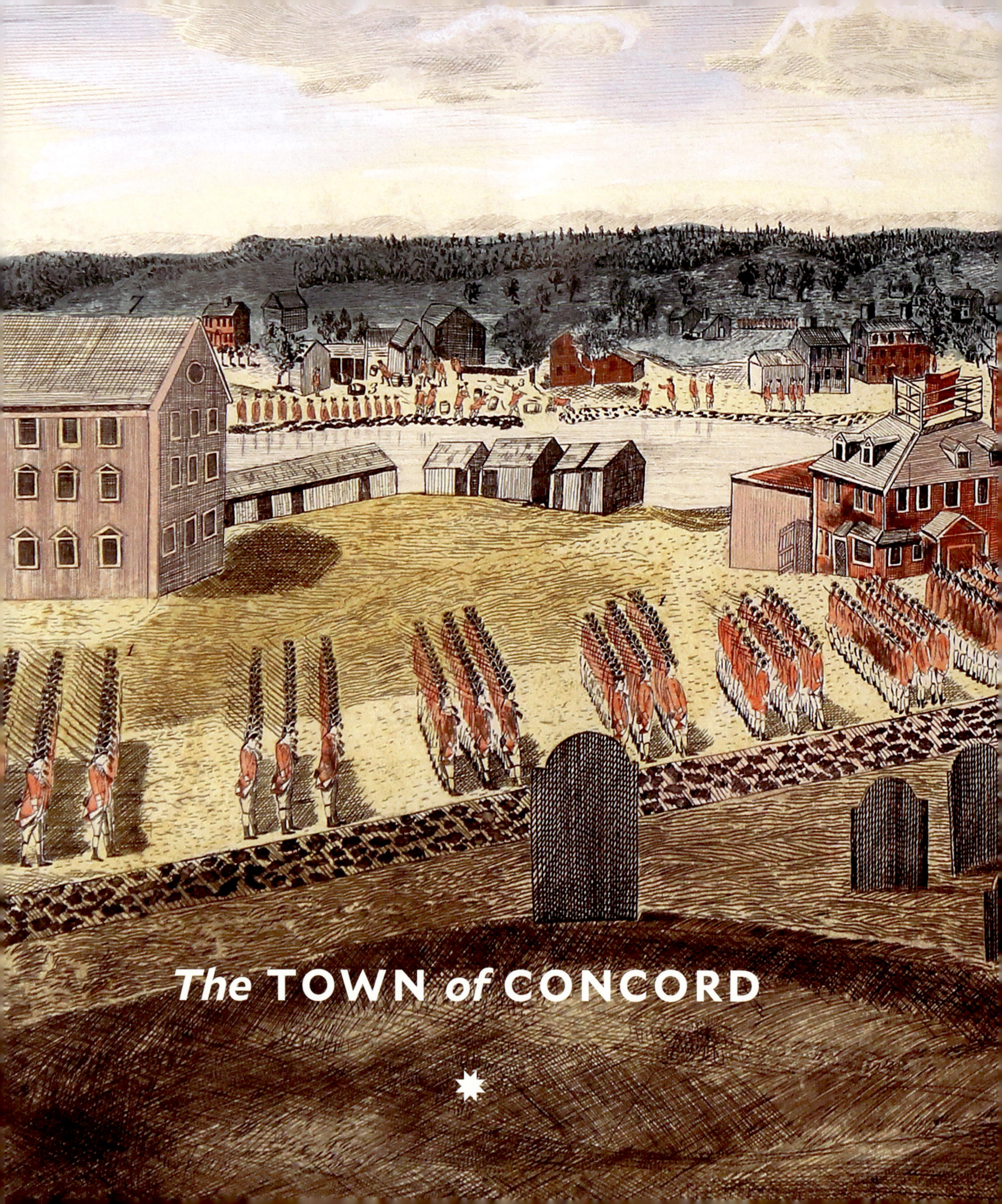

The TOWN of CONCORD

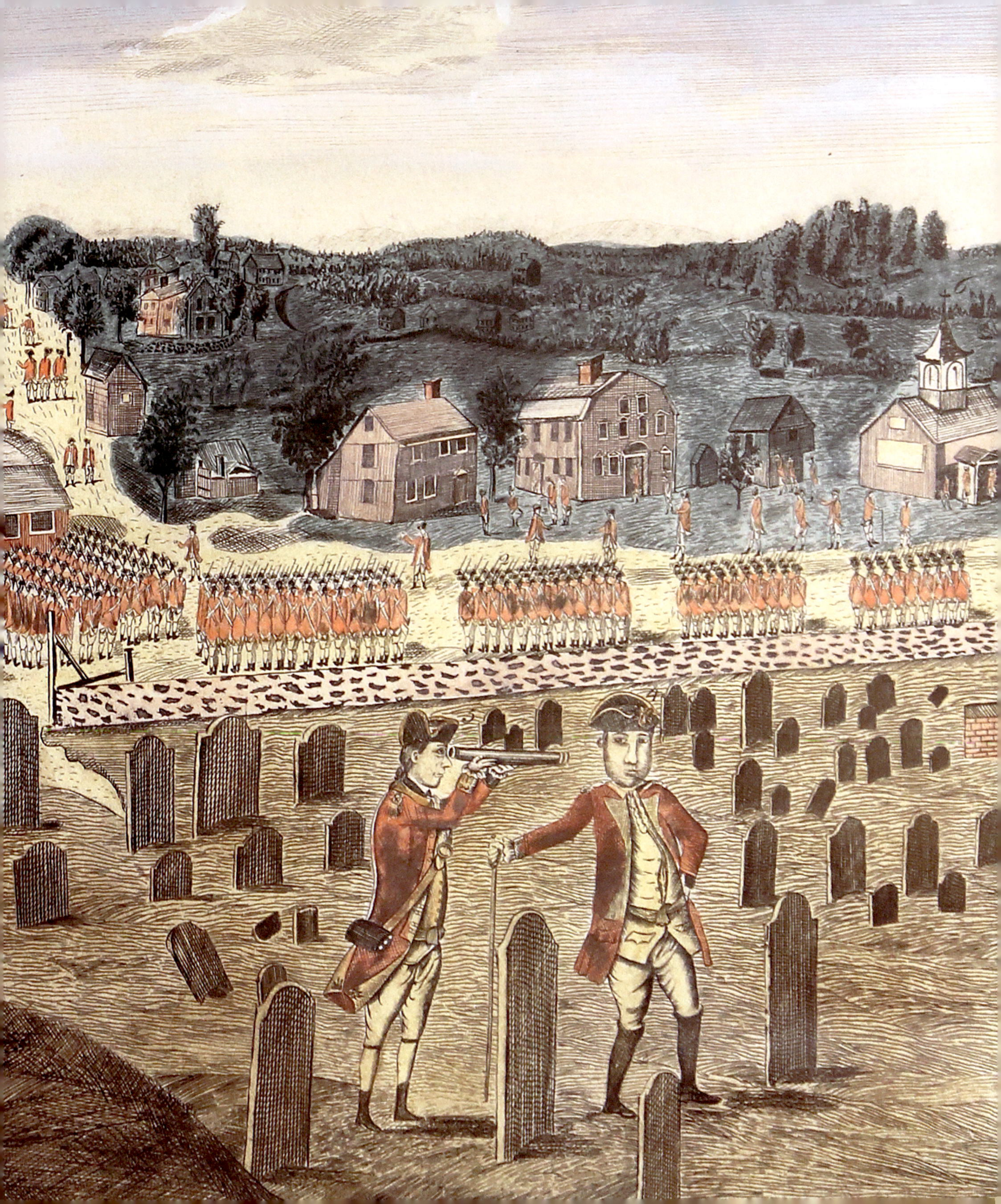

I N CONCORD preparations to receive the raiding party had been going on for hours [nos. 25–28]. *"This Morning between 1 & 2 O'clock we were alarmed by the ringing of ye Bell,"* William Emerson wrote in a journal entry dated April 19, *"and upon Examination found that ye Troops, to ye No. of 800, had stole their March from Boston.... This intelligence was brought us at first by Samuel Prescott who narrowly escaped the Guard that were sent before on Horses, purposely to prevent all Posts and Messengers from giving us timely information."*

On hearing that the column of Regulars was near, Emerson continued, *"a Number of our Minitute Men belonging to ye Town & Acton and Lyncoln, with several others that were in Readiness, marched out to meet them."* Amos Barrett, a twenty-three-year-old corporal in Captain David Brown's minute company, one of two minute companies in Concord, remembered that march fifty years later: *"I think better than I can remember things 5 years ago.... The Bell Rong at 3 o Clock for alaroum as I was then a minnit man I was soon in town and found my Capt and the Rest of my Compny at the post."* The post Barrett mentioned was the usual place of parade for the Concord militia, the open common that lay between the meeting house and the town house. *"Before Sunrise thair was I beleave 150 of us and more of all that was thair. We thought we would go and meet the British. We marched down towards Lexington about a mile or mile half and we see them acomming, we halted and stayd till they got within about 100 Rods* [one-third of a mile] *then we was orded to the about face and marchd before them with our Drums and fifes agoing and also the British. We had grand musick."*

The *"grand musick"* that Amos Barrett remembered vividly fifty years later was played on fife and drum. The fife and drum not only provide the cadence for marching but also communicate messages over relatively long distances. Not every minute and militia company that responded to the April 19 alarm had a fifer, but the names of fifer Luther Blanchard of Acton and fifers Joseph and Elijah Mason of Lincoln, as well as Jonas Welch and David Lane of Bedford are known. Concord fifers included Samuel Darby in Charles Miles's

25. *A VIEW OF THE TOWN OF CONCORD, PLATE II*
(PRECEDING PAGES)

After Amos Doolittle
Engraved by Sidney L. Smith
Boston, Massachusetts, 1903
Engraving on paper, hand-colored
Height: 19³⁄₁₆"; Width: 23¼"
Gift of Charles E. Goodspeed. P1403

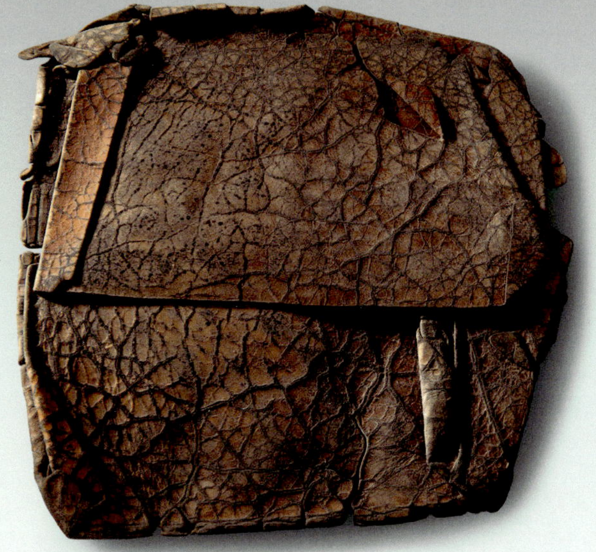

26. POCKET BOOK MADE
FROM A DRUMHEAD

New York City, New York, 1776
Animal skin, possibly calf
Height: 3⁷⁄₁₆"; Width: 3¼"
Gift of Miss Mary Washington Ball.
2006.352

One drumhead burst perhaps in
an urgent circumstance became a
favored personal souvenir, a pocket
book, or wallet. A note that accom-
panies this pocket book reads: *"a
pocket Book made out of a Drum head
that burst in the american army while
stationed at Kings bridge & has been
worn daily by the doaner ever since up
to the present year 1834 being a space
of 60 years."* Mary Washington Ball
believed the handwriting to be that
of ancestor Gideon Ball but Gideon
died in 1826, eight years before the
note was written.

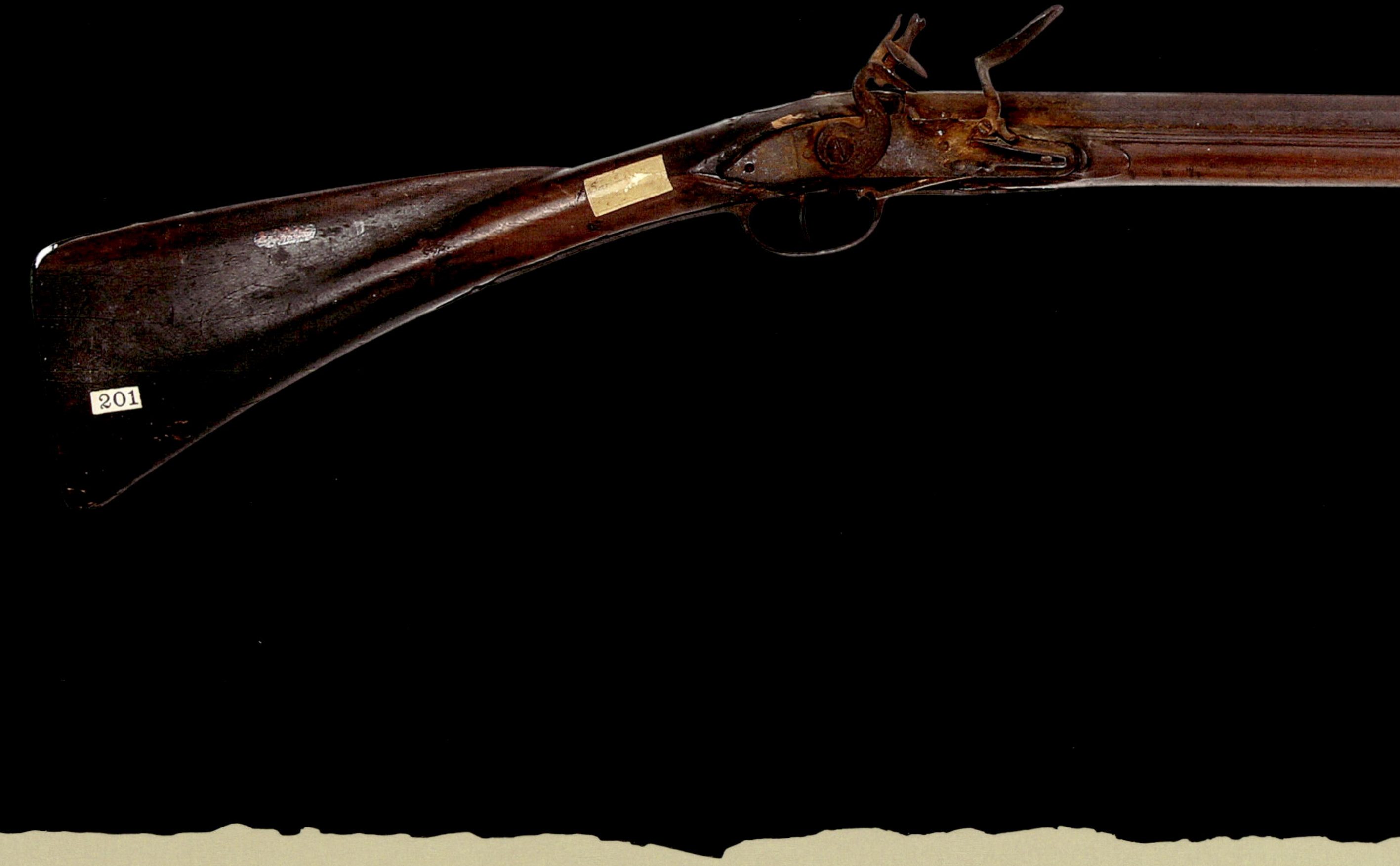

27. FOWLER BELONGING TO SAMUEL DAKIN

France, about 1730
Steel, walnut
Overall Length: 52";
Barrel Length: 36¼"; Bore: ½"
(approximately .50 caliber)
Gift of Cummings E. Davis. A2006

Samuel Dakin, Jr. (1744–1811) was a private in Captain William Smith's company of Lincoln minutemen, part of Colonel Abijah Pierce's regiment, and was paid for four days' service in response to the April 19 alarm. The Lincoln minutemen, alarmed by Samuel Prescott around midnight of April 18, were in Concord well before sunrise and joined with the Concord companies on the march out to meet the British Regulars. Samuel Dakin was armed with a fine French fowler made about 1730. It may have belonged to Samuel Dakin's father, also named Samuel, who died in service during the Seven Years' War. The fowler was never converted to percussion as many flintlocks were, but the barrel was reduced in length. The iron butt plate on the stock is a replacement for the original, the change made while the firearm was still in use. The main spring broke through the floor of the lock mortise, which may have been what put an end to the working life of the firearm. The small powder horn, undecorated apart from the engraved *"SD"* on the wooden plug, may also have originally belonged to the senior Samuel Dakin.

Tolman 1911, 201: "FOWLING PIECE, used as a musket by Samuel Dakin at Concord North Bridge, April 19, 1775."

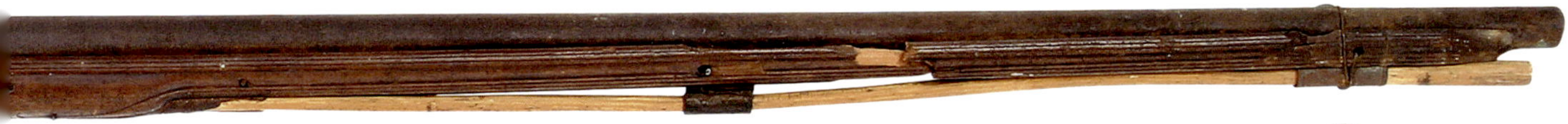

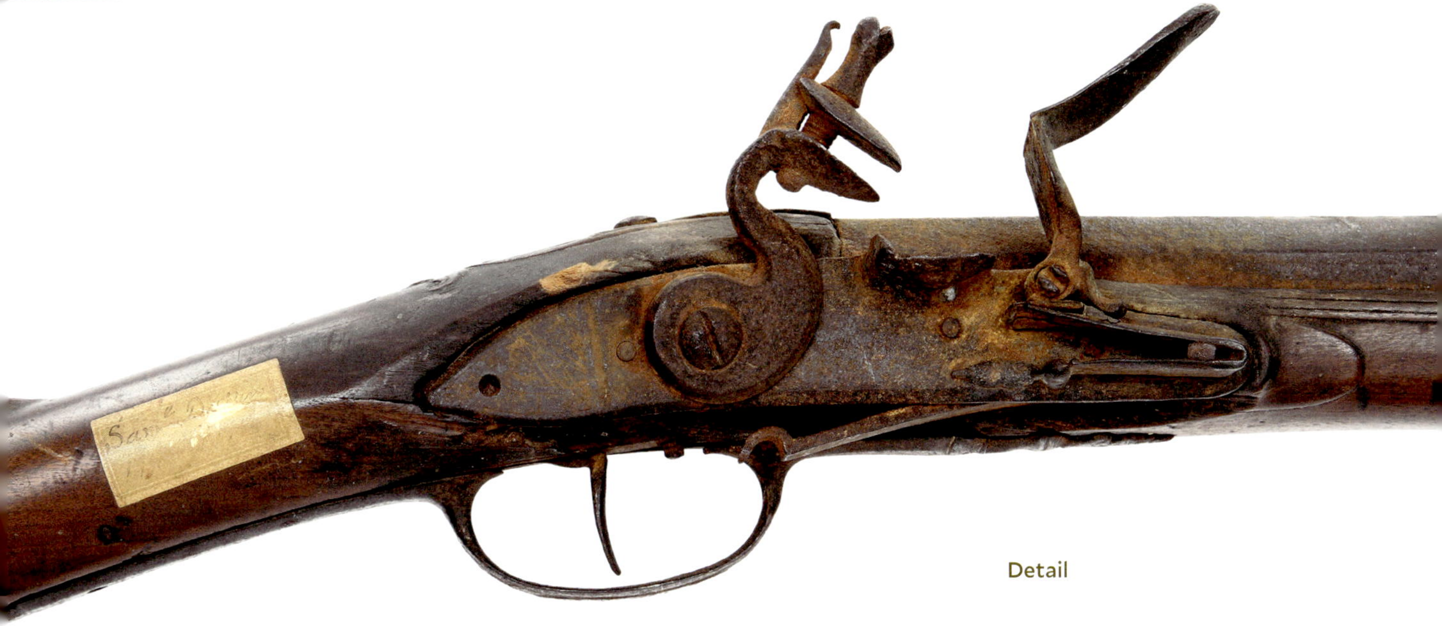

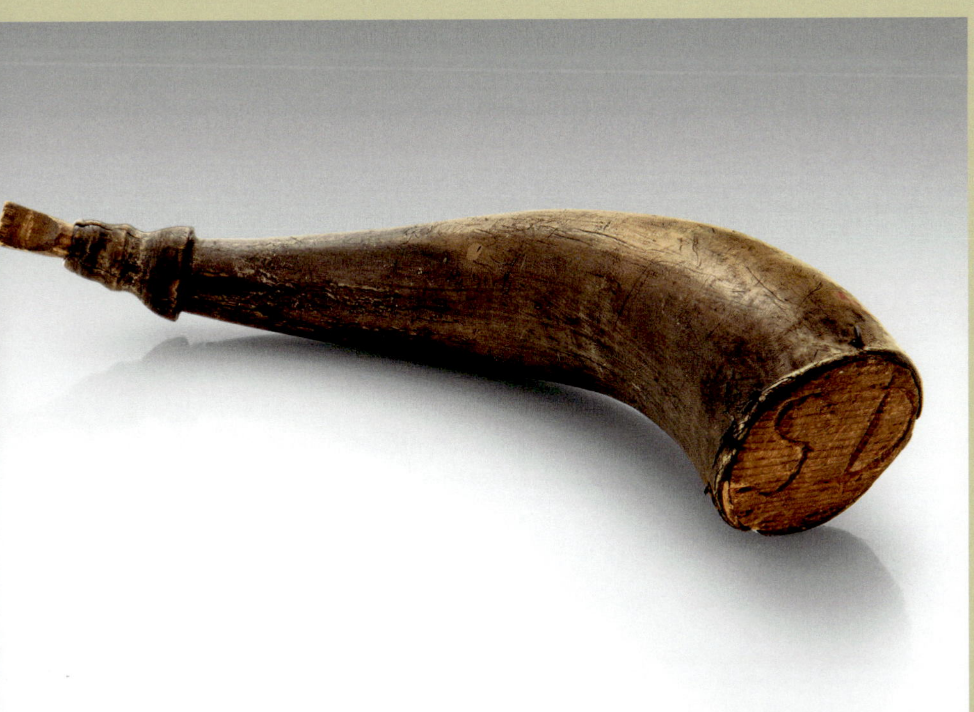

Detail

28. POWDER HORN OF SAMUEL DAKIN

Lincoln, Massachusetts, 1750–1770
Horn, pine
Length: 8¼"; Width: 2"
Gift of Cummings E. Davis. A300

Tolman 1911, 509: "SMALL POWDER HORN. Samuel Dakin, 1775."

company and John Buttrick, Jr. in David Brown's company. Fifers, though generally privates, received the pay of corporals, reflecting the importance of their function, although, like drummers, they went into action unarmed.

While the minutemen went out to meet the advancing column of Regulars William Emerson stayed in town with the "alarm Company," Concord's militia companies. *"Capt. Minot who commanded them thought it proper to take Possession of the Hill above the Meeting house as the most advantageous situation."* The "Hill above the Meeting house" is a ridge of terminal moraine left behind by the glacier that had covered the area twelve thousand years ago. It was atop this ridge that a "Liberty Pole" had been erected, though when that happened is not recorded. *"We then retreated from the Hill near Liberty Pole,"* Emerson continued, *"& took a new Post back of ye Town, upon a rising Eminence, where we formed, before we saw ye brittish Troops at ye Distance of ¼ of a Mile, glittering in Arms, advancing toward us with the greatest Celerity."*

A young British officer of the 10th Regiment, Ensign Henry DeBerniere, reported that as the column approached Concord *"the light-infantry marched on the hills that lay the length of the town,"* corroborating what another officer, Lieutenant William Sutherland, reported to General Gage: *"On our approaching Concord we saw upon the height above the Town, what appeared to me to amount to 12 [1,200] or 1500 people, On which we halted a little on this side of the first Bridge to make a Disposition to go up the Hill."*

By *"the first Bridge"* Sutherland meant the bridge over the stream that fed the mill pond in the center of town at the point where it crosses the road to Lexington, just over a mile from the pond. It was this action by the light infantry that dislodged the Concord militia as William Emerson witnessed, though they were far fewer than Lieutenant Sutherland imagined, perhaps no more than 200. *"Some were for making a Stand, notwithstanding the superiority of their Numbers, but others more prudent thought best to retreat till our Strength be equal to the Enemy's, by Recruits from neighboring towns that were continually coming to our Assistance. Accordingly we retreated over the Bridge* [the North Bridge] *when the Troops came in the Town,"* Emerson wrote. The minute companies who had gone out to meet the Regulars did the same, according to Amos Barrett, who recalled *"We marched into town and then over the North Bridge a little more than half a mile and then on a Hill not far from the Bridge whair we could see and hear what was agoing on."*

On our approaching Concord we saw upon the height above the Town, what appeared to me to amount to 12 or 1500 people, On which we halted a little on this side of the first Bridge to make a Disposition to go up the Hill.

— BRITISH LIEUTENANT WILLIAM SUTHERLAND

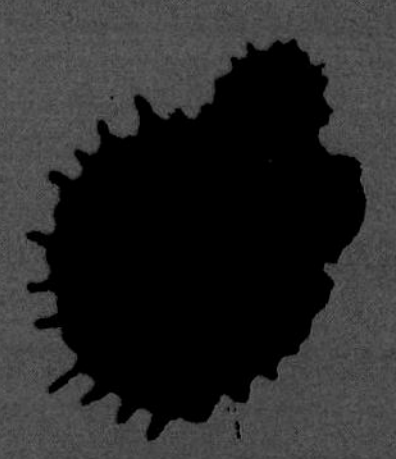

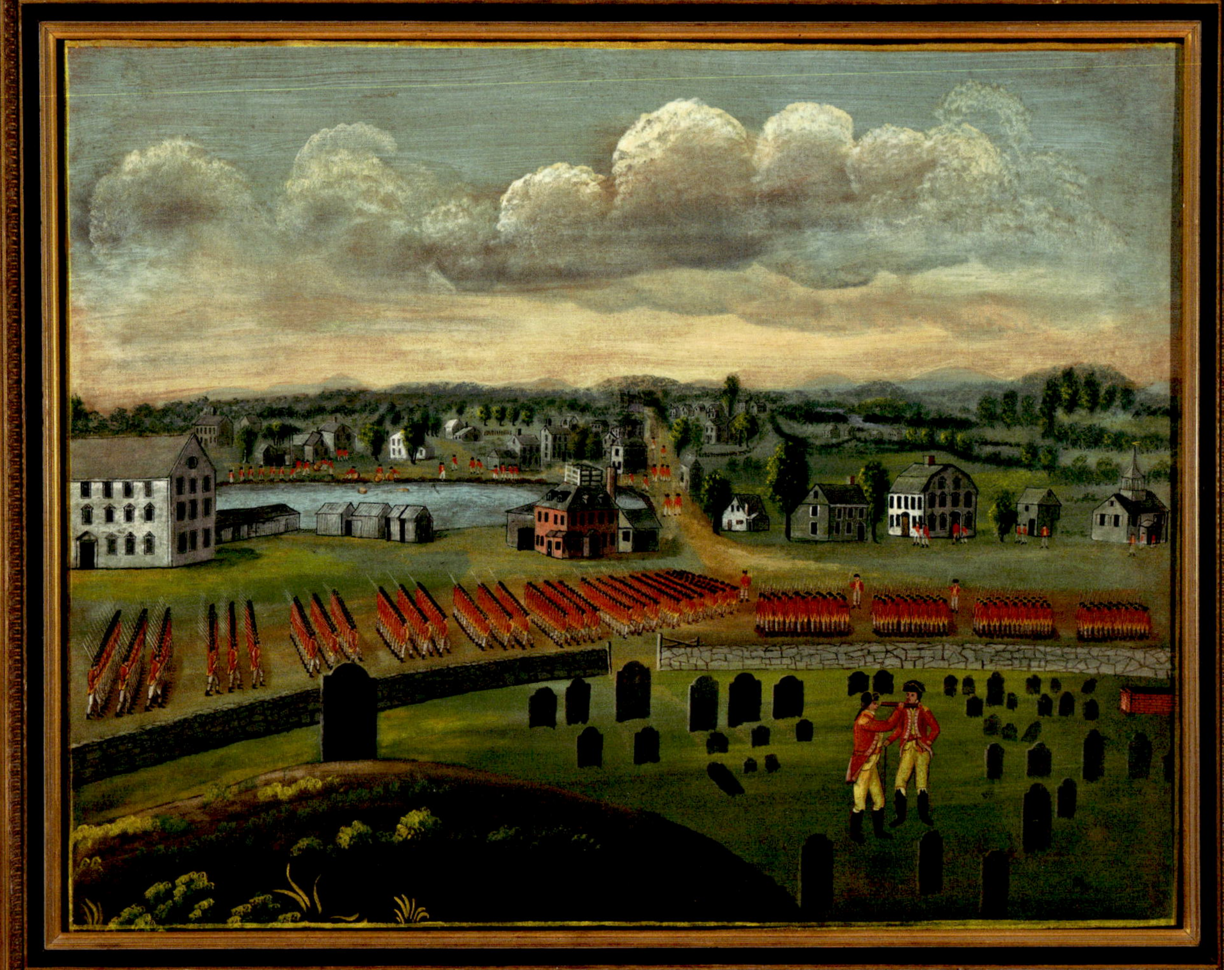

Amos Doolittle's *A View of the Town of Concord*, reproduced in a painting of about 1825, shows the center of town at about 8:30 a.m. when the British column had arrived, and the Provincial forces had moved on to the North Bridge. The painting was for many years attributed to Ralph Earle, the Connecticut artist who provided Amos Doolittle with the topographic views of the April 19 battle that Doolittle engraved. It is now thought to have been painted by ornamental painter Timothy Martin Minot [no. 29].

On the left in the painting is the meeting house; in the center is Mr. Taylor's house, more familiarly known as the Wright Tavern, and between them is the mill pond. On the far right is the town house with a belfry for the church bell that had sounded the alarm. On the far bank of the mill pond a party of grenadiers roll some of the sixty-eight barrels of flour stored in the barns of Ebenezer Hubbard to the water's edge to be "shook out." The grenadiers also found a quantity of cannon balls and threw them in, some of which were recovered sixty years later [no. 30]. In the center of the image is the road leading south. The near end of the road by the Wright Tavern runs along the top of the mill dam that forms the pond; the grist mill can be seen on the right. The soldiers on the road may be some of the company of British grenadiers sent to hold the South Bridge and search for supplies. The house furthest south along the road is the home of Samuel Jones where there were fifty-six barrels of flour stored. Near the grist mill, in the yard of the jail, were three iron cannon, the trunions of which were dutifully knocked off by the members of the artillery company who with their tools had accompanied the raid, although two were later salvaged and repaired. The road to the right leads to the North Bridge; Major Pitcairn with a spyglass is looking at the North Bridge where the militia from surrounding communities continued to increase their numbers. To Major Pitcairn's right is the figure of Lieutenant Colonel Smith. Beyond the figures of the two officers are companies of light infantry drawn up and facing their officers, awaiting orders.

Martha Moulton, a widow of seventy-one years, lived in the gambrel-roofed house two doors from the town house and was a witness when the army *"entered the town, and drawed up in form before the door of the house where I live; and there they continued on the green, feeding their horses within five feet of the door."* The house Martha Moulton lived in was that of Doctor Timothy Minot, the father of the painter Timothy Martin Minot who may not have been at home at the time. In a petition for a pension Mrs. Moulton recorded fetching water for some of the men and *"chairs for Major Pitcairn and four or five more officers, who sat at the door viewing their men… when all on a sudden they had set fire to the great gun carriages just by the house, and while they were in flames your petitioner saw smoke arise out of the Town House higher than the ridge of the house."*

The supplies for the army of fifteen thousand that General Gage knew to be stored in Concord were to be utterly destroyed, with particular care paid to the especially dangerous cannon. Colonel Smith's orders from General Gage had been detailed:

> You have a Draught [map] of Concord, on which is marked the Houses, Barns, &c., which contain the above military Stores [ammunition, provisions, artillery, tents, and small arms]. You will order a Trunion [an axle that attaches the gun tube to the carriage] to be knocked off each Gun, but if it is found impracticable on any, they must be spiked [the touchhole for the fuse disabled], and the Carriages destroyed. The Powder [gunpowder] and flower [flour] must be shaken out of the Barrels into the River, the Tents burnt, Pork or Beef destroyed in the best way you can devise. And the Men may put Balls of lead in their pockets, throwing them by degrees into Ponds, Ditches &c., but no Quantity together, so that they may be recovered afterwards. If you meet any Brass Artillery, you will order their muzzles to be beat in so as to render them useless.

Ensign Henry DeBerniere of the 10th Regiment in a report to General Gage noted that *"Capt. Parsons of the 10th, was dispatched with six light-companies to take possession of a bridge that lay three quarters of a mile from Concord, and I was ordered to shew him the road there, and also to conduct him to a house where there was some cannon and other stores hid."* It was Ensign DeBerniere who provided the draught, or map, that General Gage cited in the orders for the expedition. DeBerniere had in February scouted the area west of Boston as far as Worcester for General Gage, creating a map on that occasion, and returned in March to map the exact locations of the supplies that the Committee of Safety was stockpiling in Concord. DeBerniere had good inside information on those locations, provided in part by Dr. Benjamin Church, a member of the Committee of Safety who was being paid by General Gage for information. The first draft of General Gage's orders for the expedition refers to *"Four Brass Cannon and two Mortars or Cohorns with*

England, 1755–1775
Iron
Left: Diameter: 9¼″ (three pound)
M409
Right: Diameter: 11¼″ (six pound)
Gift of Cummings E. Davis. M410

Two cast-iron cannon balls recovered from the mill pond in the center of Concord in 1835, one weighing three pounds and one weighing six pounds, were unquestionably part of the material gathered by the Committee of Supplies. The balls are neatly finished and are almost certainly of English manufacture. They were cast in a two-part mold; the casting seam is just visible on one of them. Henry Thoreau recorded in a journal entry the recovery of three more cannon balls from the mill pond in 1857.

Tolman 1911, 30–31: **"TWO REVOLUTIONARY CANNON BALLS, thrown into the mill pond by the British soldiers, April 19, 1775, and recovered by Cyrus Stow about 1835."**

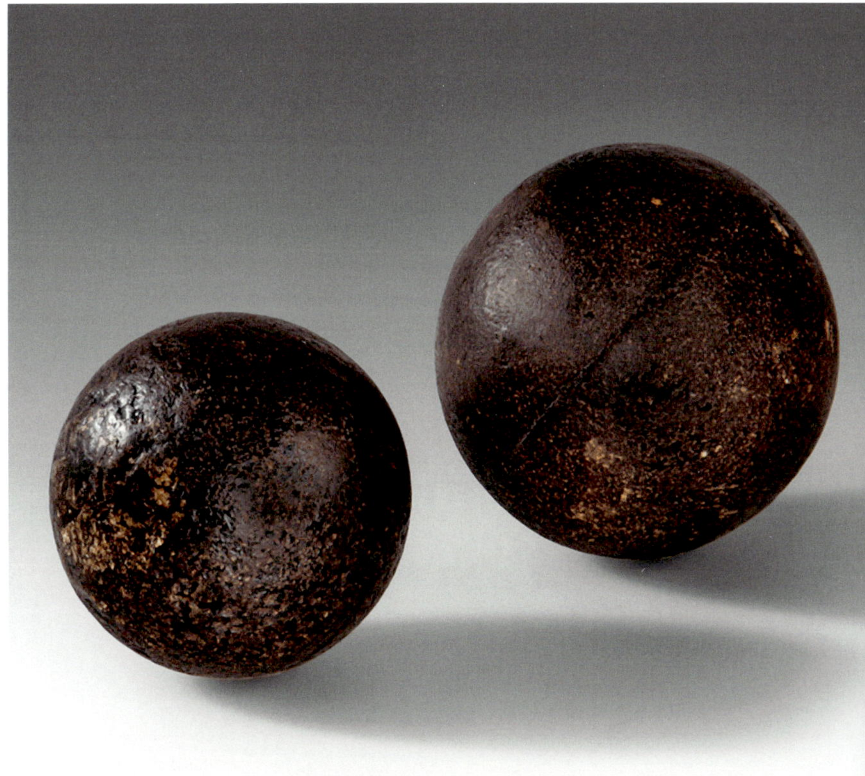

a Number of small arms in the cellar or out Houses of Mr. Barrett a little on the other side the Bridge where is also lodged a Quantity of Powder & Lead," intelligence that apparently came from DeBerniere.

The intelligence was good, but not perfect. Ensign DeBerniere had last visited Concord on March 20, 1775. On April 5, the same day that the Provincial Congress ordered the printing of *Rules and Regulations for the Massachusetts Army,* the Committees of Safety and Supplies, meeting in Concord, ordered an *"exact account in writing, of all the provisions and stores, and the places of their disposition."* Over the next two weeks the places of disposition for the provisions, like flour and rice, and for the military stores changed. On April 18 the committees voted for the relocation out of Concord of hundreds of barrels of provisions, including beef, flour, rice, molasses, and rum. The committees also voted to relocate thousands of iron pots, wooden bowls, spoons, and canteens, as well as two thirds of the *"spades, pick-axes, bill-hooks, shovels, axes, hatchets, crows, and wheelbarrows, now at Concord."*

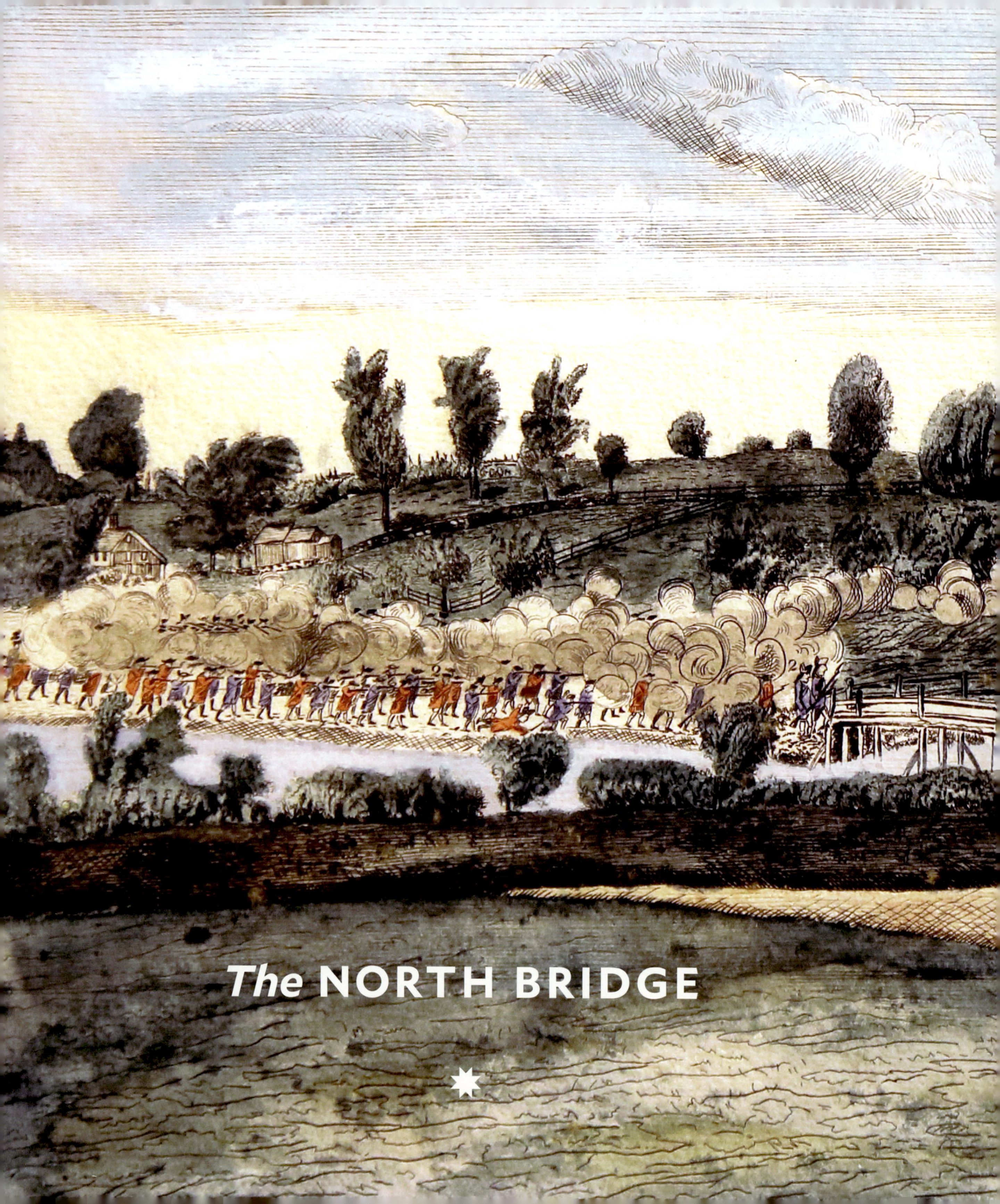

The NORTH BRIDGE

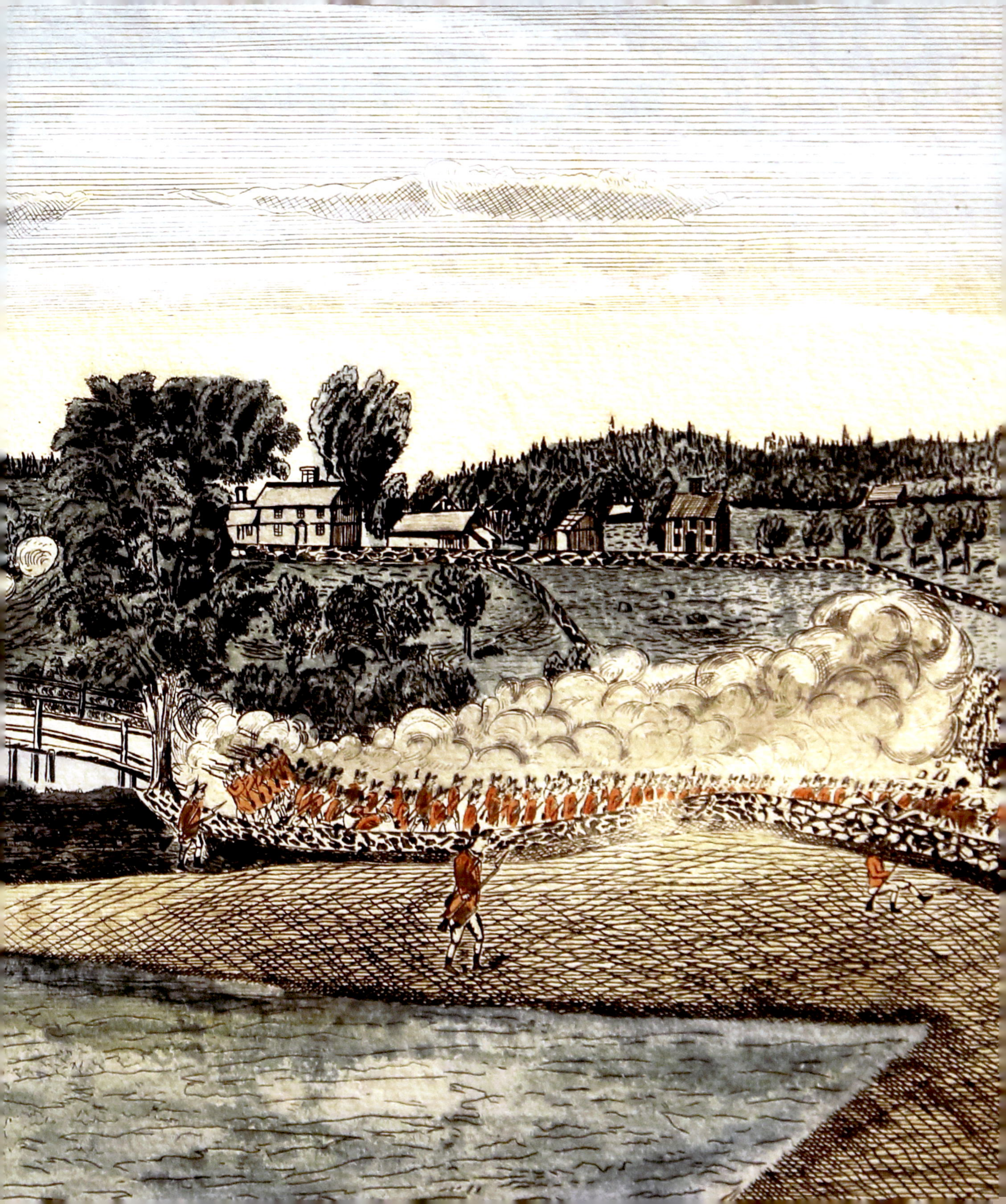

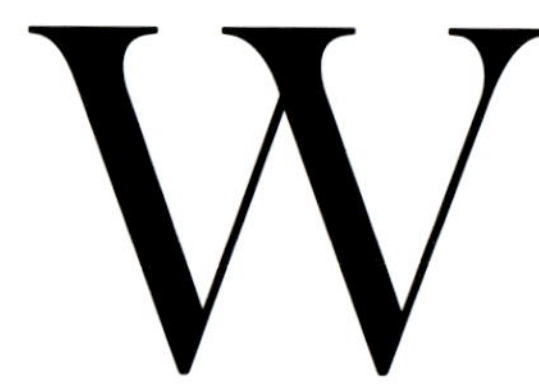

W*hen we arrived at the bridge,"* DeBerniere reported, referring to the North Bridge, *"three companies under the command of Capt. [Laurie] of the 43d, were left to protect it, these three companies were not close together, but situated so as to be able to support each other; we then proceeded to Col. Barrett's where these stores were."*

The North Bridge crosses the Concord River about three quarters of a mile north and west of the center of Concord [no. 31]. From the 1650s to the 1790s this was the main route leading west of town, the old Groton road. Colonel James Barrett's house was about two miles west of the bridge on the Groton road. This is what brought six companies of British Regulars to the North Bridge on April 19, with three of the companies proceeding over it to the Barrett house and three of them remaining on the west side in defense.

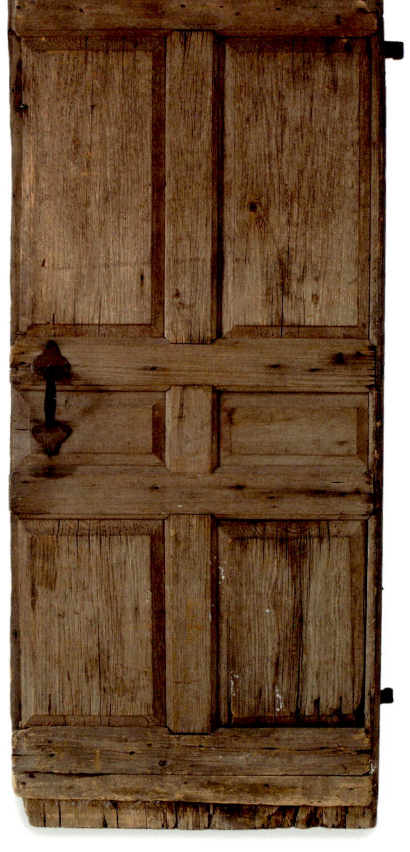

Colonel James Barrett was not at home when the three companies of light infantry arrived there but was with the hundreds of Provincial soldiers who continued to gather in response to the spreading alarm and were now on Punkatasset Hill half a mile from the North Bridge. The colonel's wife, however, was at home. The James Barrett house was built in about 1705 and a surviving door appears to be part of a major renovation undertaken about 1760 [no. 32]. It is the exterior door to a kitchen ell added to the west side of the house, and it was to this door, not the front door, that the Regulars came. Rebecca Barrett (1717–1806), who was fifty-seven in 1775, left no first-person account of what it was like to open the door and see 100 soldiers with fixed bayonets in the yard. Something very like the violence that Colonel Barrett had been stockpiling tons of supplies for since the previous fall had come home to Concord. One or more of the Barretts' children may have been at home, and fourteen-year-old Philip, who was enslaved in the household, may have been as well. All had probably been engaged for the past day and night in removing stored material to other locations; Rebecca Barrett knew precisely what the soldiers were there for.

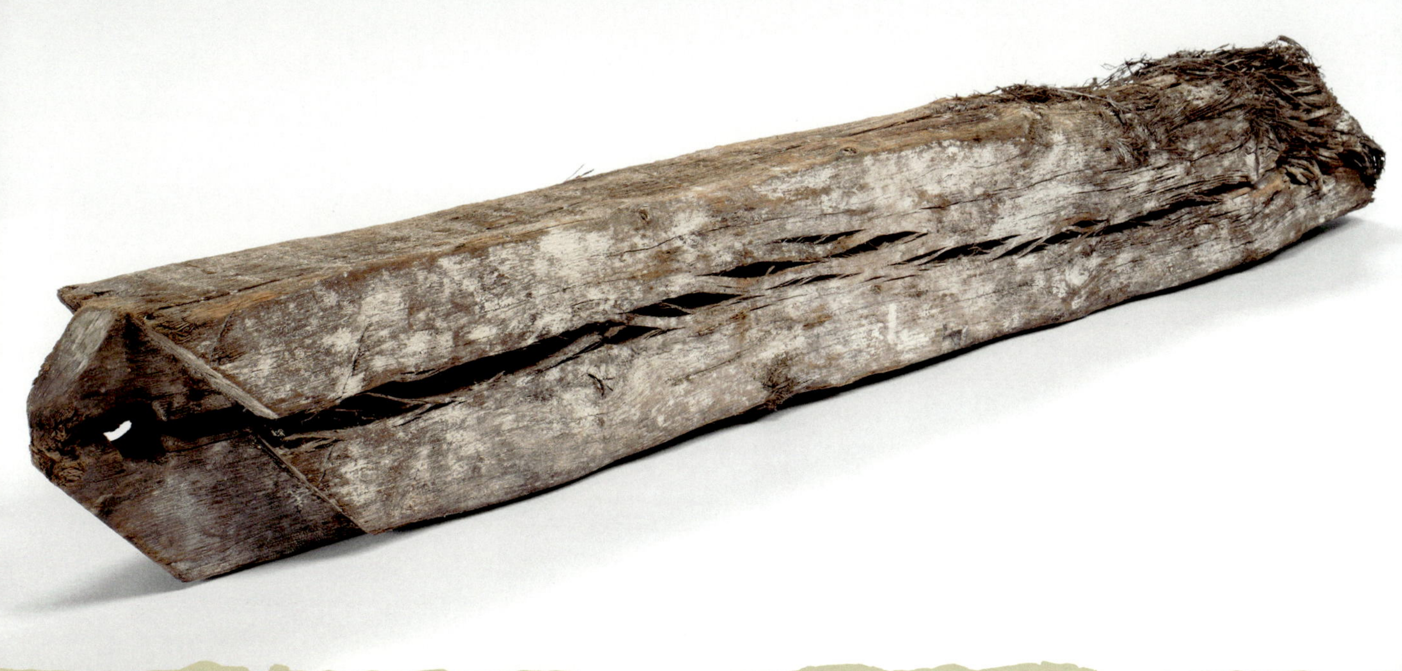

31. DIAGONAL BRACE FROM THE NORTH BRIDGE

Concord, Massachusetts, about 1760
Oak
Length: 53½"; Width: 5¾"; Depth: 6⅝"
Gift of the Town of Concord. M2130.3

Bridges, like boats, are in constant need of maintenance and the North Bridge was replaced several times over the 150 years of its active use. The bridge depicted in Amos Doolittle's view of the engagement at the North Bridge was built in 1760. One rod (sixteen feet) wide and 100 feet long, the *"rude bridge"* in fact *"arched the flood"* just as Emerson wrote, being higher in the center than at either end. Three large fragments of structural elements from the North Bridge survive in the Concord Museum collection. They were salvaged from the site in 1956 during construction of the present recreation of the North Bridge. Two of those pieces are cut at one end with tenons indicating that they were used as angled support elements, like the two diagonal braces visible in the Amos Doolittle view. The North Bridge was substantially rebuilt in 1788 then removed entirely to a new position just downstream in 1793. Two men, their names not presently known, who helped build the North Bridge in 1760 were at the time enslaved by members of the Billings family. In 1788, Brister Freeman and Cesar Robbins who had been enslaved and served in the Continental Army, along with two men named Samson and Reuben with no surnames given, worked with Captain David Brown to rebuild the North Bridge as free men.

32. EXTERIOR DOOR OF THE COLONEL JAMES BARRETT HOUSE

Concord, Massachusetts, about 1760
Pine, iron
Height: 70"; Width: 32"
Gift of the Medford Historical Society.
2018.7.1

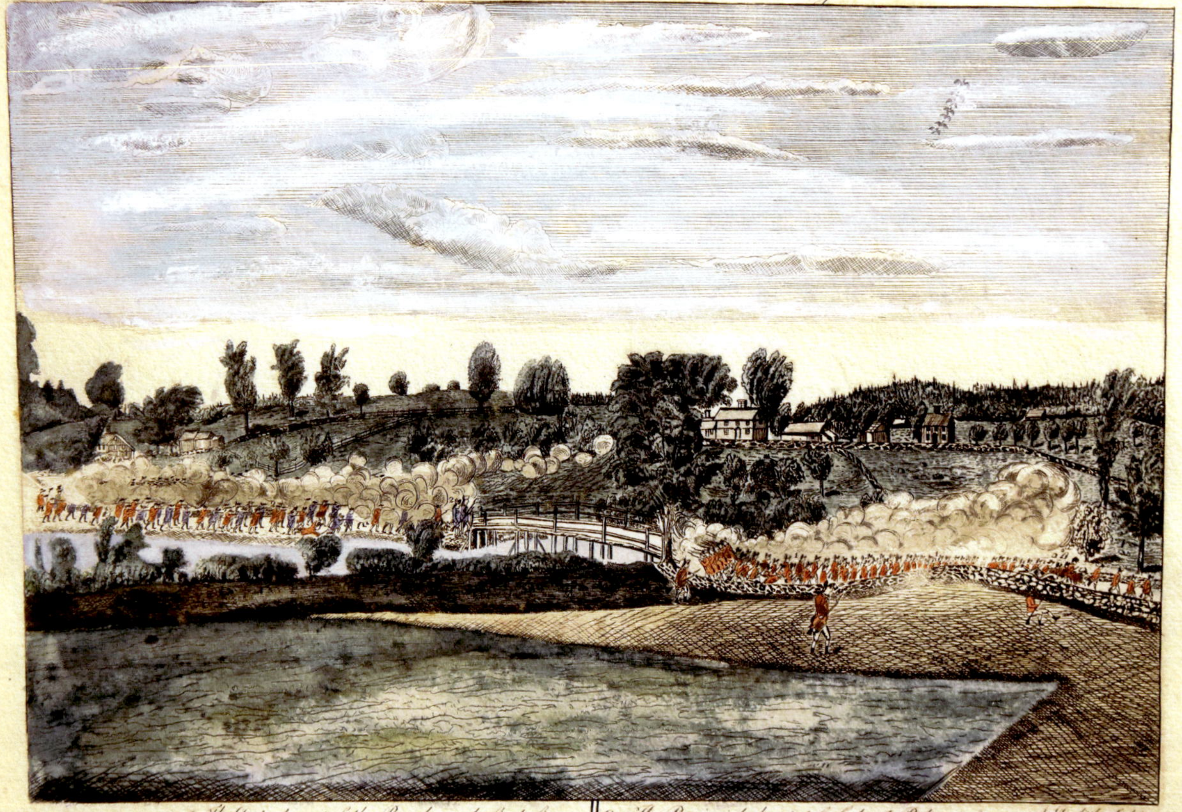

1 The Detachment of the Regulars who fired first on the Provincials at the Bridge
2 The Provincials headed by Colonel Robinson & Major Buttrick 3 The Bridge

A. Doolittle Sculpt.

The British Regulars searched the Barrett property but as Ensign DeBerniere noted *"we did not find so much as we expected."* They had expected to find four iron cannon that fired six-pound balls, but the Committee of Safety meeting in Concord on April 17 had *"Voted, That the four six pounders be transported to Groton, and put under the care of Col. Prescott."* The Regulars may have expected to find a quantity of gunpowder that Colonel Barrett had been asked on April 14 to make into cartridges for the cannon, but that probably had not yet arrived. They also may have expected to find *"a ton of musket balls now arrived at Concord"* that the Committee of Safety voted on March 23 *"be there lodged with Col. Barrett"* and on April 18 voted *"be buried under ground, in some safe place."* The raiding expedition, much as Paul Revere had predicted the night before, seemed to *"miss their Aim."*

While the companies of British Regulars searched the Barrett property, the Acton minute company, responding to the alarm delivered by Samuel Prescott, nearly encountered them on their way to Concord. The Acton minutemen had been paid to drill twice a week since January. As Reverend Webster had warned the Groton minute companies in February, if conflict came, they would be facing the Regulars, professional soldiers who trained constantly. The captain of the Acton company was Isaac Davis, a blacksmith then thirty years old. Davis's company, having evaded the Regulars, returned to the road that led to the North Bridge which they reached at about 9 a.m.

Amos Doolittle depicted the military engagement at the North Bridge in a view looking west [no. 33]. In the foreground is the newly plowed field of Concord minister William Emerson. All three companies of British Regulars are present at the moment Doolittle portrays on the east side of the bridge but a few minutes earlier they had been on the west side. The company from the 4th Regiment was on the high ground around the home of David Brown on the far left [nos. 34, 35]. The company from the 43rd Regiment was near the west end of the bridge and the company from the 10th Regiment was not far away on the right, near the home of John Buttrick that shows prominently on the horizon above the east end of the bridge.

British Captain Laurie described the scene: *"I saw their whole body Moving towards me, and as they came nearer the Light Compy of the 4th. Regt. posted on a height immediately retreated to me at the Bridge, as did likewise the Lt. Compy of the 10th. Regt. who also had been at no great distance."*

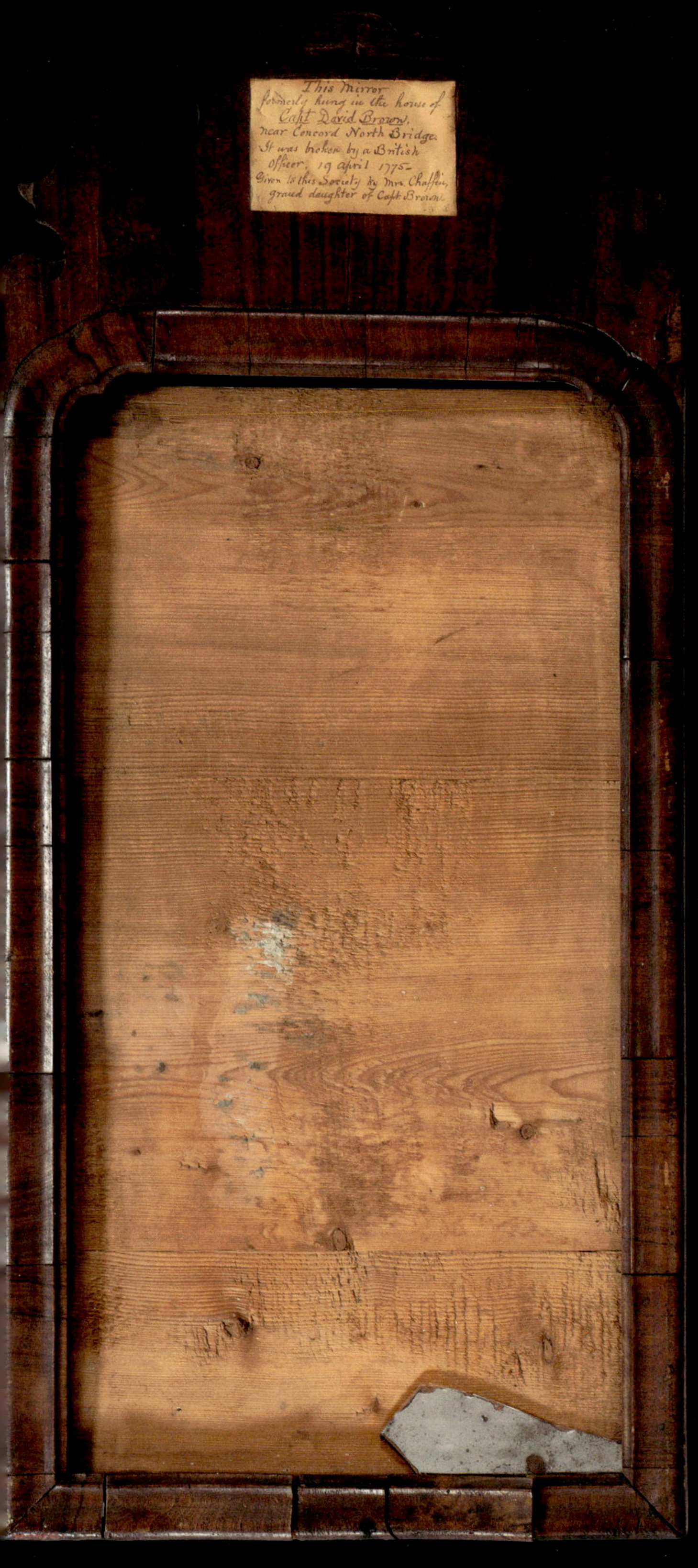

34. LOOKING GLASS FROM THE HOME OF CAPTAIN DAVID BROWN

England, about 1770
Walnut veneer, pine, mirrored glass
Height: 31⅜"; Width: 14⅝"
Gift of Mrs. Chaffin. M401

A paper label glued to the crest in the nineteenth century reads: *"This Mirror / formerly hung in the house of / Capt David Brown, / near Concord North Bridge: / It was broken by a British / officer, 19 April 1775 – / Given to this Society by Mrs. Chaffin, / grand daughter of Capt. Brown."*

The home of David Brown, captain of one of Concord's minute companies, may be seen on the left in Amos Doolittle's engraving of the engagement at the North Bridge. It was located on the western shore of the Concord River, on the road that led to James Barrett's house. The light infantry company of the 4th Regiment posted themselves around the house awaiting further developments before being ordered back to the east side of the North Bridge just before the firing began. In the interim, someone smashed David Brown's looking glass. A Brown family tradition that the damage was the result of good-natured scuffling on the part of two officers is not plausible; it was instead a casual act of vandalism of a sort repeated many times that day. A quick stroke of the butt of a firearm cost David Brown the equivalent of a month's wages. Imported looking glasses like this one were readily available for sale in Boston. Their value did not lie in the walnut-veneered frame but in the glass (one fragment remains), which had to be polished to a perfect flatness before being silvered. The technology to do that was not available in America in the mid-eighteenth century. The last image the intact glass reflected would have been that of a member of the 4th Regiment.

Tolman 1911, 353: "MIRROR, broken by a British officer in the house of Capt. David Brown on the morning of April 19, 1775. Presented by his granddaughter, Mrs. Chaffin, of Acton."

35. LOOKING GLASS THAT BELONGED TO CASE FEEN

England and America, eighteenth century
Glass, painted pine
Height: 7⅝"; Width: 6⅝"; Depth: ⅝"
Gift of Cummings E. Davis. F2521

The frame of this looking glass that once reflected the image of Case Whitney is probably American and the glass probably English. The glass was re-silvered at some time in the nineteenth century, a coating that has since failed, and at that time was re-backed with a recycled page from a copy book.

Henry Thoreau knew George and Mary Minot, from whom Cummings Davis apparently acquired the looking glass, and from the Minots learned some of the history of Whitney (later going by Feen), a former Continental soldier. Five feet five inches tall and with black hair, Case was born in Guinea (on Africa's west coast) about 1744 and was kidnapped into slavery about twenty years later. Casey, as Thoreau spelled the name, would dream of home, and *used to weep in his latter days when he thought of his wife and two children in Africa from whom he was kidnapped.*

Case Whitney, with occupation noted as farmer, enlisted in the Continental Army in 1781. The Whitney surname comes from Samuel Whitney, muster master of Concord's militia, in whose household the enlistee was enslaved. It is likely that Case Whitney was at the North Bridge with Samuel Whitney, and with the other militia and minutemen would have lined up, changed flints, marched down to the North Bridge, and fired when ordered to. In subsequent military records Case took the surname Feen. Case Feen returned to Concord after service in the Continental Army. Case Whitney, the name Case Whitney bore before 1781, was listed as a single head of household in the 1790 Concord census; in the 1800 census the name was given as Case with no surname. In 1816 Case, again with no surname indicated, was in need of assistance from the town for subsistence, care which was provided initially by Cesar Robbins, who like Case was almost certainly at the North Bridge and was also enslaved. The care was later provided by Jack Garrison, the son-in-law of Cesar Robbins. Garrison had escaped slavery in New Jersey and come to Concord not long after Case returned from military service. Case died in 1822.

36. PORTRAIT OF JOSEPH HOSMER

Ethan Allen Greenwood (1779–1856)
Concord or Boston, Massachusetts,
1819
Oil on canvas
Height: 23⅛"; Width: 19½"
Gift of descendants of Joseph Hosmer:
Van Sant Hosmer and Susan Hosmer.
2018.1.1

Joseph Hosmer's distinguished record of service to Concord and to Massachusetts includes serving on Concord's committee of correspondence. Hosmer rose in service to become captain of the Concord Light Infantry and afterward rising to the rank of major. Hosmer was elected a representative for Concord in the General Court and for fourteen years was sheriff of Middlesex County. Ethan Allen Greenwood, a prolific itinerant painter, painted the aging Joseph Hosmer in 1819. The painting descended in Hosmer's family for six generations before being made a gift to the Concord Museum.

Captain Laurie seems to be describing the approach of the companies from Concord, Bedford, and Lincoln that had been on Punkatasset Hill half a mile away and now drew up in a field just west of the North Bridge and overlooking it. They were soon joined by the Acton minute company. As the companies arrived, they were organized by Lieutenant Joseph Hosmer who had been appointed adjutant, which is an officer assigned to communicate between officers and soldiers [no. 36].

Joseph Hosmer began forming the arriving companies into two lines in the field above the bridge that has come to be called the Musterfield, with minutemen in one line and militia in the other. The senior officers, including Colonel John Robinson (1735–1805) from Westford and Colonel Barrett of Concord, gathered to confer. Concerned that the Provincials were going to attack, Captain Laurie sent for reinforcements from Colonel Smith who in response sent two companies of grenadiers toward the North Bridge. *"By this time the Body of the Country people,"* Laurie continued, *"arrived on the heights, which the Company of the 4th Regt. had occupied, and there drew up with Shouldered Arms to the Number of about Fifteen hundred."* Laurie's official report and perhaps perception as well multiplied the number of Provincial soldiers present by about four.

Before they shouldered their arms, the Provincial soldiers had gotten another order, probably from Lieutenant Hosmer, to change their flints. The order is not recorded in any of the written accounts of the events that transpired at the North Bridge but is documented solely by artifactual evidence. In the fall of 1934 local avocational archaeologist Benjamin Lincoln Smith walked over the Musterfield, which had recently been plowed for the first time in years, hoping to find Indigenous archaeological items. Instead Smith found seven gun flints [no. 37]. The next day, after a heavy rain, *"Gun flints seemed to be everywhere,"* Smith later wrote in an address delivered at the North Bridge in 1961, *"and they stood out against the dark, wet ground like glittering jewels."* Smith found them *"in two long lines about fifty feet apart and running Northeast to Southwest across the slope of the hillside, roughly facing the North Bridge roadway."*

The meaning of the discovery was evident. After being formed in lines, in nearly unobstructed view of the companies of Regulars, the Provincial soldiers, formed up in two lines, had changed their flints. Flints are a necessary part of the ignition system of a flintlock musket,

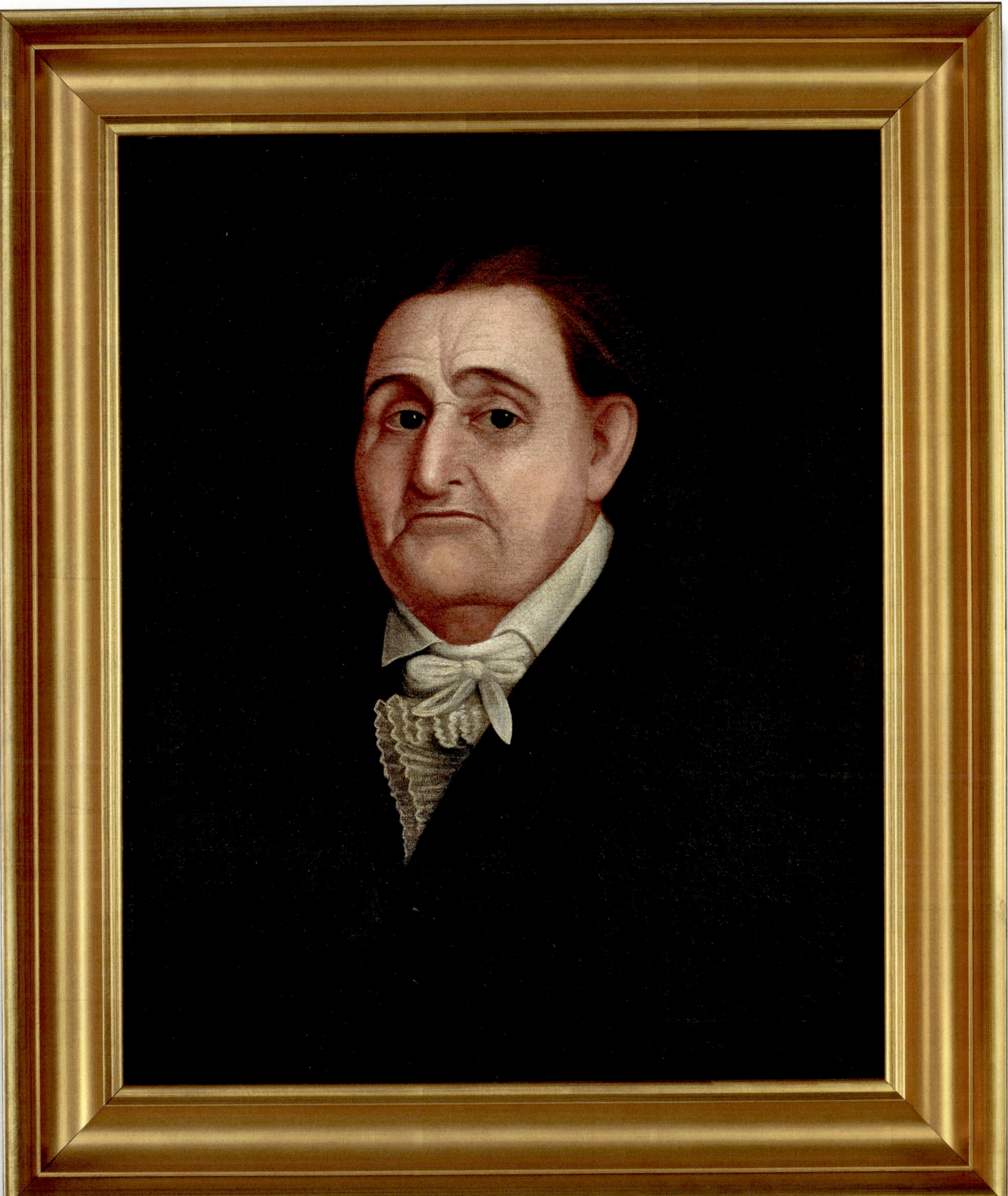

37. GUN FLINTS

England and possibly France,
1770–1775
Flint
Width: approximately 1⅓"
Concord Museum collection, Gift of
Mrs. Frederick Mears, in memory of
Frederick Mears; Bequest of Benjamin
Lincoln Smith. M412, M2263, M2279

which is what both the Regulars and the Provincials carried. They produce a shower of sparks when the trigger is pulled and the hammer falls, and the sparks ignite the gunpowder that propels the lead bullet out of the barrel. The more a flint is used the less efficient it becomes at creating sparks, and misfires become more likely. Installing fresh flints to improve their weapons' ability to fire was about as audacious and provocative an action as the minutemen and militia could well have performed.

Captain Nathan Barrett testified that it was the smoke that the Provincial forces could all plainly see rising from the town that caused them to act: *"We then, seeing several fires in the town, thought our houses were in danger and immediately marched back towards* [the] *bridge."* Joseph Hosmer is credited with asking the conferring officers, *"Will you let them burn the town down?"* The smoke was rising from the fire at the town house that Martha Moulton managed to get extinguished, as well as a fire at the shop of saddler Reuben Brown and the burning Liberty Pole just above Brown's house on the ridge overlooking the center of town. The order to march came from Nathan Barrett's senior officer (and father) James Barrett: *"I ordered said militia to march to said bridge and pass the same, but not to fire on the King's troops unless they were first fired upon."*

Captain Laurie reported that when the Provincial companies *"then moved down upon me in a Seeming regular manner … I determined to repass the Bridge with the three Companys, retreating by Division to check their progress, which we accordingly did."* On the east side of the bridge the British Regulars formed into the column that Amos Doolittle depicted, with the 4th Regiment company at the front.

Laurie's comment on the *"Seeming regular manner"* with which the Provincials moved was echoed by others. *"The Rebels begun their march from the hill we before had retired from with as much order as the best disciplined troops,"* Ensign Jeremy Lister of the 10th Regiment later recalled. Lieutenant Sutherland of the 38th Regiment also reported that the Provincial companies came down *"in a very Military manner."* The months of intensive training that the minute companies had undertaken had been effective.

"We then want loded," Corporal Amos Barrett recalled, *"we was all orded to Load and had strickd orders not to fire till they fird firs, then to fire as fast as we could — we then marched on."* [no. 38]

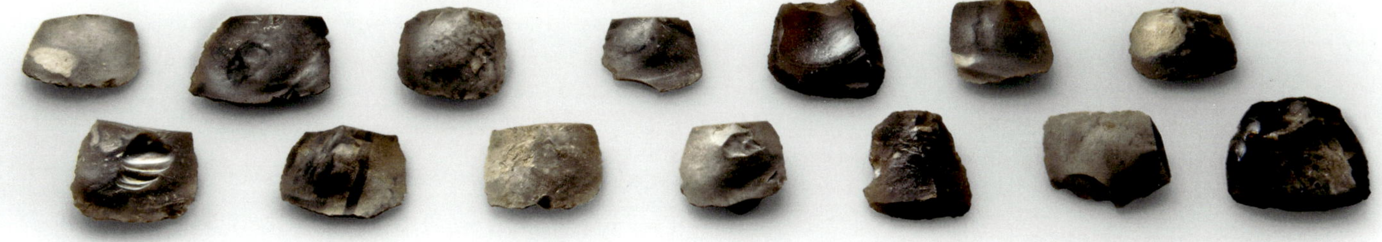

38. NINE-ROUND CARTRIDGE BOX

England, 1765–1770
Leather, pine
Dimensions not recorded
Gift of Cummings E. Davis. A400

Loading a flintlock firearm was more quickly accomplished with the use of paper cartridges, also called cartouches. Cartridges are paper tubes with the ball at one end and the pre-measured powder behind with the open end twisted shut. In use the cartridge would be torn open and the powder poured down the barrel, followed by the ball. All the British Regulars were provided with carriers for cartridges, either pouches worn over the shoulder or boxes worn around the waist. Pouches and boxes could carry between eighteen and thirty rounds.

A 1771 British Army ordinance called for nine-round boxes to be carried by light infantry soldiers and one such box was recovered after the Concord fight. In 1856 Henry Thoreau gave this box to Cummings Davis for Davis's collection of historic Concord items, and in 1861 mentioned it in a journal passage that laments the loss of an ancient tree in the center of town: "*We cut down the few old oaks which witnessed the transfer of the township from the Indian to the white man and commence our museum with a cartridge-box taken from a British soldier in 1775!*" Thoreau's phrase "*taken from a British soldier*" suggests the possibility that it came from a wounded soldier. The cartridge box disappeared from the Concord Museum in about 1973.

Tolman 1911, 502: "BRITISH CARTRIDGE BOX OF 1775. Presented by Henry D Thoreau to C. E. Davis."

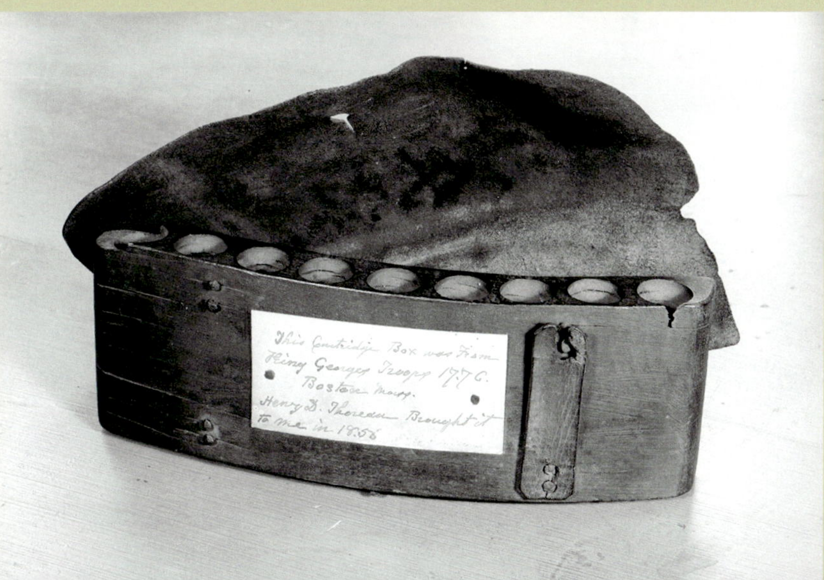

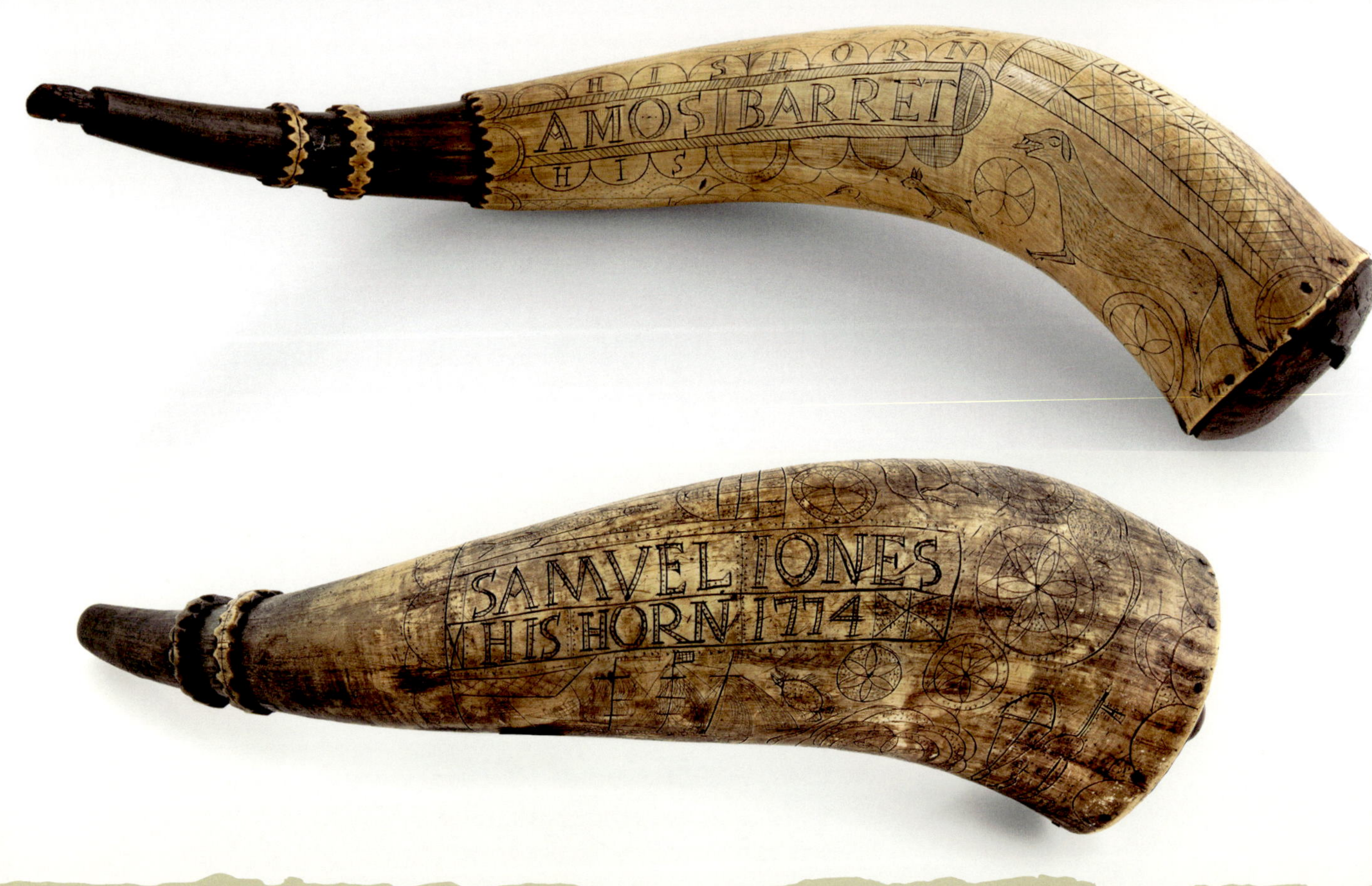

39. POWDER HORN OF AMOS BARRETT

Carving attributed to Samuel Jones (1741–1812)

Concord, Massachusetts, 1775

Horn, pine

Length: 15⅞"; Width: 3⅛"

Gift of Frederick S. Richardson, Peter H. Richardson, and Joan R. Fay. 1994.63

Engraved: *"HIS HORN / AMOS BARRET / HIS"; "APRIL XIX"; "1775"*

40. POWDER HORN OF SAMUEL JONES

Carving attributed to Samuel Jones (1741–1812)

Concord, Massachusetts, 1774

Horn

Length: 13⅛"; Width: 3⅜"

Gift of Cummings E. Davis. A101

Engraved: *"SAMUEL JONES / HIS HORN 1774"* and on the reverse in a small reserve *"SI"*

To carry out the order to load Amos Barrett used a powder horn, pouring a measured amount down the barrel and a little more in the pan on the lock [no. 39]. Powder horns were made of water-resistant cow horn and were worn over one shoulder suspended by a strap. A tab for attaching the strap to the broad end of the horn has been removed from the Barrett horn but may have been present on April 19.

Samuel Jones also used a powder horn to follow the order to load [no. 40]. A member of one of the two Concord militia companies, Samuel Jones was a blacksmith. Although most soldiers did not engrave their own powder horns Samuel Jones may have been an exception. The horn Jones used is competently but not professionally engraved, something a blacksmith might have the tools and skills to accomplish, and in addition to the full name bears the initials of the owner. The redundant initials can be read as a signature. In addition to taking up arms on April 19, Samuel Jones had fifty-six barrels of flour stored at home which the raiding party did not discover.

The muskets that the Provincial soldiers loaded were their own for the most part and they varied in age, origin, and caliber more than the weapons carried by the British Army. Many of them were the long-barreled "fowlers" favored by New England farmers for hunting.

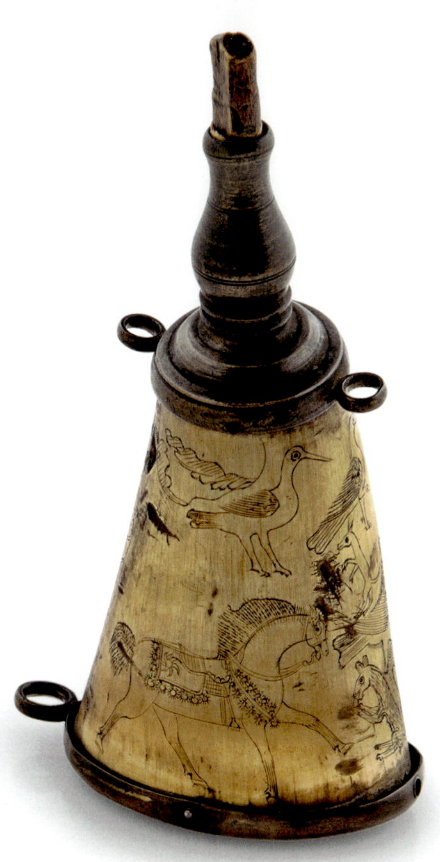

41. POWDER HORN OF STEPHEN PARKS

Horn and mounts probably
England, 1690–1710
Engraving attributed to
Stephen Parks (b. 1721)
Concord, 1747
Horn, bronze
Length: 6½"; Width: 3¹¹⁄₁₆"
Gift of Cummings E. Davis. A102

Number 137 of the five hundred or so watercolors of American engraved powder horns by Rufus Grider (1817–1900) now at the New York Historical Society depicts both sides of the Stephen Parks horn. An inscription on the drawing reads *"The/ CONCORD BRIDGE/ Powder Horn."* It is not clear what Rufus Grider heard about the horn that would account for the identification with the North Bridge fight. In 1890 when Grider drew the horn Cummings Davis had already died, so it was presumably George Tolman who provided the information. The exact connection is lost but there were seven members of the Parks family at the North Bridge on April 19, among them Willard Parks, the son of Stephen.

The horn is inscribed *"JOSEPH GAR/ GIFT TO/ STEPHEN/ PARKS"* Nothing is known about Joseph Gar but Stephen Parks lived in a part of Concord that in 1754 became part of Lincoln. One way to read the inscription would be that Joseph Gar gave Stephen Parks an undecorated small priming or flask horn, and Parks engraved it with birds and beasts and the dedicatory inscription.

Tolman 1911, 510: **"SMALL POWDER HORN. Parks, of Lincoln."**

42. POWDER HORN OF STEPHEN PARKS

Engraving attributed to
Stephen Parks (b. 1721)
Concord, Massachusetts, about 1747
Horn
Length: 13⁹⁄₁₆"; Width: 2¹⁵⁄₁₆"
Gift of the Cummings Davis Society,
The Philip and Betsey C. Caldwell
Foundation, Mr. Charles N. Grichar,
and an anonymous donor. 2007.266

A substantial group of powder
horns dated to the 1740s that seem
to represent the first generation of
American engraved military powder
horns are engraved by the same hand
as the 1747 horn, including another
undated but contemporary horn also
owned by Stephen Parks. Prominently
engraved on this horn is a double
standing portrait of the Duke and
Duchess of Cumberland. The Duke of
Cumberland played a prominent role
in suppressing the 1745 Scottish
rebellion at the Battle of Culloden and
was consequently a military hero in
England. The story of this distinctive
group of powder horns has yet to be
fully told but it seems that Stephen
Parks should be given credit for the
innovations in decoration they intro-
duce, some of which were picked up
and modified by later horn engravers.

43. FOWLING PIECE

Worcester County, possibly
Marlborough, Massachusetts,
about 1760
Steel, cherry, brass
Overall Length: 71"; Width: 5¹⁄₁₆";
Barrel Length: 55"; Bore: ⅝"
(about .64 caliber)
Gift of Dr. Benjamin Ferris, Jr.
A2210

This fowling piece was converted to
percussion ignition in the nineteenth
century, then reconverted back to
flintlock using an ill-fitting lock
by the Ketland firm of gunsmiths.
Engraved on a silver wristplate is
"R. Chaffin," probably for Robert
Chaffin of Acton.

44. TRADE GUN

Possibly London, England, 1730–1760
Walnut, iron, cast and engraved
brass sideplate
Overall Length: 69"; Width: 5";
Barrel Length: 53½"; Bore: 1¹⁄₁₆"
(about .69 caliber)
Gift of Cummings E. Davis.
M400a2

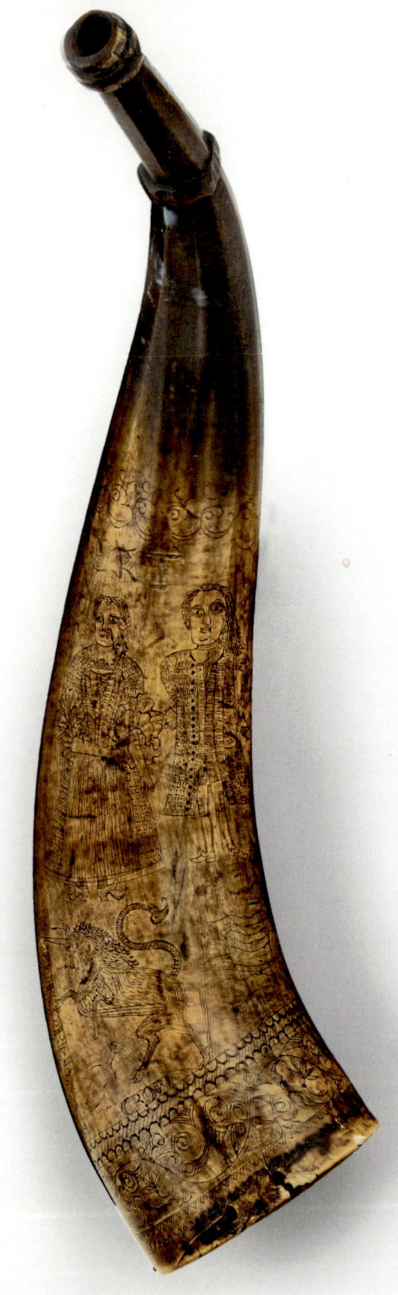

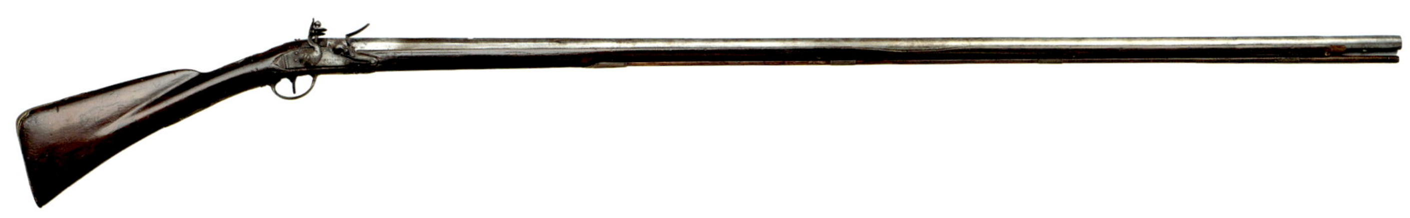

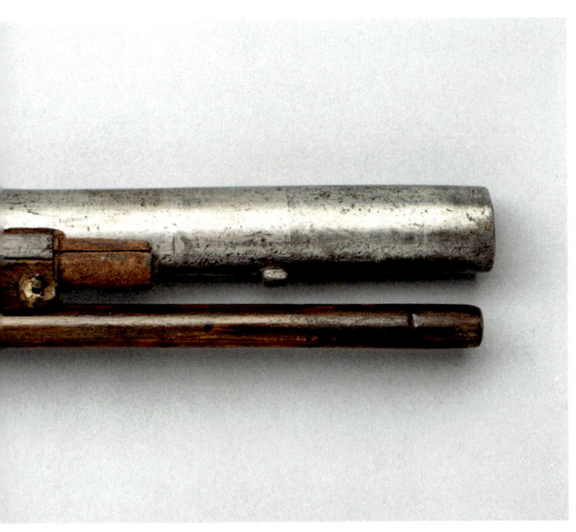

Detail

A fowling piece survives with a history of use at the North Bridge by Ezekiel Davis, brother of Captain Isaac Davis and a member of the Acton minute company [no. 43]. Originally it was a firearm of the type now known as Worcester County fowlers, arms produced through the middle of the eighteenth century by such makers as Barnabas Mathis of Marlborough, Massachusetts. Though many of its details such as the carefully molded stock and the intricately modelled trigger guard have worn nearly away through constant use, it was once a fine piece. The fowler bears a significant mark that speaks to the historic moment; it is fitted with a bayonet lug [detail]. Bayonets were an integral part of organized combat in the eighteenth century but had no place in the civilian world. Militia members armed themselves with domestic firearms, and fowlers fitted with bayonet lugs indicate use in the militia.

Another fowler fitted with a bayonet lug has an intriguing history, part of which cannot possibly be true. That history states that Abijah Pierce (1727–1800) of Lincoln, recently appointed colonel of the regiment of minutemen that included the Lincoln companies, responded to the April 19 alarm armed only with a "stout cane" and procured the weapon from one of the British Regular soldiers killed at the North Bridge. However, it is not remotely a British military long arm. It is instead a trade gun of the type made in quantity in England for sale to Indigenous and other hunters involved in the American fur trade [no. 44]. The oversized trigger guard, "club butt," and serpentine side plate are characteristic of these relatively cheaply made arms. While perhaps not the "first trophy of the Revolution" as its history excitedly claims it could certainly have been used on April 19, 1775, and may even be the "stout cane" that Colonel Pierce carried from Lincoln to the North Bridge.

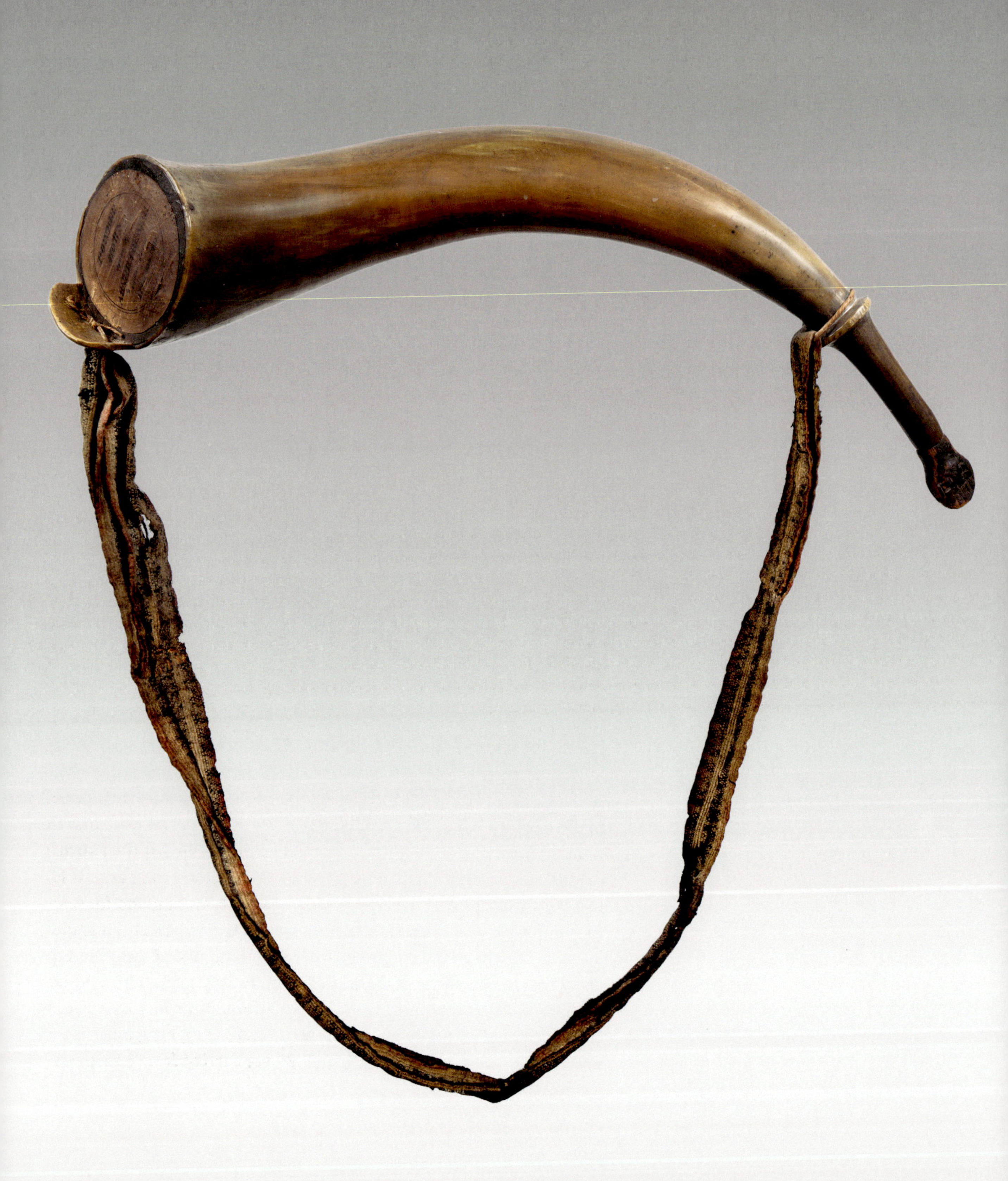

After the Provincial soldiers changed their flints and loaded their firearms they marched down to the North Bridge. *"Capt Davis minit Compney marched first,"* Corporal Amos Barrett recorded, and reported that Captain Davis was about eighty yards from the bridge *"when they fird 3 guns one after the other. I see the balls strike in the River on the Right of me, — as soon as they fird them they fird on us."* Amos Barrett's account agrees with that of Nathan Barrett (a second cousin) who deposed, *"The troops who were stationed there, observing our approach, marched back over the bridge, and then took up some of the planks; we then hastened our steps towards the bridge, and when we had got near the bridge, they fired on our men, first, three guns, one after the other, and then a considerable number more."*

The importance of only acting defensively, stated in the Suffolk Resolves, reiterated by the Continental Congress in 1774, and repeated emphatically by Reverend William Emerson in the sermon to the troops just a month before, was also stressed at the North Bridge. William Emerson recorded that the Provincial soldiers were *"advancing with Special Orders not to fire upon ye Troops, unless fired upon."* Nathan Barrett also reported *"having orders from our commanding officers not to fire till we were fired upon."*

But they had been fired upon. *"We then was all orded to fire that Could fire and not Kill our own men,"* Amos Barrett wrote. William Emerson left a similar account: *"We received the Fire of the Enemy in 3 several and separate discharges of their Pieces, before it was returned, by our commanding Officer."* The commanding officer at that moment, Colonel Barrett having departed, was Major John Buttrick, whose home is near the center of the Doolittle view of the North Bridge. *"The firing then became general for several minutes,"* William Emerson continued, *"in which Skirmish two were killed on each Side, and several of the Enemy wounded."* Captain Laurie described the Provincial fire as a *"general popping,"* rather than a massed volley.

In the firing at the North Bridge, *"Capt Davis was kild and mr osmore and a number wounded,"* as Amos Barrett wrote. Captain Isaac Davis was one of the highest-ranking American officers killed in the fighting on April 19. "Mr osmore" was Abner Hosmer, a twenty-one-year-old private in Captain Davis's Acton minute company. Abner Hosmer's powder horn was carefully preserved by the family, as the surviving original woven wool strap attests [no. 45]. The horn is undecorated, as most powder horns were, and retains its original tab for securing

---

45. POWDER HORN OF ABNER HOSMER

Acton, Massachusetts, 1745–1755
Horn, pine
Length: 17"; Width: 2¾"
Gift of Miss Elizabeth S. Hosmer.
A2053

A paper label attached to the plug in the nineteenth century reads *"Powder Horn worn by Abner Hosmer April 19 1775."*

> *By the rude bridge that arched the flood*
> *Their flag to April's breeze unfurled*
> *Here once the embattled farmers stood*
> *And fired the shot heard round the world.*

— Ralph Waldo Emerson, 1837

In 1837 Ralph Waldo Emerson wrote "An Original Hymn" to be sung by participants at the dedication of the granite obelisk commemorating the North Bridge fight. In the lyric Emerson used a term—embattled—that has come generally to be misinterpreted to mean something like "besieged." However, Emerson used the term the way that Shakespeare did, meaning drawn up in military order. Farmers drawn up in military order is a far more powerful image than farmers besieged and it fittingly captures the disciplined behavior of the Massachusetts minute and militia companies at the North Bridge.

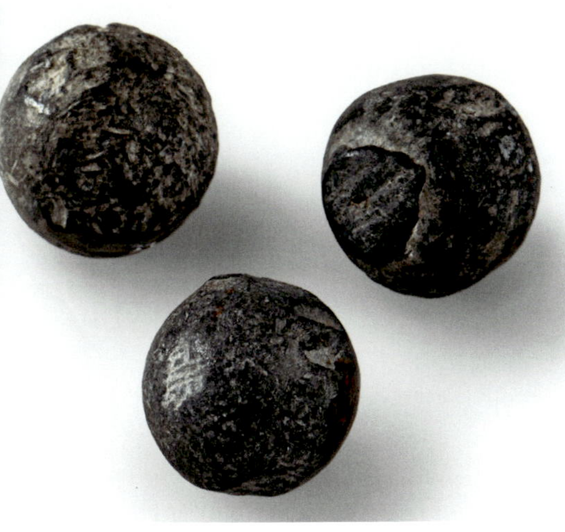

the strap at the wide end. The wooden stopper is engraved *"IH"* which indicates that the horn was made for Jonathan Hosmer ("I" was used to represent the letter "J" in the eighteenth century), father of the slain Abner. In a terrible irony, nine days earlier Jonathan Hosmer had written a letter (collection of Dr. Gary Milan) telling a family member about a false alarm (an alarm carried by Paul Revere, who made it all the way to Concord on that occasion) predicting that if the Regulars did turn out *"there will be bloody work."*

In the nineteenth century, the field depicted in the lower left of Amos Doolittle's view of the North Bridge was known as "The Battlefield." This field is between William Emerson's house and the Concord River. Three musket balls were recovered from it by Henry Thoreau in around 1850 [no. 46]. The bullets range in size from about .66 to .69 caliber and they have been fired. Visible on each of them is a characteristic band of wear that incurred when the bullet travelled down the barrel. The bullets' relatively small size (under .70 caliber; standard British military arms are about .75 caliber) and the variety of sizes—three balls of two different sizes—are characteristic of the arms carried by the Provincial minutemen and militia. Lieutenant Sutherland was in the field when the firing broke out and reported being spun around by a bullet strike to one shoulder. The musket balls that Henry Thoreau found give every appearance of having been part of the firing that William Emerson's grandson would one day refer to as *"the shot heard round the world."*

When Captain Isaac Davis fell in the firing at the North Bridge the second in command of Davis's Acton minute company, Lieutenant John Hayward, became captain. Hayward carried a small sword, the sort of sword a gentleman in London or Boston might carry when dressed formally [no. 47]. In the militia the small sword was an indicator of rank rather than an offensive weapon; officers carried small swords, but privates generally did not. Almost all the swords with histories of use on April 19, with the exception of a few with silver hilts, were brass-hilted small swords like this one. Hayward's sword has a blade triangular in profile. Alternatively, eighteenth-century small swords might have a flat blade, like that carried by Captain Nathan Barrett [no. 48].

The firing at the North Bridge hardly lasted for more than a minute, with perhaps a few hundred shots fired by both sides together. Captain Laurie's three companies, in the words of William Emerson, *"soon quitted their Post at the Bridge and retreated in the greatest Disorder and*

46. MUSKET BALLS

Massachusetts, 1774–1775
Lead
Diameters: ⅝" (about .66 caliber),
1¹⁄₁₆" (about .69 caliber), and 1¹⁄₁₆"
(about .69 caliber)
Gift of Mr. Walton Ricketson and
Miss Anna Ricketson. TH69a-c

A cardstock label inscribed in a nineteenth-century hand identifies these as *"Three bullets / Supposed to have / come from the battle / -field at Concord / Thoreau Collection."*

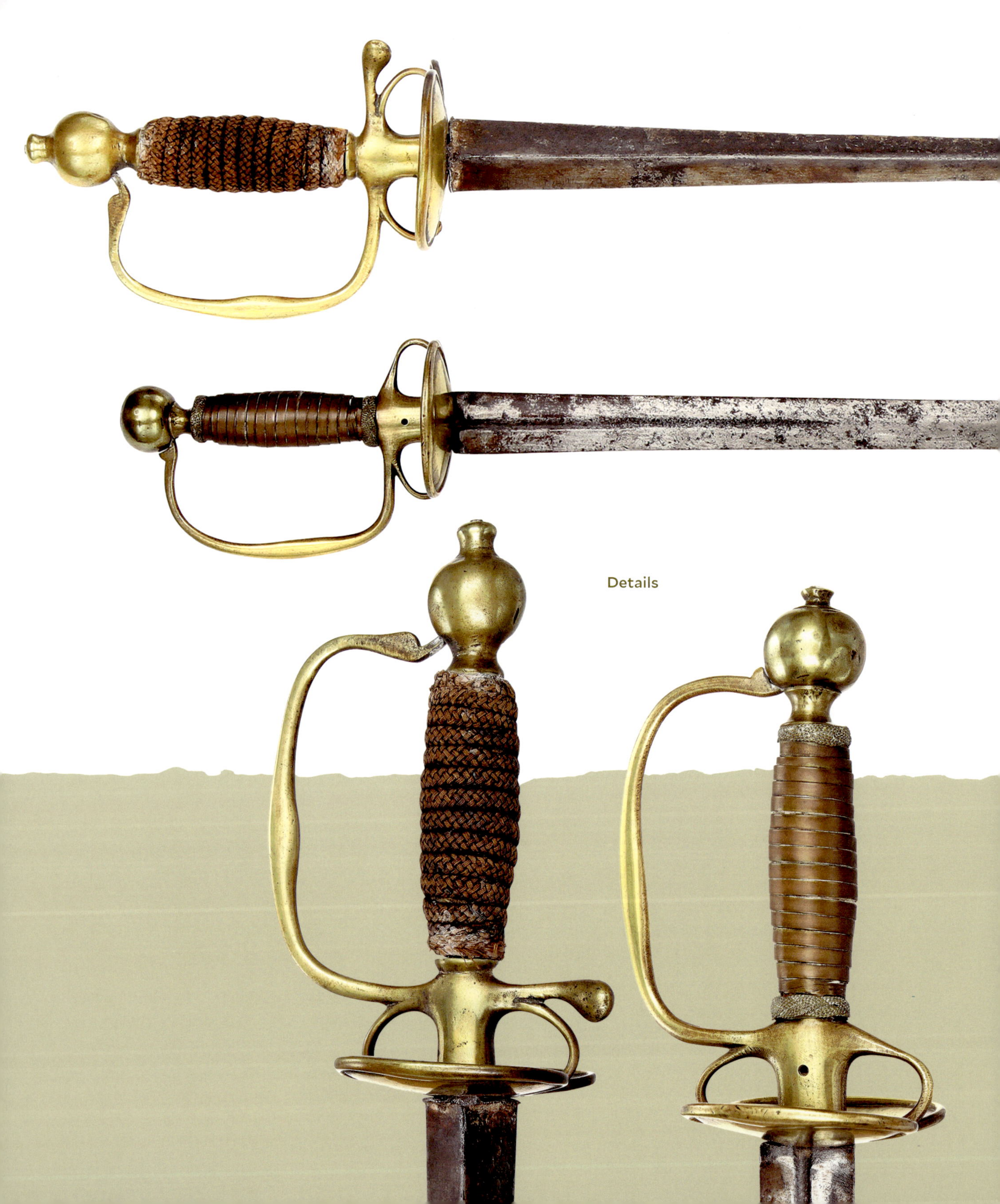

Details

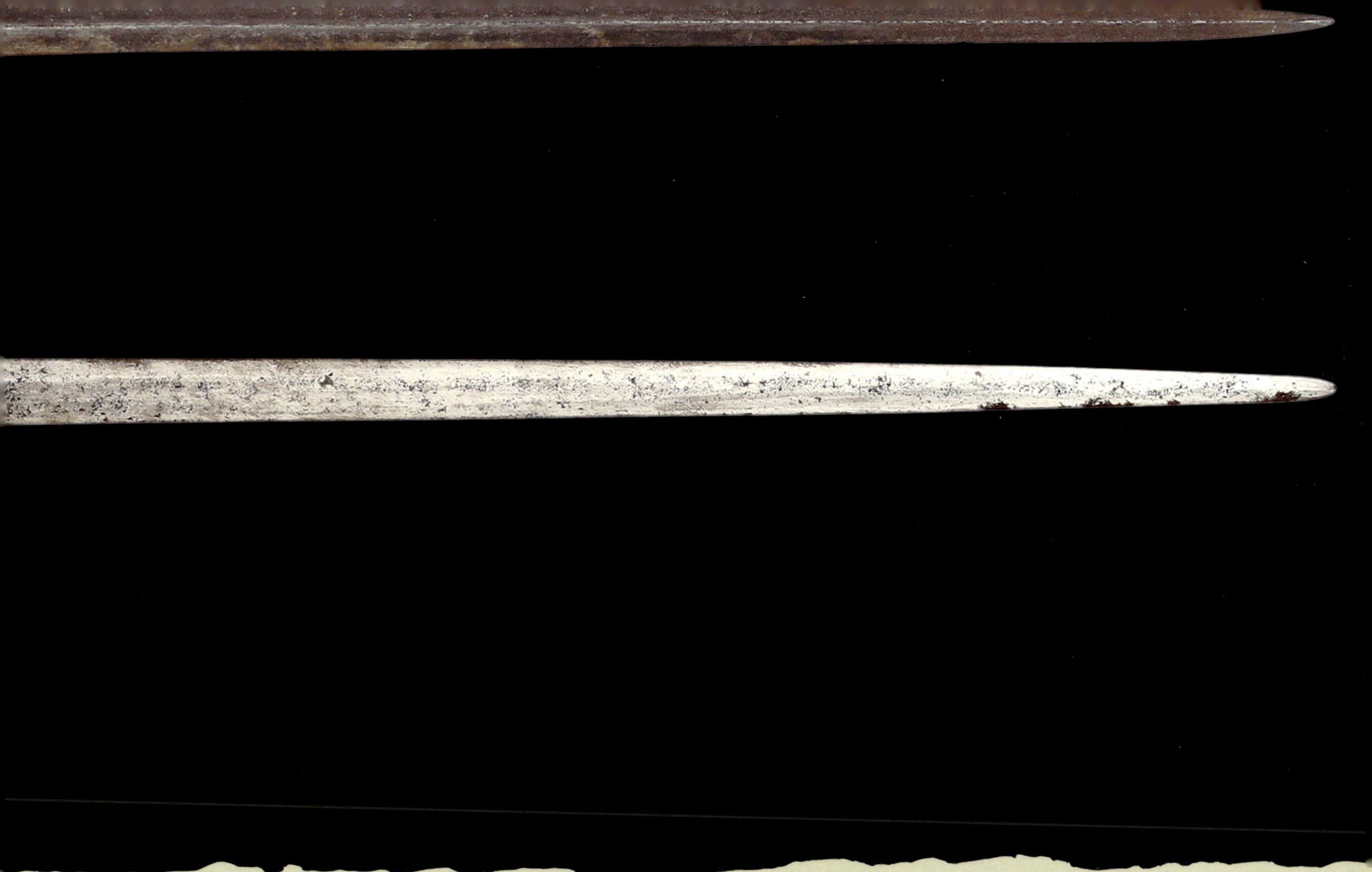

47. SMALL SWORD THAT BELONGED TO JOHN HAYWARD

England, 1750–1770
Steel, brass. Hilt wrappings replaced
Length: 28 9/16″; Width: 3 13/16″;
Depth: 2 7/8″
Gift of Carolyn C. Baldwin. 2000.82

48. SMALL SWORD THAT BELONGED TO NATHAN BARRETT

England, 1750–1770
Steel, brass. Hilt wrappings replaced
Length: 23 7/16″; Width: 4 5/16″;
Depth: 3 5/16″
Gift of Carolyn C. Baldwin. 2000.83

William King (active about
1785 to after 1806)
Boston, 1804–1806
Paper
Image Height: 5½"; Width: 4"
Gift of Cummings E. Davis. Pi1302

Mary Jones [see also no. 7] **had
fourteen brothers, one of whom,
Josiah, was taken captive in Maine
on suspicion of being on a mission
to supply hay to the British soldiers
besieged in Boston. Henry Thoreau
recorded in a journal entry that Josiah**
*"was confined in Concord 4 months
& a fortnight,"* **that Mary brought
every meal he had from Weston—**
*"He was afraid he might be poisoned
else"*—**and that on** *"17th June '75
she brought over ripe cherries in her
chaise."* **Josiah Jones and two other
prisoners** *"secreted knives furnished
them with their food sawed the
grates off & escaped to Weston."* **This
oral history of a jailbreak confirmed
for Thoreau the oral tradition that
spring came early to Massachusetts
in 1775:** *"Can we believe when behold-
ing this landscape—with only a few
buds visibly swollen on the trees &
the ground covered 8 inches deep
with snow—that the grain was wav-
ing in the fields & the appletrees
were in blossom Ap. 19th 1775. It may
confirm this story however—what
Grandmother said that she carried
ripe cherries from Weston to her
brother in Concord jail the 17th of
June the same year."*

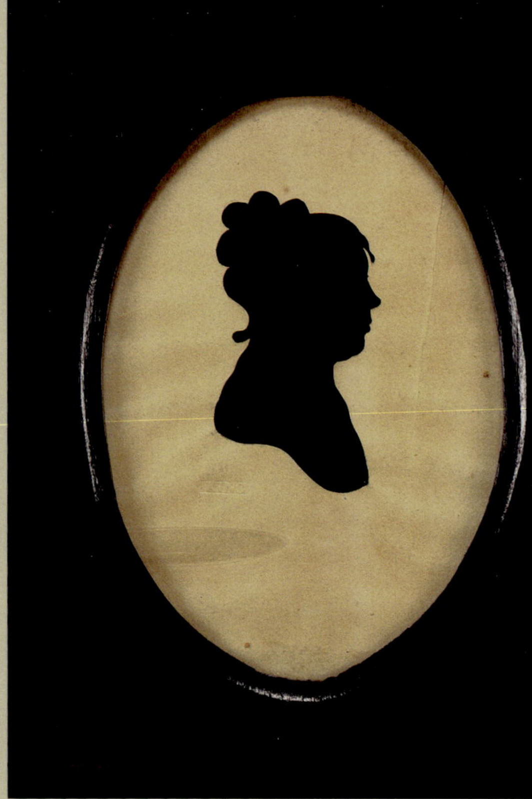

Confusion to ye Main Body, who were soon upon ye March to meet them."
Just before the engagement at the bridge, Captain Laurie had sent
a messenger to Colonel Smith requesting reinforcements and it was
these reinforcing troops (the 47th Regiment grenadiers, according to
Jeremy Lister, who was with Laurie's companies at the North Bridge)
that William Emerson saw meeting up with the captain's companies.
The *"Disorder and Confusion"* among the Regulars that Emerson noted
was corroborated by Lister who wrote that under forceful Provincial
fire *"we was oblig'd to give way then run with the greatest precipitance."*

Some of the Provincial soldiers stayed on the west side of the river
and attended to the dead and wounded but about half of them, Amos
Barrett and John Buttrick among them, crossed the North Bridge, on
Major Buttrick's order posting themselves behind a stone wall that
ascended a hill on the east side of the road leading into town.

The Regulars spent some time in the center of Concord arranging for
the treatment and transport of several who were wounded at the North
Bridge. Some of that care was provided by Dr. Timothy Minot [no. 50]

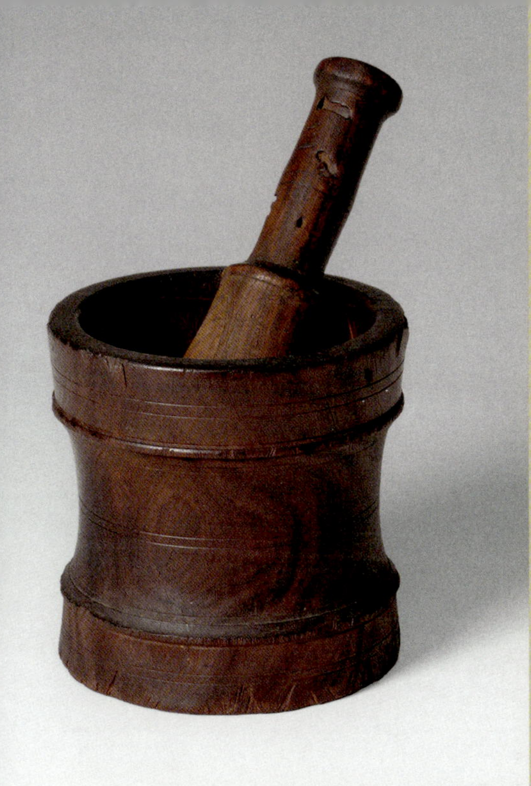

On April 19, while treating the British soldiers who had been wounded at the North Bridge, Dr. Minot might have found the mortar useful for tasks like crushing yarrow to make into a poultice to stanch bleeding. The tropical species lignum vitae is one of the densest and hardest of all woods which makes it a good choice for fashioning mortars. The mortar and pestle shown here, which appear to belong together, might have been made in Boston using imported wood, or they might have been made in the West Indies for export. The wood used for the pestle had been damaged by insect infestation before the piece was turned on the lathe, a cosmetic flaw that both the maker and buyer must have noticed but chose to ignore, which is suggestive of the high value placed on lignum vitae for its durability.

who lived in the gambrel-roofed house depicted in the Amos Doolittle view of the center of Concord.

The infantry and grenadiers [no. 51] maneuvered in the road for about ten minutes, sending the officers to the front of the column, Corporal Amos Barrett recounted, while *"we Lay behind the wall about 200 of us with our guns Cockd Expecting every minnit to have the word fire."* Major Buttrick never gave the order, which Barrett thought would have meant the death of almost all the officers, *"and their want* [wasn't] *a gun fird."*

They were joined by the three companies of light infantry who had gone to Colonel James Barrett's house. Those companies had returned over the North Bridge unimpeded by the hundreds of Provincial soldiers who remained on the west side of the river. The light infantry saw the bodies of the Regulars who were killed at the bridge and saw that one of them had been struck in the head with a hatchet. That awful sight spawned a rumor that the Provincials were scalping the wounded, a rumor that found its way into the official reports of the action.

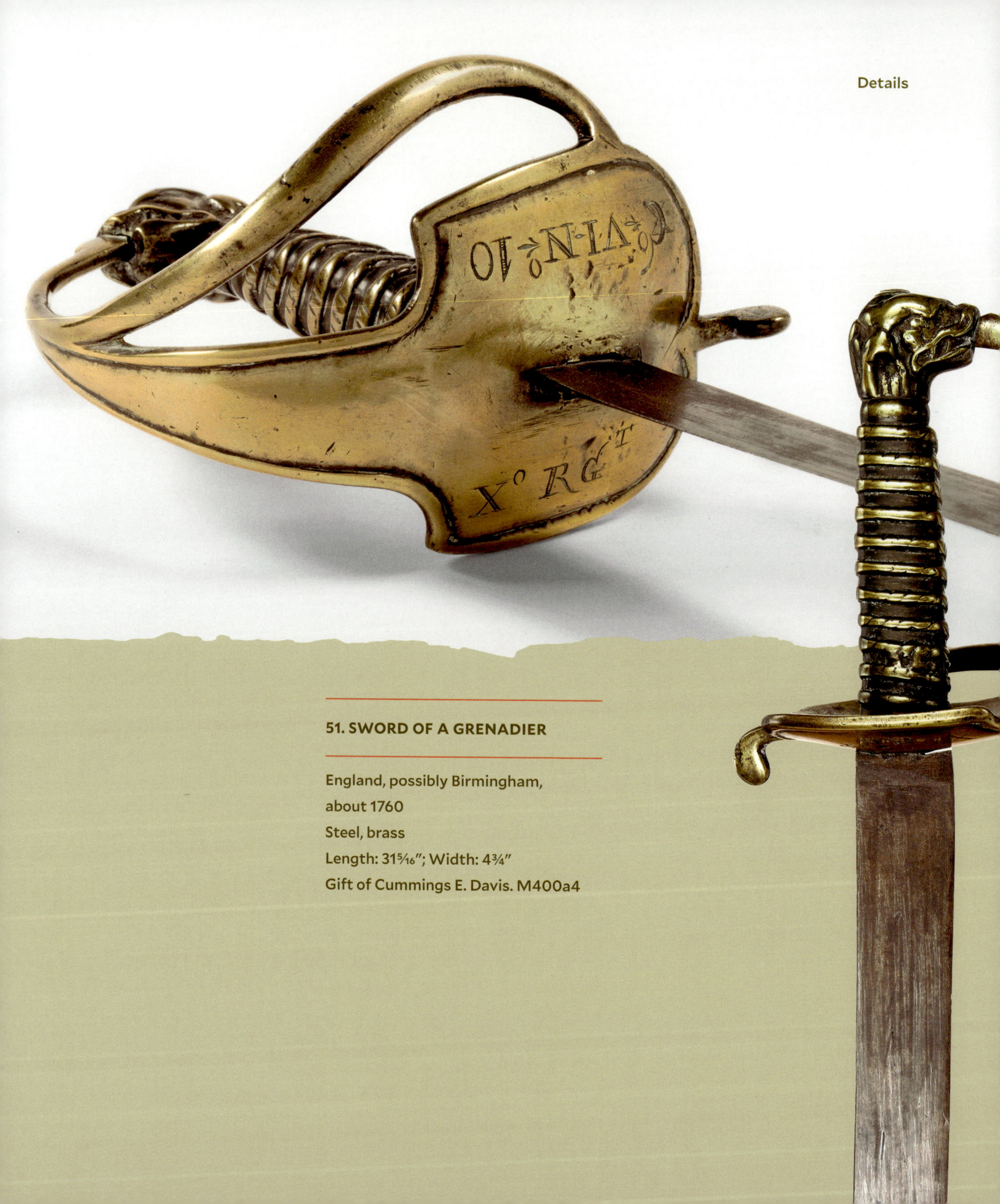

51. SWORD OF A GRENADIER

England, possibly Birmingham,
about 1760
Steel, brass
Length: 31⁵⁄₁₆"; Width: 4¾"
Gift of Cummings E. Davis. M400a4

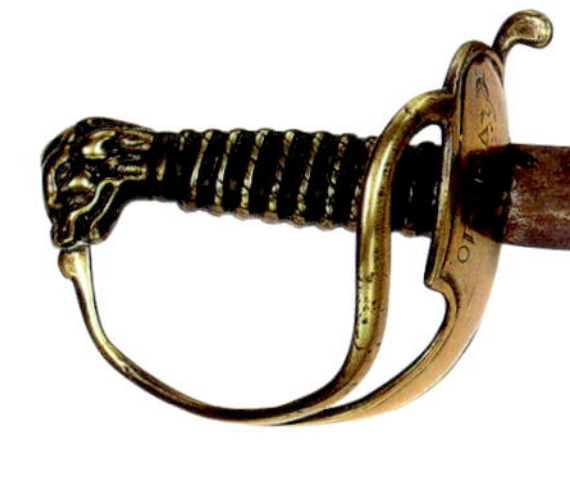

The engraving on the brass hilt of this sword, of the type known as a hanger rather than a cutlass, identifies it as the sword of private number 10 of the 6th Company of the 10th Regiment. Company Six was a grenadier company. Although other privates in the British Army had stopped carrying swords by 1768, grenadier privates continued the practice for a few more years. The sword is one of the more famous relics of April 19, 1775. It made its first print appearance in *Harpers Weekly* in 1875 and was among the relics displayed in the dinner tent at Concord's Centennial celebration. In its earliest appearances as a relic the sword was identified as an officer's sword and was associated with Marine Lieutenant Isaac Potter who was held prisoner for some time at the home of Reuben Brown in Concord. In a 1911 catalog, Concord Antiquarian Society secretary George Tolman identified the sword with Samuel Lee, who was taken prisoner on April 19, 1775 and even claimed to be the first prisoner taken on that day. Cummings Davis apparently got the sword from George Minot along with the information that it *"Came from Mr. Ephraim Minott who married Abegail Prescott one of the daughters of Doct Abel Prescott."* Although the private who carried the sword has not been identified it seems to have been left in Concord on April 19, a relic possibly of one of the wounded soldiers treated by Doctor Timothy Minot in the gambrel-roofed house in the center of town.

Tolman 1911, 153: "CUTLASS OF SAMUEL LEE, a grenadier of the 10th British Regiment, made prisoner at Concord on the 19th of April, 1775; the first British sword taken in the war of the Revolution. Lee was never exchanged, but remained all his life in this town, where he married Mary Piper, and set up in business as a tailor in the double house nearly opposite the house of the Concord Antiquarian Society. He died in 1790, leaving several children."

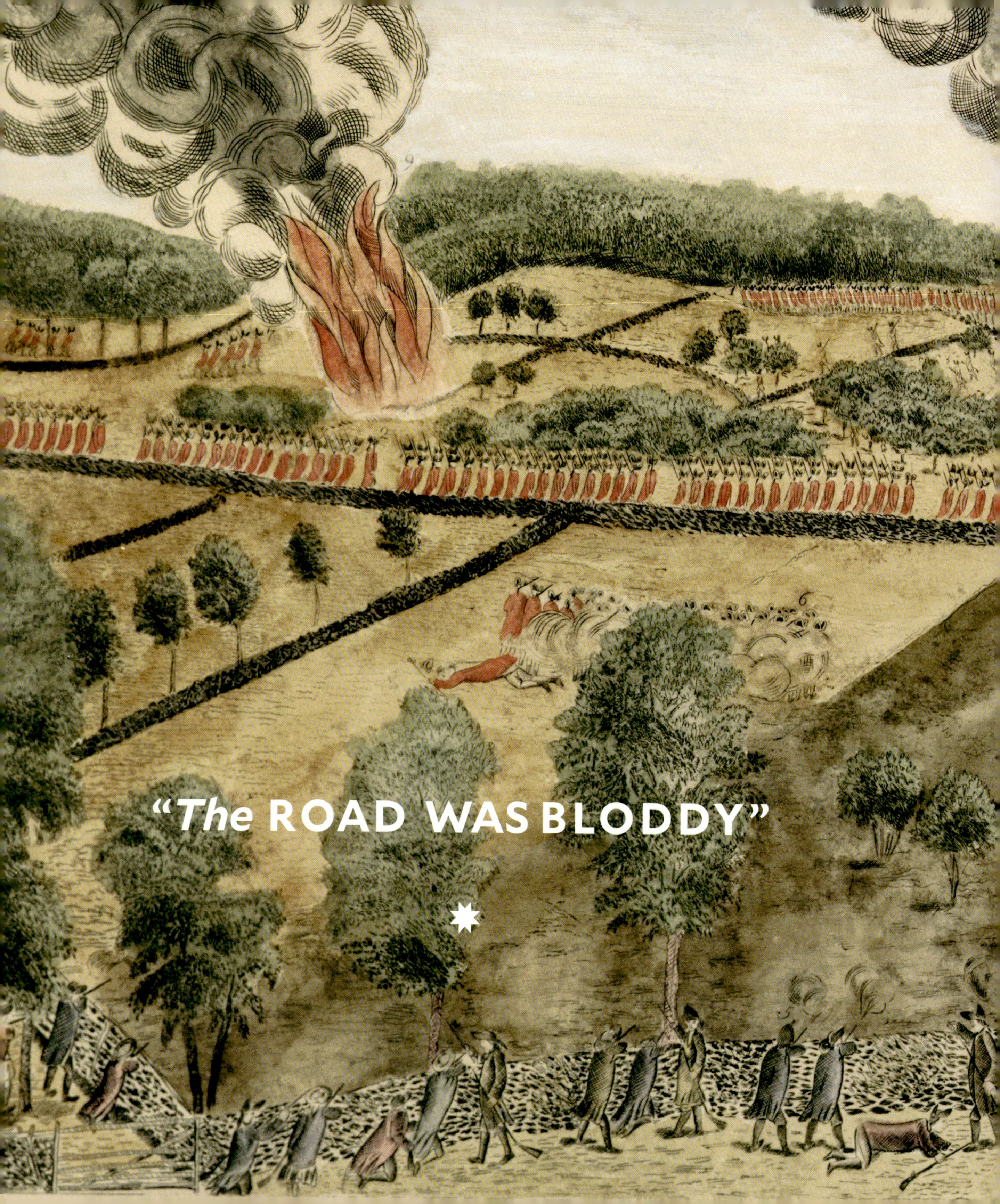

"The ROAD WAS BLODDY"

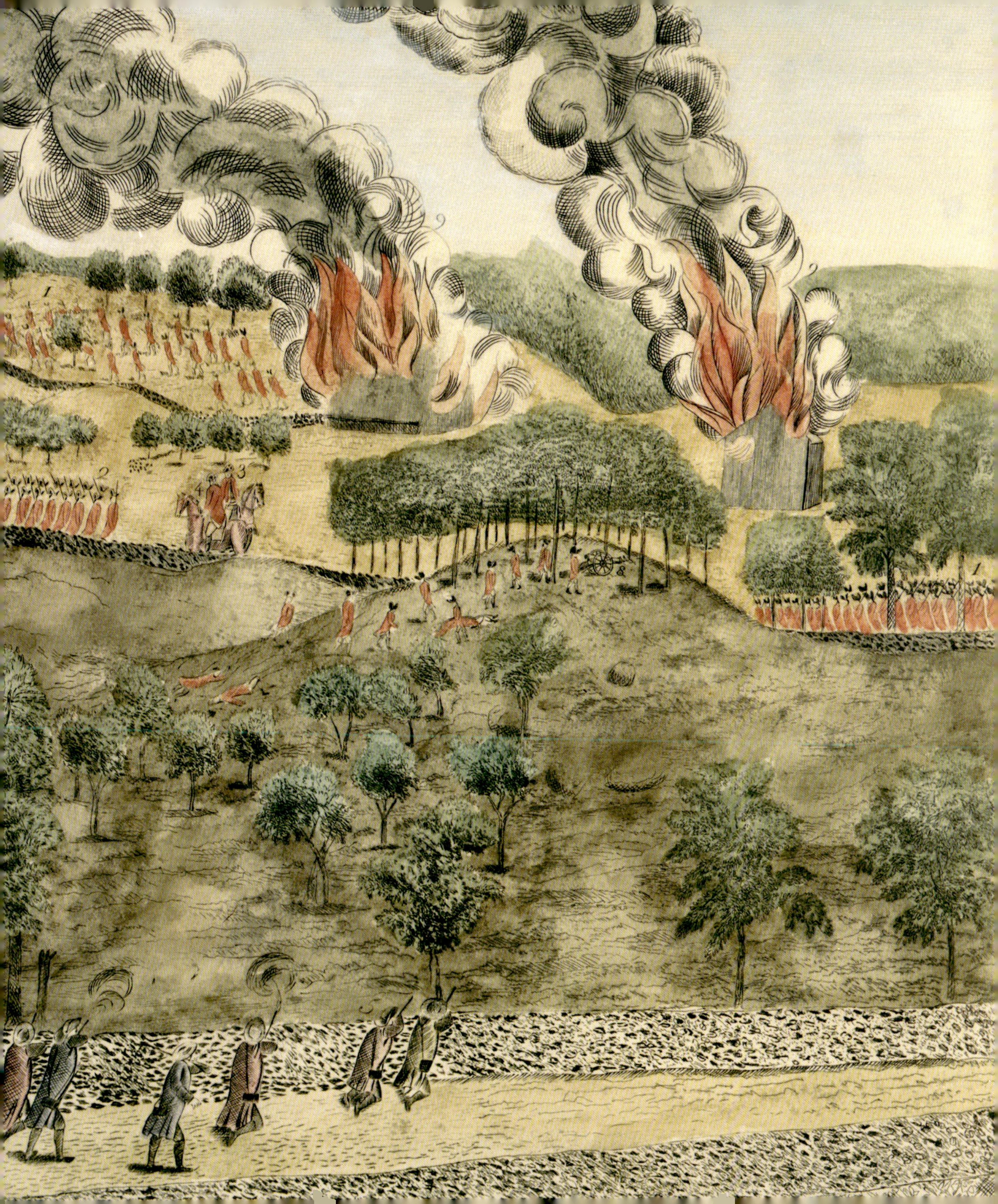

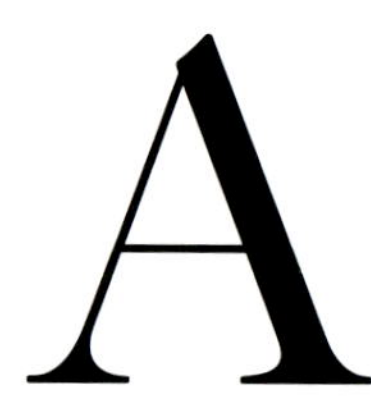

52. MUSKET BALL

Massachusetts, 1774–1775
Lead
Diameter: ⁹⁄₁₆″ (about .50 caliber)
Gift of Joseph Palumbo, Farmer
2016.12.1

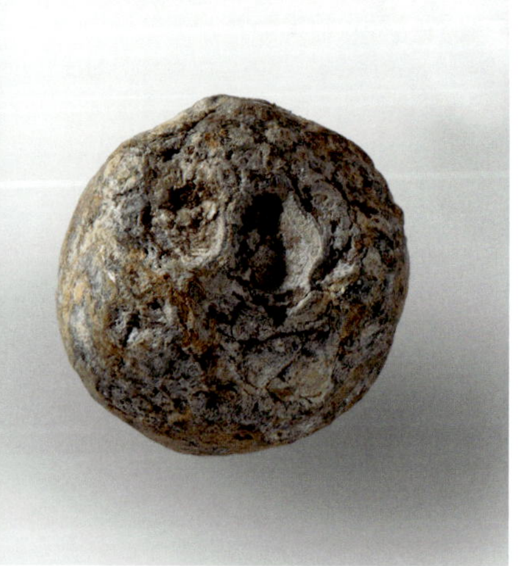

A BOUT NOON the column of Regulars formed up and began their return to Boston. As they had done on the way in, the light infantry took a path along the top of the ridge and the grenadiers marched in the road. Amos Barrett with about two hundred others followed along on the back side of the ridge, catching up to the column at the point where the ridge ends.

The glacial ridge that overlooks Concord ends near a home that had been occupied by members of the Merriam family since the seventeenth century. Located about a mile and a half east of the center of Concord, this is also the location of the small bridge that carried Lexington Road over the mill stream feeding the mill pond in Concord center. A 1775 English map of the events of April 19 depicts the bridge and identifies the spot as *"Bridge where the attack began."* From the British perspective it was not the firing on Lexington Common at dawn nor the firing at the North Bridge at about 9 a.m. that marked the real beginning of hostilities on April 19, it was the firing at Merriam's Corner just after noon. By the time that Amos Barrett and other Provincials who had been at the North Bridge got to the Merriam house, the attack had already begun. *"When they got about mil half to a Road that Comes from Bedford and Billerica,"* Amos Barrett reported of the column of Regulars, *"they was way Laid and a grait many killd when I got thair a grait many Lay dead and the Road was bloddy."*

A .50-caliber musket ball recovered from the field across Lexington Road from the Merriam house is smaller than those used in British military arms, but like the balls Henry Thoreau found in the field between the home of William Emerson and the North Bridge is of a size that would fit the fowlers typically carried by the Provincial militias [no. 52]. The ball had not been dropped but had been fired from a point a few hundred feet along the road toward Bedford and Billerica. Companies of soldiers from the Massachusetts towns of Westford, Stow, Billerica, Chelmsford, Reading, Woburn, Sudbury, Wilmington, and Framingham, none of whom had been at the North Bridge, joined

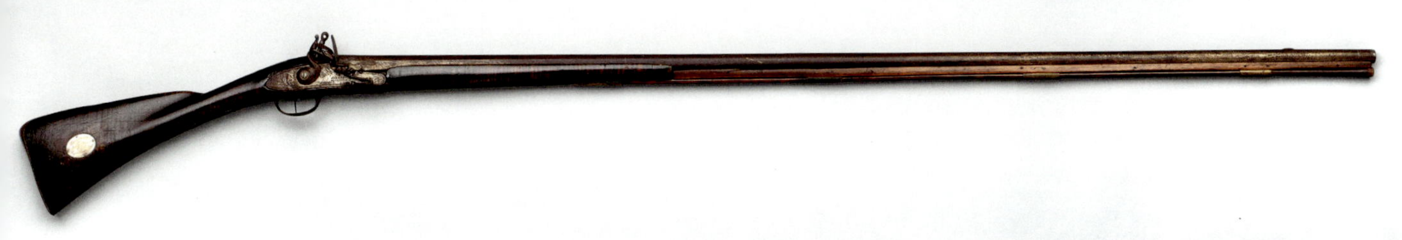

in the attack on the British column at Merriam's Corner and at points a little further east along the Lexington Road.

General Thomas Gage in a letter written to Connecticut governor Jonathan Trumbull a few weeks after the event graphically described the situation the returning column of British foot soldiers encountered:

> Except upon Captain Laurie at the bridge, no hostilities happened from the affair at Lexington, until the Troops began their march back. As soon as the Troops had got out of the Town of Concord, they received a heavy fire on them from all sides — from walls, fences, houses, trees barns, &c., which continued, without intermission.

53. FOWLING PIECE

Unidentified maker

Massachusetts, about 1770

Iron, steel, cherry

Overall Length: 70"; Width: 5¾";

Barrel Length: 54¹⁄₁₆"; Bore: ⅜"

(about .69 caliber)

Gift of Lt. Colonel Philip A. Moore.

A113

Captain Micajah Gleason's Framingham minute company encountered this returning column of Regulars at a point about a mile east along the Lexington Road from the Merriam house. To do that the company had to march north for thirty miles after receiving the alarm, a march of at least eight hours. Given that they were at the Lexington Road in Concord not long after 1 p.m. it is evident that the three companies of soldiers sent by Framingham did not pause to deliberate but set off immediately. Roger Brown (1749–1840) was a corporal in Micajah Gleason's minute company and was credited with ten days' service in response to the alarm. The fowler that Roger Brown carried was made in about 1770 and had been militarized with the addition of a bayonet lug [no. 53]. The fowler was converted to percussion, probably while owned by James W. Brown, and later reconverted. It was also half-stocked, meaning the wooden stock was cut down and a thin rib added under the barrel, probably when converted to percussion.

Even before the firing on Lexington Common, Lieutenant Colonel Smith of the 10th Regiment, alerted by the ringing of bells and firing of alarm guns that the expedition was no longer a secret, had sent a request back to General Gage in Boston that a relief column be sent out in support immediately. Misplaced orders led to delays and the relief column, commanded by Brigadier General Hugh Percy, did not set out over Roxbury Neck until 9 a.m., about the time of the engagement at the North Bridge. The relief column met the returning column of Regulars in Lexington, which is the scene depicted in the last of the four views engraved by Amos Doolittle [no. 54]. General Percy had brought along two six-pound cannon, one of which can be seen firing in the direction of the Lexington meeting house. The cannonfire halted the persistent attack of the pursuing Provincials long enough to grant a respite to the returning column, which had already lost perhaps two dozen killed and many more wounded. To secure the resting soldiers General Percy ordered three houses overlooking their position to be burned. The middle of the three depicted is the house and shop of the widow of clockmaker Nathaniel Mulliken, whose son was among the militia on Lexington Common. It was the Mulliken house that Samuel Prescott had been visiting, paying court to young Lydia Mulliken, before joining Paul Revere and William Dawes in spreading the alarm.

After about an hour the entire column, now numbering about eighteen hundred formed up again and marched on toward Cambridge, with the relief column at the back and light infantry flankers to the left and right. The next few miles saw the worst fighting of the day. The thirty companies of militia and minutemen from a dozen towns that had pursued the column through Lexington were joined by forty more companies from ten more towns. The Provincials attacking the returning column around Menotomy (present-day Arlington) outnumbered the Regulars two to one.

The militiamen who awaited the drum signal in Buckman's Tavern heard the tense seconds ticked away and the small hours of the morning struck on the eight-day clock made for tavern keeper John Buckman in 1769 [no. 23].

The town of Danvers twenty-five miles north of Boston received the alarm at about 9 a.m. from one of the many couriers that were spreading the news of the raid in every direction. Like Framingham, Danvers wasted no time sending off their companies, eight of them. A rapid march brought them to Menotomy just as the Regulars arrived late in the afternoon. They marched into a literal hail of gunfire around the Jason Russell house. Twelve Provincial soldiers were killed at the Russell house, including the owner, who was shot and then bayoneted eleven times, and seven of the newly arrived Danvers soldiers, the worst losses in any single engagement that day.

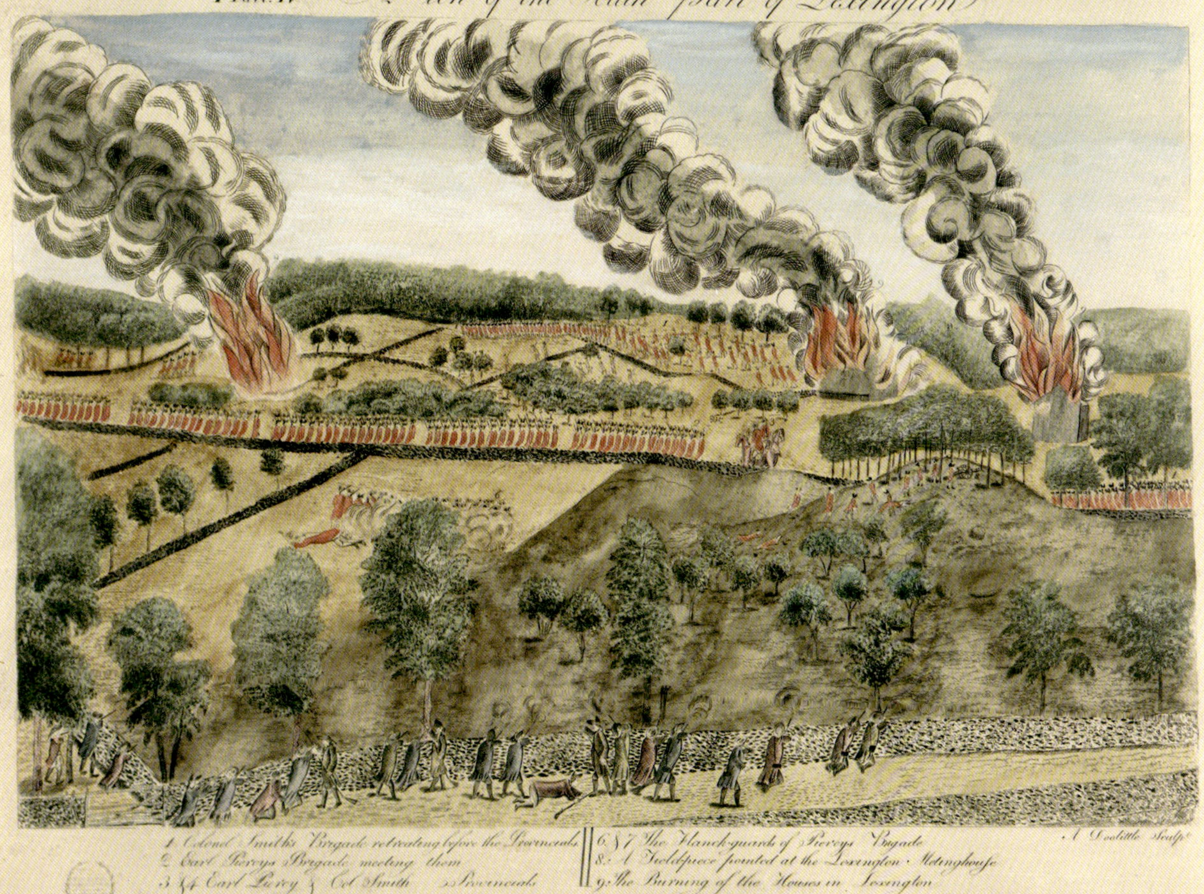

Plate. IV. A View of the South Part of Lexington
1 Colonel Smith's Brigade retreating before the Provincials.
2 Earl Percy's Brigade meeting them
3 & 4 Earl Percy & Col Smith   Provincials
6 & 7 The Flanck-guards of Percys Brigade
8. A Fieldpiece pointed at the Lexington Metinghouse
9. The Burning of the Houses in Lexington
A. Doolittle Sculp

55. WATCH

Movement engraved
"H. Morris / London / 1046"
London, England, 1761
Brass, steel, silver, enamel
Diameter: 2"
Gift of Howard Whitmore. Per2194.1.1

This watch became a favored relic of the Marsh family for its association with April 19 and with the Battle of Bunker Hill, where Ezekiel Marsh also served. It has a watch paper in the inner case, one of those engraved by Paul Revere for Aaron Willard, who cleaned the watch in Boston in 1823. Around 1825 it was engraved with the initials *"THM"* (Thomas Hartshorn Marsh, the son of Ezekiel Marsh, Jr.) and the date *"1776"* by an itinerant engraver in exchange for a meal. Late in life, Ezekiel Marsh retained the traditional dress of the eighteenth century as Lucius Marsh recalled: *"My grandfather as I remember him, was a tall and very straight* [man]. *He wore a queue, also breaches, knee and shoe buckles and walked with a staff."*

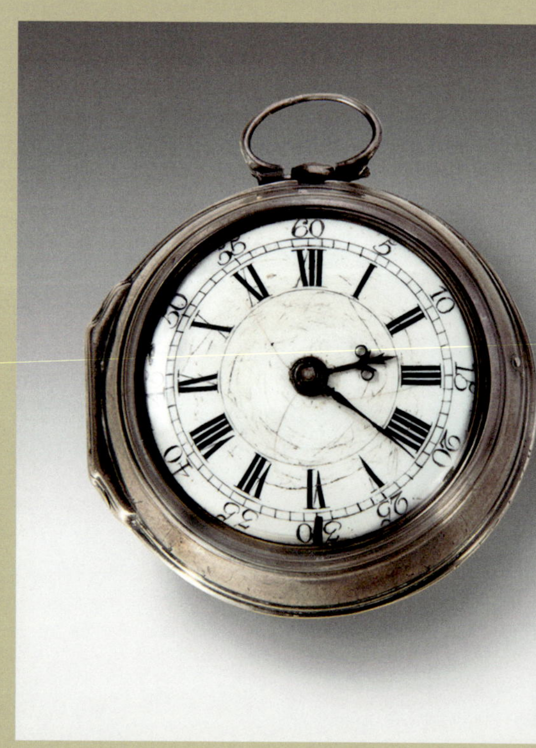

Ezekiel Marsh, Jr. (1740–1822) marched with the Danvers company captained by Caleb Low. Marsh was a lieutenant, commissioned by Governor Thomas Hutchinson in June 1773. Lucius March, his grandson, wrote in 1897, *"My grandfather had this watch in his pocket on the 19 of April, 1775 at the battle of Lexington, his father, my great grand father was with him, then 65 years old, and marched to Cambridge."* [no. 55] As an officer, Ezekiel Marsh may have had use for a watch, but it is also the case that the soldiers who set off on the alarm tended to dress as formally as they could. Charles Miles, captain of one of the two Concord minute companies, later told Concord minister Ezra Ripley of going to the alarm with the same attitude as going to church. Some of the Acton men reportedly powdered their hair before setting off.

The captured arms of a British Regular officer testify to the state of the returning column in the late afternoon on April 19, 1775. Two brothers from Watertown recovered a musket and sword in Menotomy. When the pieces were exhibited in the dinner tent at the 1875 centennial of the April 19 battle, they were identified as *"A sword taken by Nathaniel Bemis of Watertown from a British officer whom he shot; and the gun, marked 'David Bemis, 1775,' with which he shot him."* Nathaniel Bemis was not enlisted on April 19 but apparently accompanied brother David Bemis who marched as a private in the Watertown minute company captained by Samuel Barnard.

The captured sword has a German blade and silver mounts with hallmarks for Paris [no. 56]. The ivory handle is carved with a motif that is common to military swords of this period and is variously referred to as "lion head," "dog head," or "monster head." The hilt of the 10th Regiment grenadier's sword [no. 51] features a similar creature. British officers were responsible for providing their own swords and the one Nathaniel Bemis picked up had been expensive to acquire. The silver mounts indicate that the sword was carried by an officer in a company that had silver tape on the facings (cuffs, collar, and lapels) of their uniforms. There were two British Regular officers killed at Menotomy but neither one was from a silver-faced company. Nathaniel Bemis did not shoot the owner of the sword with the musket picked up by David Bemis and later that year engraved on the butt plate *"David Bemis Jr. / 1775."* The musket is of the type called a fusil. Fusils are a lighter-weight version of the standard long arm carried by enlisted troops and were the shoulder arms that officers carried. The muskets of junior officers were supplied by the colonel of the regiment and could vary in quality depending on the generosity of the colonel. The musket David Bemis picked up is of middling quality [no. 57]. The lock is marked *"Grice"* for the gun manufactory of William Grice (1715–1790) of Birmingham, England. The rack number *"5"* is engraved on the wrist plate. A crack in the stock was later repaired with a plate of thin copper.

Whatever its quality the officer who carried the fusil was responsible for its return. Given the circumstance of their recovery it seems likely that musket and sword were carried by the same officer, and since no officer from a silver-faced company was either captured or killed in Menotomy it appears that the officer discarded them. By the time the column reached Menotomy the ammunition for the cannon was depleted as was most of the ammunition for muskets. Half of the Regulars had been marching for twelve hours, half of that time under fire, with little rest, rations, or water. Desperation seems to have driven one officer to jettison useless, but expensive, weight.

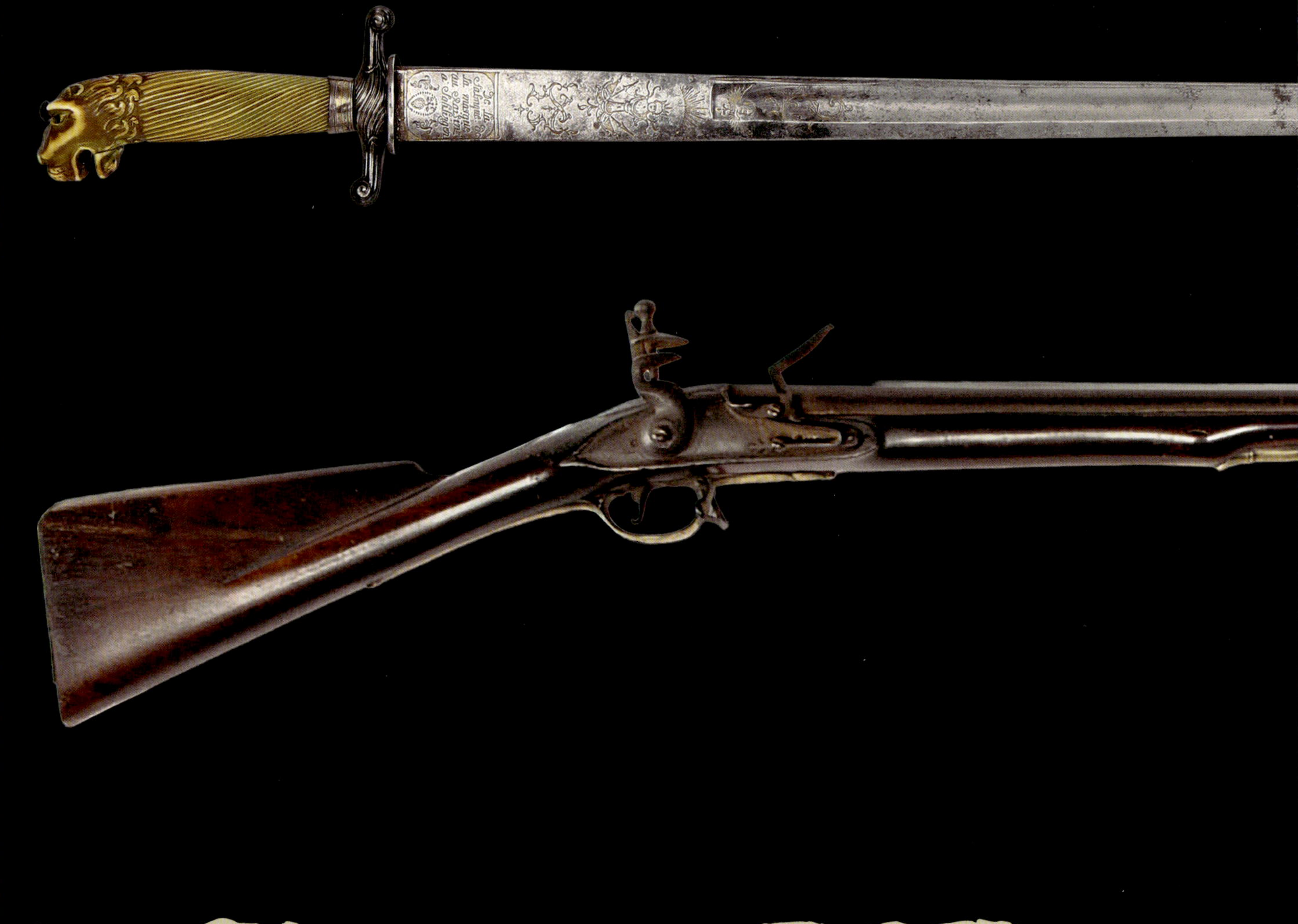

56. OFFICER'S SWORD

Paris, France, 1760–1761
Steel, silver, ivory, gilding
Length: 31⅜"; Width: 3"
Gift of Mrs. Chandler. A2060.1

57. OFFICER'S FUSIL

William Grice, Birmingham, England,
1765–1770
Walnut, steel, brass
Overall Length: 57⅜"; Width: 4⅝";
Barrel Length 42"; Bore: ⅝"
(about .63 caliber)
Gift of Mrs. Chandler. A2075

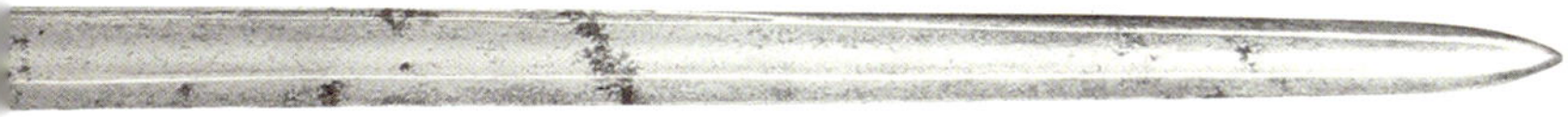

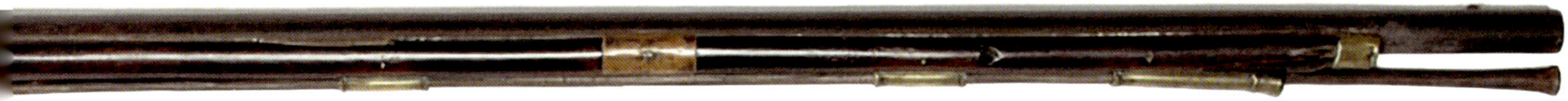

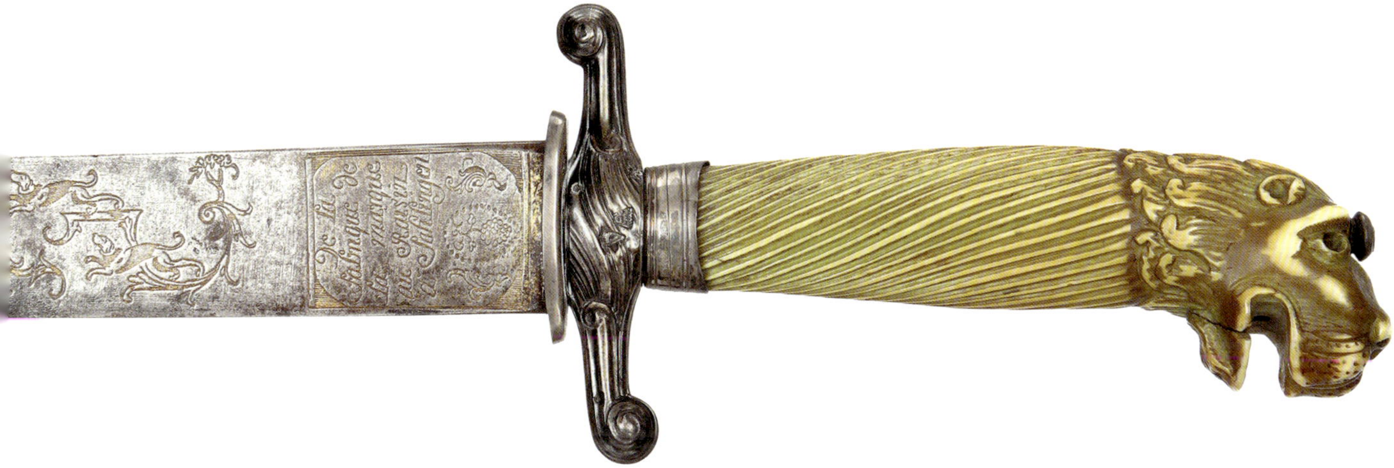

Details

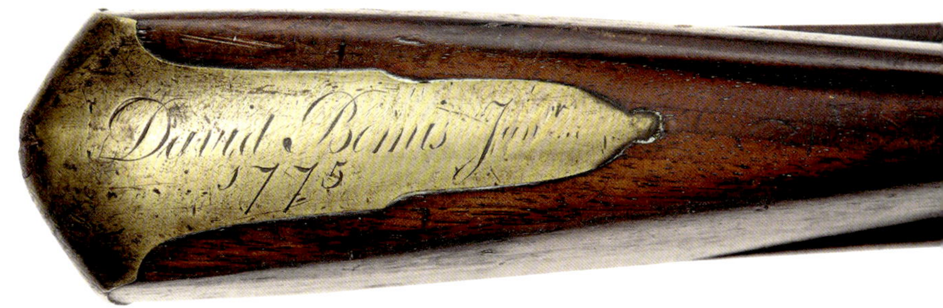

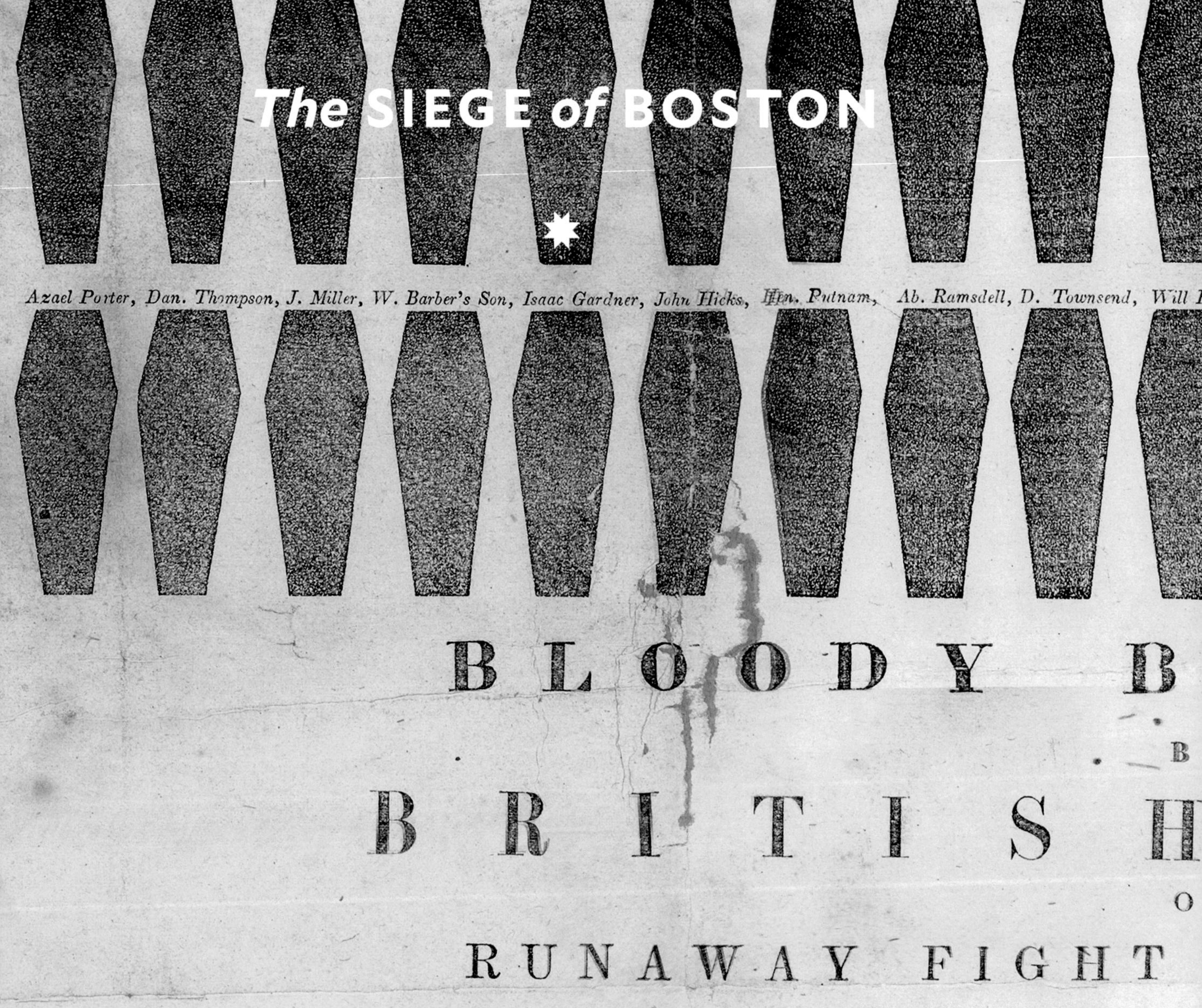

The SIEGE of BOSTON

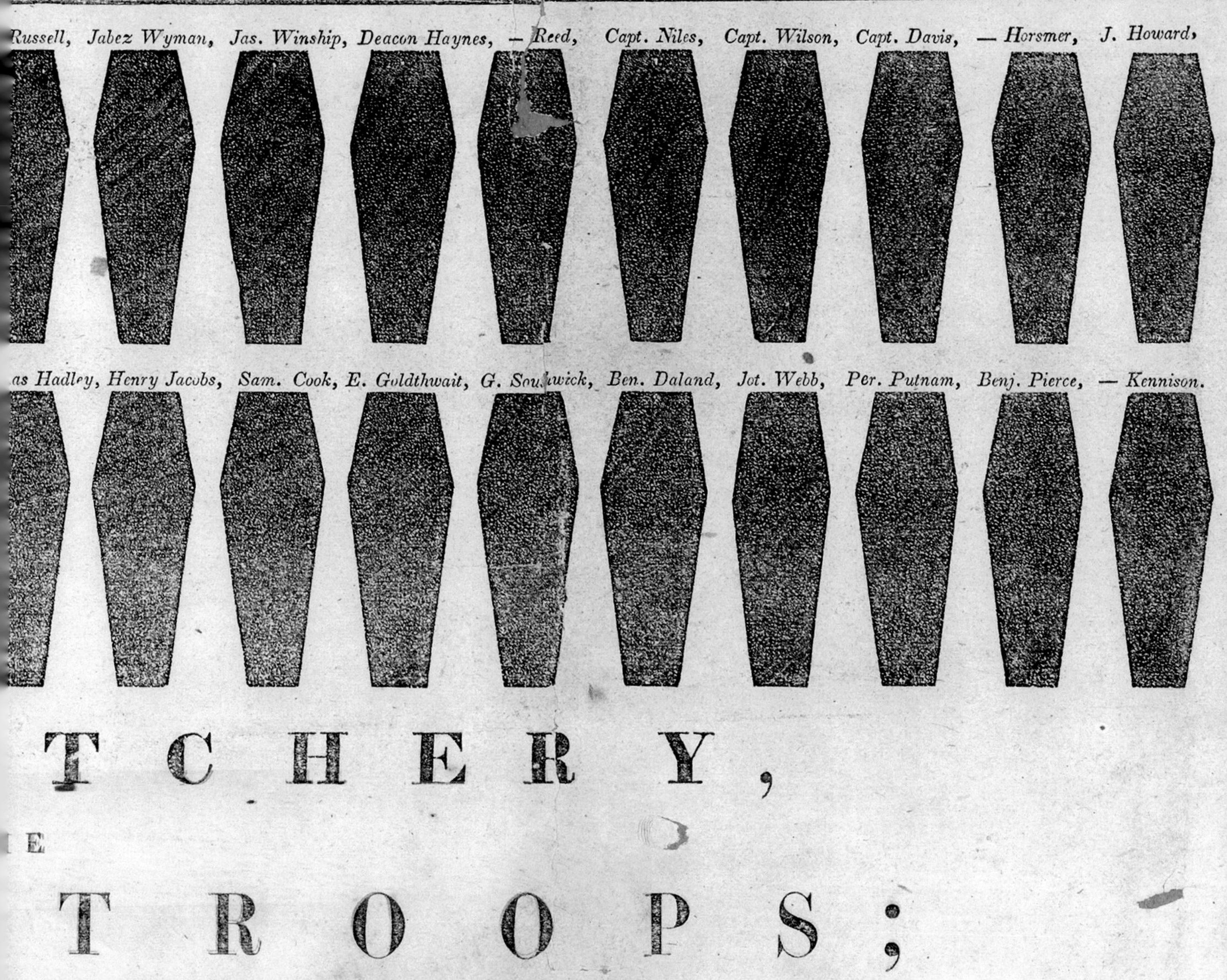

TCHERY,

E

TROOPS;

HE

F THE REGULARS.

CONCORD, situated Twenty Miles from Boston, in the Province of the Mas-
c Majesty, and a few Hundred Provincial Troops, belonging to the Province of
5, when it was decided greatly in favor of the latter. These particulars are
IES, who died gloriously fighting in the CAUSE OF LIBERTY and their COUNTRY,
re well-wishers to America, may be possessed of the same, either to frame
ude to the memory of the Deceased Forty Persons, but as a perpetual me-

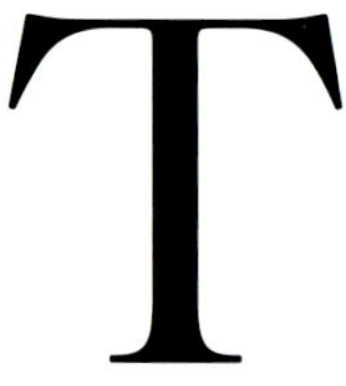

THE SUN HAD JUST gone down on April 19, 1775 when the column of British soldiers arrived in Charlestown twenty hours after the expedition had begun. The sun rose the next day on Boston besieged. Five days later the *Essex Gazette* published an account of what had happened on April 19 and the account was soon reprinted in a broadside titled *"BLOODY BUTCHERY, by the BRITISH TROOPS"* printed by Samuel and Ebenezer Hall of Salem, perhaps that same week [no. 58]. In that narrative the raiding column of British Regulars was eight or nine hundred strong and encountered about a hundred militia mustered near the meeting house in Lexington. The British commanding officer (meaning Major Pitcairn) ordered the Provincials to disperse; the troops huzzaed, one or two officers fired pistols followed by firing from four or five troops, then a general discharge from the Regulars that killed eight.

Speaking of Concord, the account notes the firing at the North Bridge that killed two Provincials and reports a limited success for the raid: some gun carriages and carriage wheels burned, and about twenty barrels of flour were destroyed. The account includes preliminary casualty figures. The forty known Provincial soldiers killed were represented by forty coffins in the first edition of the *"BLOODY BUTCHERY"* broadside, an indicator of how quickly the broadside came out. The second edition of the broadside issued soon after included forty-two coffins. The final reckoning was forty-nine Provincials killed, forty-one wounded, and five missing. By contrast the British Regulars lost seventy-three killed, 174 wounded, and twenty-six missing. More than twice as many Regulars were wounded as were killed, but more Provincials were killed than wounded. That disparity has long been viewed as evidence that the Regulars were killing the wounded, which was the fate of Jason Russell. It was an accusation first leveled in the text of the broadside: *"Not content with shooting down the unarmed, aged, and infirm, they disregarded the cries of the wounded, killing them without mercy, and mangling their bodies in the most shocking manner."*

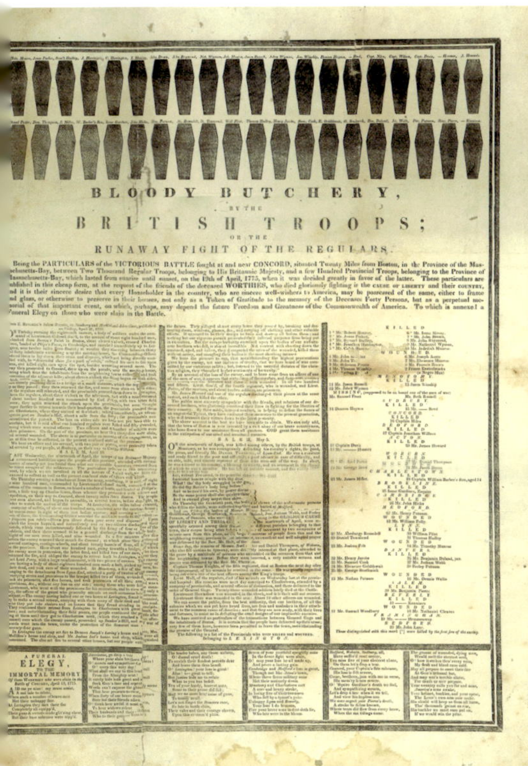

The account in the *Essex Gazette* mentions that the Provincial soldiers killed at the Jason Russell house in Menotomy were buried on April 21. The stone erected at the grave itself reads like a polemical broadside, with a text almost as shocking as a double line of coffins:

> Mr JASON RUSSELL was barbarously murdered in his own House by GAGES bloody Troops on ye 19th of April 1775 Aetats. 59. His body is quietly resting in this Grave with Eleven of our Friends, who, in Like manner, with many others, were cruelly slain on that fatal day.

William Emerson recorded an alarm in Concord on April 20, 1775, when the sight of some returning Provincial soldiers raised fears of a renewed attack from the British Regulars. The fear on that occasion turned out to be unfounded, but the perception of Concord as a target for further hostility was real enough; the supplies were still there in quantity. The Provincial Congress met in Concord on the morning of April 22, having been reconvened as arranged a week earlier, then adjourned to Watertown that afternoon to be closer to Boston. Francis Faulkner (1728–1805) on that same day wrote orders for the two militia companies from Acton to guard the stores still in Concord, undiscovered by the raiding party [no. 59]. Those supplies of ammunition and provisions, which had cost the Provincial Congress thousands of pounds to acquire, were needed immediately by the thousands of soldiers continuing to gather outside Boston. Essential to the success of the Provincial military, the supplies were an obvious target for another attack from the Regulars.

---

59. ORDERS FOR GUARD DUTY

Francis Faulkner (1728–1805)
Concord, Massachusetts, April 22, 1775
Manuscript on paper
Height: 6½"; Width: 7⅝"
Gift of Mr. Russell Hawes Kettell. D1125

*"To Capt Joseph Robbins
Sir our Regiment is Dismist from Duty at / Present at Cambridge in order to Gard the / stores at Concord and the two Militia Company / in Acton are to Gard with fifty men / tomorrow night the Gard to be Mounted at / Six of the Clock in the Eveing the one half / to be Dismissed at Six of the Clock in the / Morning the Remainder to be Relieved at / Six of the Clock on monday Evening / and you are Required to go or Send an / officer with 24 men to Attend Said Duty and / Relieve the Gard at Concord tomorrow / Eveing / Concord April ye 22 1775 Fncs. Faulkner"*

In Provincial Congress, at Watertown, *April* 23, 1775.

RESOLVED, That the following Establishment of Forces now immediately to be raised for the Recovery and Preservation of our undoubted Rights and Liberties, be as follows, viz.

	per Month.
To each Colonel of a Regiment of 1000 Men,	£. 15 0 0
To 1 Lieut. Colonel of such Regiment,	12 0 0
To 1 Major of such Regiment,	10 0 0
For a Captain of 100 Men, including Officers,	6 0 0
For 2 Lieutenants for such Company, each	4 0 0
For 1 Ensign ditto,	3 0 0
For 1 Adjutant for such Regiment,	5 10 0
For 1 Quarter-Master ditto,	3 0 0
For 1 Chaplain ditto,	6 0 0
For 1 Chirurgeon ditto,	7 10 0
For 2 Surgeon's Mates ditto, each,	4 0 0
For each Serjeant,	2 8 0
For each Corporal,	2 4 0
For each Fifer,	2 4 0
For each private Centinel,	2 0 0

RESOLVED, That besides the above, a Coat for a Uniform, be given to each of the non-commission Officers and Privates, so soon as the State of the Province will admit of it.

Also RESOLVED, That the Selectmen of the several Towns and Districts within this Colony, be desired to furnish the Soldiers who shall inlist from their respective Towns and Districts with good and sufficient Blankets, and render their Accounts to the Committee of Supplies, who are hereby directed to draw on the Colony Treasurer for Payment of the same.

President, P. T.

Mr Goodenow District Clerk Please to Insert the following articles in a warrent from your Self Directed to mr Constable Fisher to warn the Voters to meet at the Meeting house Next Fryday at two o'Clock affter noon Viz — first to Chuse a Moderator

2d to Chuse District officers in the Room of Some that are going into the Massechusets Service

3ly to See if the Inhabitants will Provide Guns and Blankets for the Soldiers that are going into the Service; that are Destitute

4ly to See if the Inhabitants will allow mr Peletiah Morse Pay for keeping Thos Nichols whear under Custody

May ye 8 1775

Ephm Jennings
Wm Boden
Oliver Bacon } Selet
Joseph Morse } Men

"Wm. Goodenow District Clerk Please to Insert the following articles / in a warrent from your Self Directed to Mr. Constable Fisher to warn / the Voters to meet at the Meeting house Next Fryday at two o'Clock / affter noon Viz—first to Chuse a Moderator / 2d to Chuse District Officers in the Room of Some that are / Going into the Masechusets Service / 3ly to see if the Inhabitants will Provide Guns and Blankets for / the Soldiers that are going into the Service: that are Destitute / 4ly to see if the Inhabitants will allow Mr. Peletiah Morse Pay for keeping / Thos Nichols when under Custody / Ephrm Jennings / Wm Boden / Oliver Bacon / Joseph Morse / Selet Men / May ye 8 1775."

On the second day of meeting in Watertown the Provincial Congress established the ranks and rates of pay for the officers and men for the army still in the process of being raised. In addition to the wages the Congress resolved that *"a Coat for a Uniform, be given to each of the noncommission Officers and Privates, so soon as the State of the Province will admit of it,"* that is, as soon as the Massachusetts Bay Colony could afford to provide them. They also resolved to ask the towns to furnish *"good and sufficient Blankets"* for their enlistees and request reimbursement from the Committee of Supplies. The broadside [no. 60] that the Provincial Congress ordered printed for distribution is signed by the *"President, P.T."* meaning the president pro tempore, who was Joseph Warren.

As the Provincial Congress was deliberating on the organization of the army they also deliberated on its composition. The February incident in Natick involving Thomas Nichols (the free Black man accused of planning an uprising of enslaved people) became part of that discussion. Because the ordinary operations of the courts in Massachusetts had been interrupted by the organized protest over the Massachusetts Government Act, Thomas Nichols and William Benson had been released in February but they were arrested again after April 19 and held by tavern keeper Peletiah Morse. Paying for that custody was one of the warrant items that the Natick town meeting intended to discuss on May 12 [no. 61].

The day after the Natick town meeting, on May 13, Thomas Nichols was imprisoned in Cambridge. One week later the Committee of Safety voted that Nichols be brought before the Provincial Congress for examination and trial. The regulations for enlisting Black soldiers into the Continental Army would change over time, but at the outset it appears that the prohibition against enlisting the enslaved came from the Committee of Safety and was a response to the allegations against Thomas Nichols. The next resolution the Committee of Safety passed that day, May 20, 1775, stipulated with respect to *"the army now raising"* that *"no slaves be admitted into this army upon any consideration whatever."* At the trial before the Provincial Congress on May 23 *"there being no evidence to prove any matters or things alleged against him,"* Thomas Nichols was returned to the custody of Natick.

On April 20, the first full day of the Siege, the four thousand Provincial soldiers surrounding Boston were from Massachusetts communities within a day's march, but their numbers were steadily augmented by soldiers arriving from more distant parts. Within a few days the minute company of the Stockbridge Band—whom the Provincial Congress had appealed to for assistance just days before the fighting began—had arrived after a 130-mile march. Concord minister William Emerson in a letter home reported enjoying a cordial meal of clams shared with the Stockbridge soldiers at their Cambridge camp.

Captain Benjamin Mann's company mustered in Concord, New Hampshire, before marching for Boston on May 23. Reuben Hosmer was a private in Mann's company and with them participated in the Battle of Bunker Hill on June 17, 1775. Later in the war, in 1777, Reuben Hosmer enlisted for three years and was engaged at the pivotal Battle of Saratoga in New York. In 1940 when the Concord Antiquarian Society bought at auction (for $9) the powder horn Reuben Hosmer carried, they apparently assumed the inscribed *"Concord"* meant Concord, Massachusetts, where Hosmer was born [no. 62]. On the other side of the horn is engraved *"Mason,"* not for the fraternal organization but for Mason, New Hampshire, where Reuben Hosmer lived.

William Emerson described the state of the camps about a week after General George Washington had arrived on July 2, 1775 to take command of the Continental Army, which the twenty thousand soldiers arrayed around Boston had become by order of the Continental Congress. The companies from Massachusetts, New Hampshire, Connecticut, and Rhode Island were intermingled, to prevent misunderstanding, as William Emerson believed. As to the camps themselves, Emerson noted:

> They are as different in their form as the Owners are in their Dress, and every tent is a Portraiture of ye Temper and Taste of ye Person that incamps in it. Some are made of Boards, some of Sailcloth, and some partly of one and partly of the other. Others are made of Stone and Turf, and others again of Brick and others Brush. Some are thrown up in a hurry & look as if they could not help it—meer necessity—others are curiously wrought with doors & windows, done with Wreaths and Withes in manner of a Basket. Some are ye proper Tents and Markees that look as ye regular Camp of ye Enemy."

Two surviving documents provide evidence that the systematic distribution of the stockpiled supplies began without delay. One of

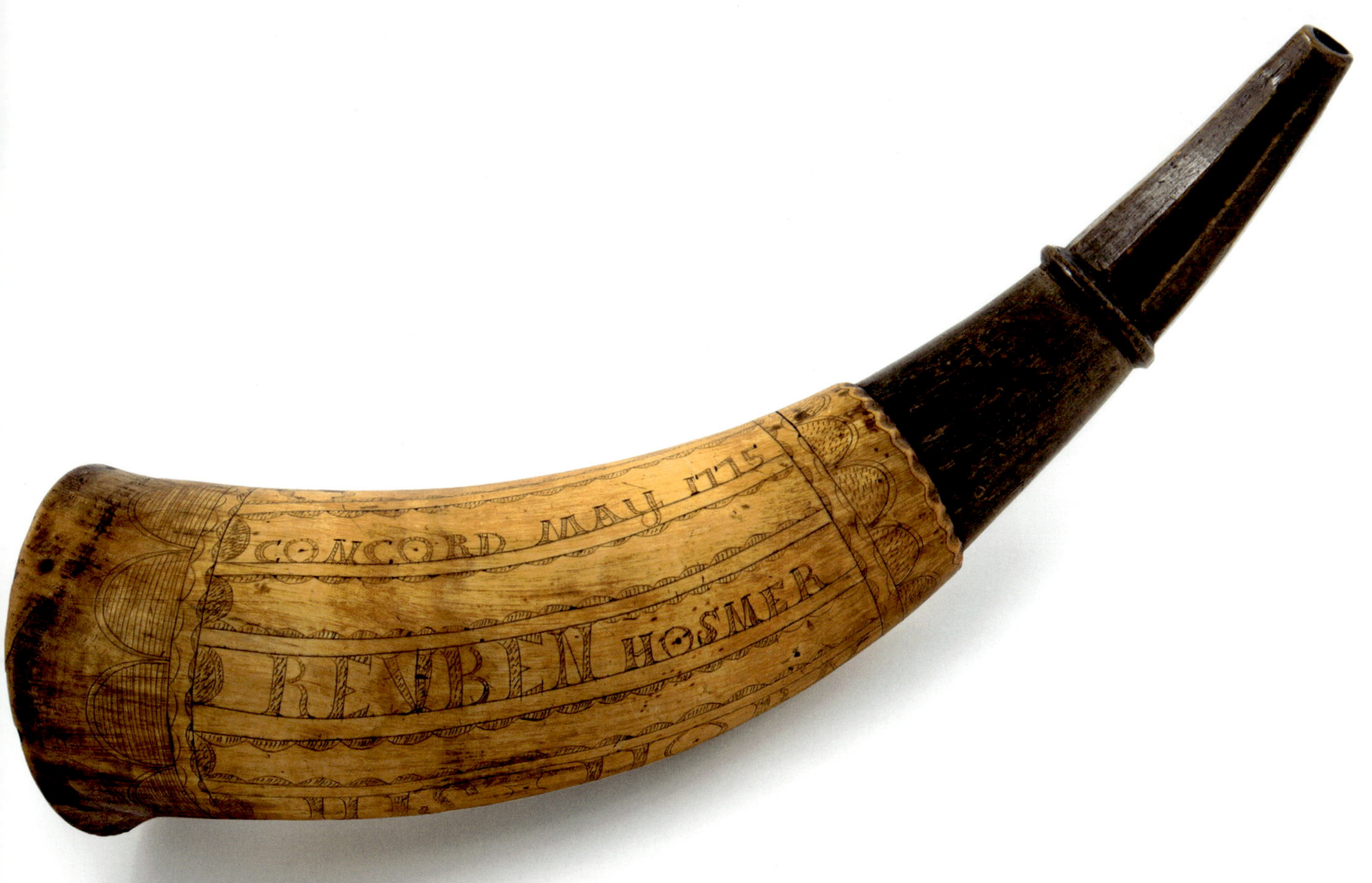

62. POWDER HORN OF REUBEN HOSMER

The Hosmer Carver
New Hampshire, 1775
Horn
Length: 12¹⁄₁₆"; Width: 3¼"
Gift of Mrs. Edward Motley. A2003.1

Inscribed *"CONCORD MAY 1775 / REUBEN HOSMER / HIS HORN"* and on the reverse *"MASON"*

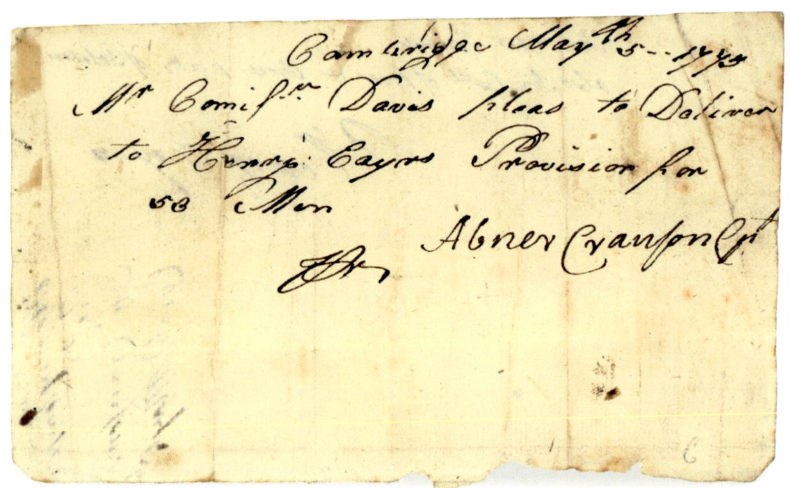

them is a request for provisions for fifty-eight men signed by Captain Abner Cranson of Marlborough, Massachusetts, and addressed to the commissary [no. 63]. The other is a receipt for provisions for eight men that is signed by Captain Benjamin Pollard [no. 64]. Pollard was from Lincoln (and later lived in Concord) and was captain of a company of artificers, that is, people who make things, which accounts for the indication that the iron pot and bowl were *"for the use of the Carpenters."* Thousands of other receipts just like these would have documented the distribution of tons of supplies to the soldiers encamped in Cambridge, Charlestown, and Roxbury, though few survive.

The Provincial Congress appointed Henry Gardner receiver general shortly after forming in October 1774, although Massachusetts already had a receiver general, Harrison Gray. The receiver general is the official who gathers money from the tax collectors for the province treasury, so the Congress was in fact seizing the provincial revenue. The money paid to Henry Gardner was immediately paid out to the Committee of Supplies that was charged with acquiring £20,000 worth of cannon, firearms, bayonets, flints, and other supplies. Early in May 1775, Henry Gardner was empowered to borrow £100,000 and from that credit to issue notes to be used for the payment of advance pay to the Massachusetts Army. The notes were issued for six, nine, ten, twelve, fourteen, fifteen, sixteen, eighteen, and twenty shillings. Twenty shillings is equal to one pound, and six shillings is about two days' wages for a skilled laborer. Paul Revere was paid five shillings a day for serving as a courier for the Provincial Congress. It was Paul Revere who was given the task of engraving and printing the notes.

With a simple economy that only in hindsight appears symbolic, Revere flipped over the copper plate used to print *The Bloody Massacre* and engraved the ten-, twelve-, and eighteen-shilling notes on the back [no. 65].

The Provincial Congress began considering the state of the Harvard campus within a month of the outbreak of hostilities and by June were arranging for the library books and scientific instruments to be removed to Concord. Part of Stoughton Hall was turned over to Samuel and Ebenezer Hall to use as a print shop, producing broadsides, pamphlets, and a weekly newspaper for the Provincial Congress. The arrangement was temporary, and the Halls relocated to Boston in 1776 before the students returned from their sojourn in Concord. The September 21–28 issue of the *Essex Gazette* includes the text of George Washington's September 14th address to the people of Canada, which was also printed as a broadside [no. 66]. The message concerned the detachment of soldiers Washington had sent under General Benedict Arnold to take Quebec, assuring the Canadian readers that they had been sent *"not to plunder, but to protect you."* The mission was a failure.

During the Seven Years' War lasting from 1756 to 1763, the military camps around Lake George in upstate New York witnessed a flourishing in artistic powder horn decoration. The seemingly infectious vogue for engraved horns was repeated in the camps around besieged Boston in 1776. Siege of Boston powder horns are among the most artistic in the tradition of American engraved military powder horns, a thirty-year tradition that ended, with some exceptions, with the conclusion of the Revolutionary War. The horn made in Roxbury for Jonathan Gardner of Sunderland, Massachusetts, is fine enough to assume that the carver was paid for the work, although no other example from this carver is currently known [no. 67]. The horn is inscribed in letters imitating typography: *"Jonathan Gardner His Horn 1776 / Liberty Property or Death."* The neat letters on scribed lines harken back to the innovations in engraved powder horn design developed by the particularly talented John Bush of Shrewsbury in 1755. Near the front of the engraved line of soldiers is an officer with upraised sword followed by a fifer and a drummer. Similar lines of soldiers occur on other Siege of Boston horns. The grim motto summarizes the issues underlying the Siege; the American colonies would either enjoy the liberties common to British subjects, among them the right not to have their property taken without consent, or they would resist with arms.

---

63. REQUEST FOR PROVISIONS

Cambridge, Massachusetts,
May 5, 1775
Manuscript on paper
Height: 3⅝"; Width: 6⅛"
Gift of the Cummings Davis Society.
2007.272.1

"Cambridge May 5th 1775 / Mr Comis.er Davis pleas to Deliver / to Henry Eayrs Provision for / 58 Men / Abner Cranson Cpt"

---

64. RECEIPT FOR PROVISIONS

Cambridge, Massachusetts,
May 5, 1775
Manuscript on paper
Height: 1⅞"; Width: 4³⁄₁₆"
Gift of the Cummings Davis Society.
2007.272.2

"Cambridge May 5th 1775 / Rec'd Provision for Six men & / also one Iron Pot & one Bowl / for the use of the Carpenters / Benja[min] Pollard Cap"

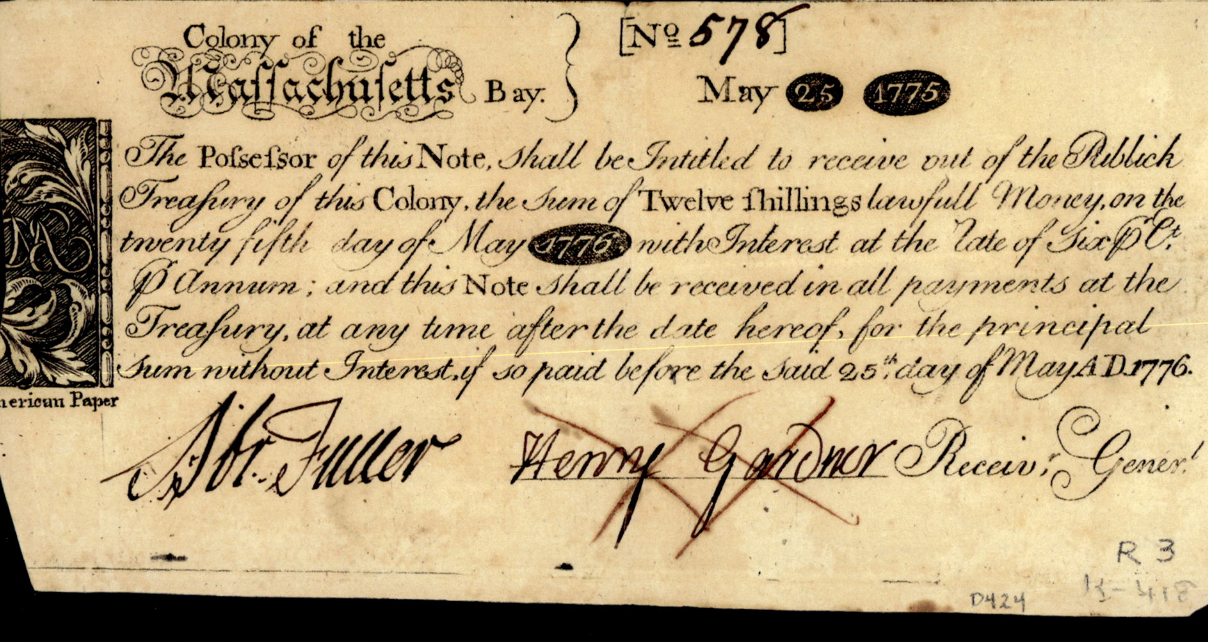

Colony of the **Massachusetts** Bay.   [No. 578]   May 25 1775

The Possessor of this Note, shall be Intitled to receive out of the Publick Treasury of this Colony, the Sum of Twelve shillings lawfull Money, on the twenty fifth day of May 1776 with Interest at the Rate of Six ♍Ct. ♍ Annum; and this Note shall be received in all payments at the Treasury, at any time after the date hereof, for the principal Sum without Interest, if so paid before the said 25th day of May A.D. 1776.

Abr. Fuller   Henry Gardner Receiv. Gener.

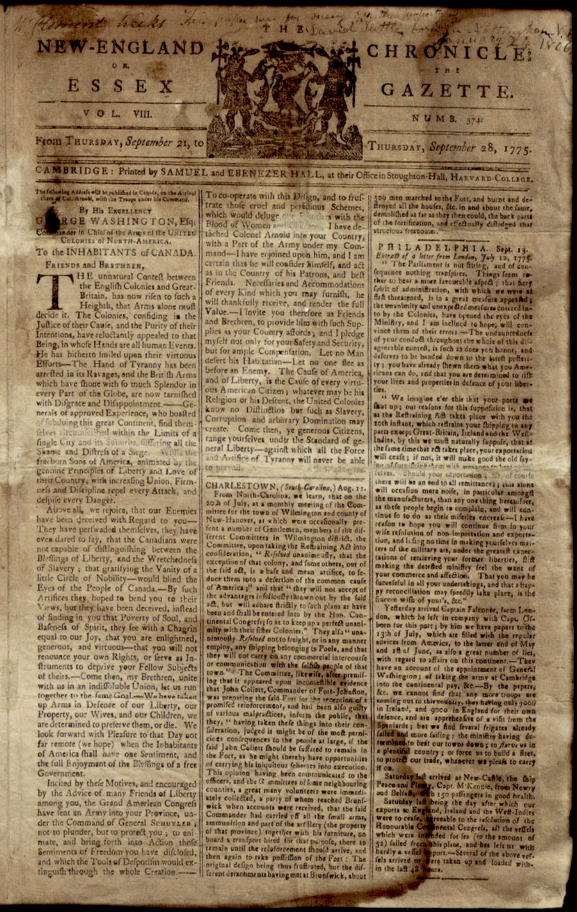

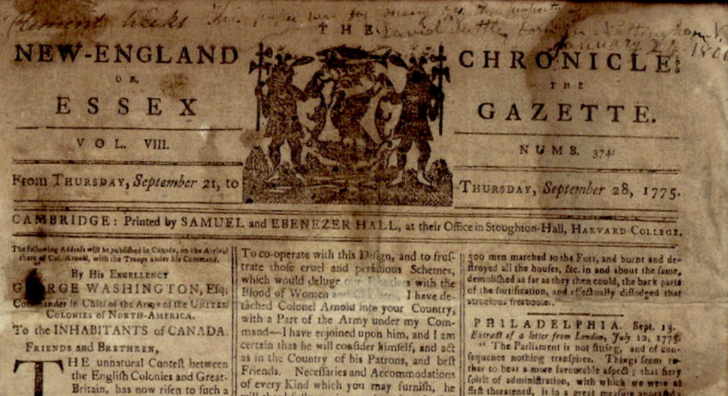

THE
NEW-ENGLAND CHRONICLE: OR, ESSEX GAZETTE.

VOL. VIII.   NUMB. 374.

From THURSDAY, September 21, to THURSDAY, September 28, 1775.

CAMBRIDGE: Printed by SAMUEL and EBENEZER HALL, at their Office in Stoughton-Hall, HARVARD COLLEGE.

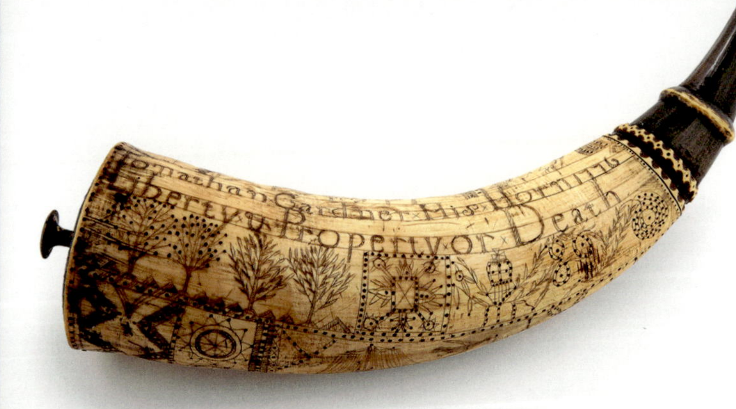

65. TWELVE SHILLING NOTE

Engraved by Paul Revere (1735–1818)
Boston, Massachusetts, 1775
Engraving and manuscript on paper
Height: 3³⁄₁₆"; Width: 6¹³⁄₁₆"
Gift of Mr. Russell Hawes Kettell.
D424

An example of a twelve shilling note in the Concord Museum collection is signed by Henry Gardner as receiver general, with the signature cancelled, indicating that it was turned in to the treasury in return for its value in silver or gold. The note is indented on the left side, meaning that it is cut irregularly. When redeemed, the irregular cut would be matched to the portion retained by the receiver general as a safeguard against counterfeiting. The indenture cuts through an engraved cypher *"CMB,"* for *"Colony of Massachusetts Bay."* Beneath it are the words *"American Paper."* Paper was one of the commodities taxed by the Townshend Revenue Act and consequently was on the nonimportation list for as long as the embargo lasted. Yet paper was a necessity for a literate society. Occasional notices in the Boston newspapers announced that a bell cart, a cart with a bell that rings constantly, would travel through the town collecting rags for the mill in Milton. Worn-out linens would be gathered, piled up to ferment for a while, shredded, and beaten to a pulp in vats of water. A screen held in a frame would be used to lift some of this pulp out and that is what became the sheet of paper. The twelve shilling note is printed on paper made in Milton out of cast-off work shirts and sheets.

In addition to the signature of the receiver general the note is counter-signed by Abraham Fuller, who was given the task of signing the twelve-shilling notes by the Provincial Congress on July 8, 1775. That would indicate that the note is one of the 667 notes Congress ordered printed from the plates in July, rather than one of those from the larger printing in May.

66. THE *NEW-ENGLAND CHRONICLE,* OR THE *ESSEX GAZETTE*

Printed by Samuel and Ebenezer Hall
Volume VIII, number 374, September 21–28, 1775
Cambridge, 1775
Letterpress on paper
Height: 19³⁄₈"; Width: 15"
Museum Purchase. 2024.14.1

67. POWDER HORN OF JONATHAN GARDNER
(SEE ALSO PAGES 68–69)

Probably Roxbury, Massachusetts, 1776
Horn, maple, brass
Length: 10"; Width: 2³⁄₁₆"
Gift of Mrs. Robert M. Bowen. A116

"GREAT BRITAIN ADIEU.
KING GEORGE *the* THIRD
ADIEU!"

✳

— *ESSEX GAZETTE,* APRIL 25, 1775

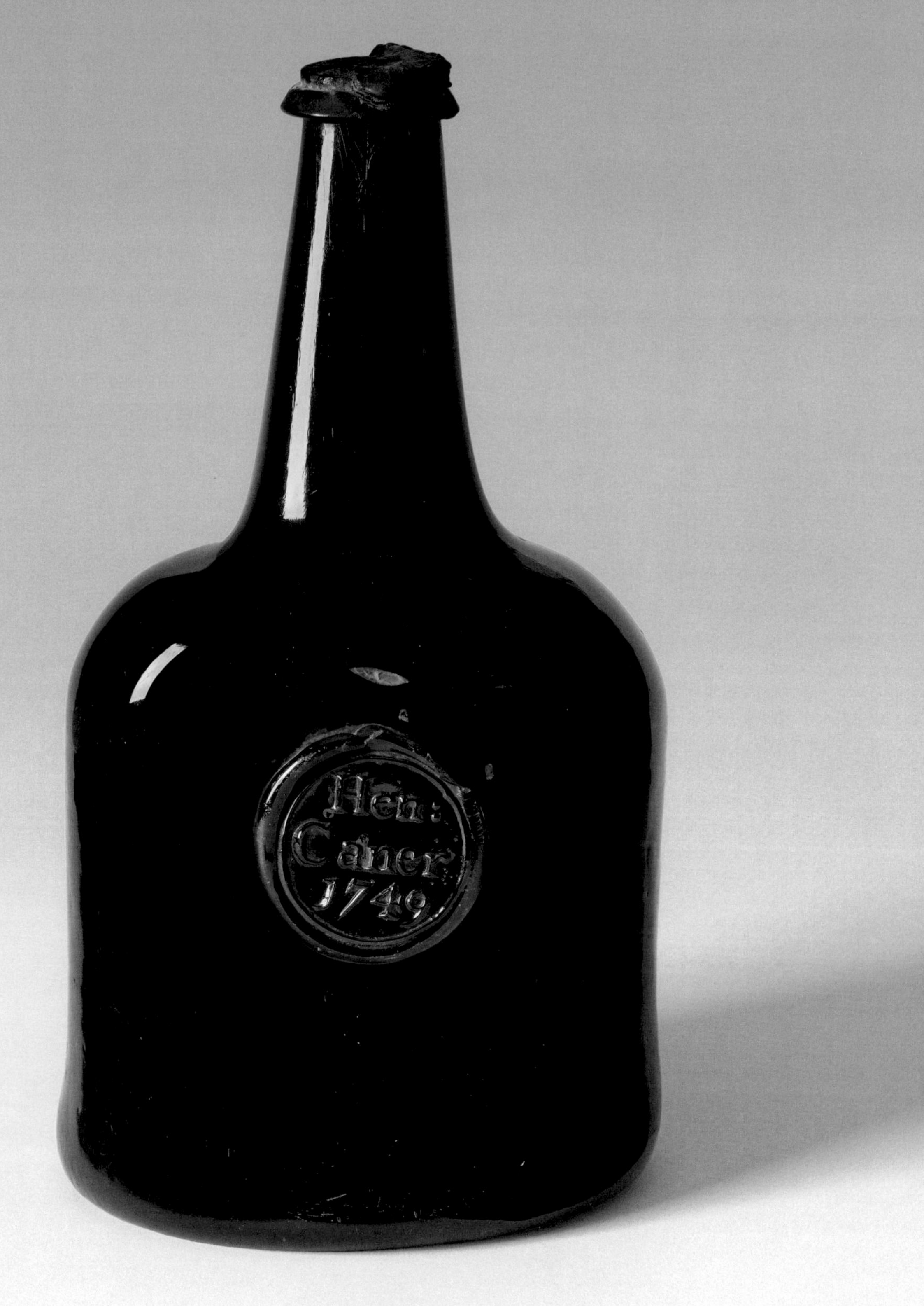
Hen:
Caner
1749

68. WINE BOTTLE

(PRECEDING PAGE)

England, 1749

Glass

Height: 9″; Width: 4¹⁵⁄₁₆″

Gift of Cummings E. Davis. G179

The applied glass seal on this bottle reads *"Hen: / Caner / 1749."*

Tolman 1911, 321: "BOTTLE from cellar of Henry Caner, Rector of King's Chapel, at Boston, who fled with the British troops and the Tories to Halifax in 1776. Bottle marked in the glass with his name and the date 1749."

T HE SIEGE OF BOSTON finally came to an end in the spring of 1776. A young Boston bookseller with deep roots in the American Revolution played a significant role. Six years earlier, on March 5, 1770, when Henry Knox was not yet twenty years old, he had heard with concern the ringing of bells and calls of *"Fire!"* Knox spoke with Captain Preston of the 29th Regiment on the steps of the Customs House just prior to the outbreak of gunfire that Paul Revere depicted in *The Bloody Massacre* engraving **[no. 8]**, advising restraint. In 1775 Knox managed the artillery for the Provincial forces at the Battle of Bunker Hill. Later that year Knox was charged by George Washington with a mission to go to Fort Ticonderoga on Lake Champlain and pick up fifty-nine cannon that had been captured the previous May. Colonel Knox's company brought the tons of artillery across the entire width of Massachusetts that winter, arriving in Cambridge at the end of January. When in early March some of the cannon were placed on Dorchester Heights overlooking Boston, General William Howe (who had replaced General Thomas Gage in command) gave the order for the British Army Regulars to evacuate Boston. They did so on March 17, 1776.

The Concord militia company of Lieutenant Ephraim Wheeler marched to Roxbury in support of this final effort to drive the British Regulars out of Boston. The muster roll for that company, prepared by the company clerk William Parkman, lists the name and rank of each soldier and officer, the number of miles travelled, the number of days of service, and allowance for rations **[no. 69]**. The clerk added at the bottom a note reading *"This Roll is Calculated according to the pay allowd by this Province,"* that is, calculated according to the pay rates established by the Provincial Congress and published in a broadside on April 23, 1775 **[no. 60]**. The estimates of the number of Massachusetts soldiers who responded to the April 19 alarm are in large part based on muster rolls much like that prepared by William Parkman.

Boston minister Henry Caner (1700–1792) was among the evacuees on March 17, 1776. Caner had assumed the pulpit of King's Chapel in Boston. The denomination of King's Chapel was Church of England,

69. MUSTER ROLL FOR THE COMPANY OF EPHRAIM WHEELER

William Parkman, clerk
Concord, Massachusetts, June 8, 1776
Manuscript on paper
Height: 15⅜"; Width: 12⁷⁄₁₆"
Gift of Mr. Russell Hawes Kettell.
D2003.2

"A list of a Company of Militia Commanded by Lieut Ephraim Wheeler of a Regement of which Eleazer Brooks Esq is Col. which Company Belongs to Concord who marchd to Roxbury March the fourth 1776 to reinforce the Army of the United Colonies on duty for our defence near Boston." The names listed are: Ephraim Wheeler, Nathanael Sterns, Amos Wood, William Parkman, John Stratton, Samuel Hubbard, John Prescott Haywood, Samuel Darby, David Hubbard, John Mullikon, Peter Wheeler, Charles Miles Junior, John Hosmer, James Coleman, Joel Hosmer, Benjamin Hosmer, Oliver Miles, Micah Balcom, Thomos Wheeler, Ephraim Hosmer, Lot Conant, Oliver Brown, Jason Hayns, Jonathan Ball, Silas Wood, Jonos Lee, Joseph Webb, Parish Miles, Jacob Caldwell, Nathanael Nutting, Jebe Hosmer, John Hosmer Junior, Willoughby Prescott, Jason Bemus, Stephen Potter, Jacob Potter, Nathan Pierce, and John Minott.

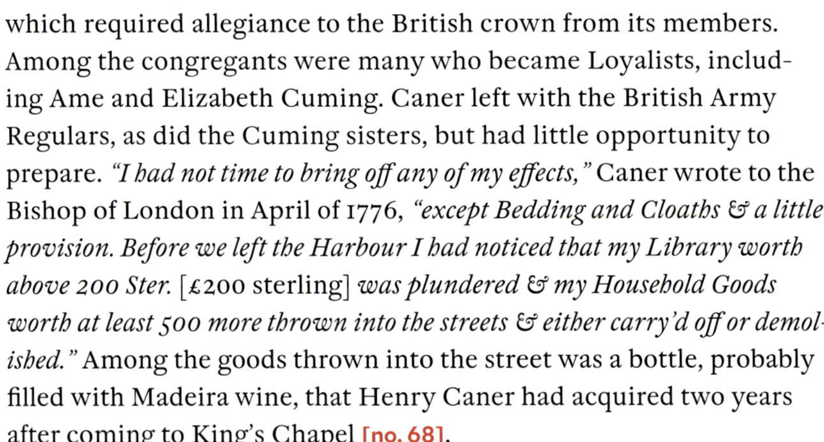

England; Virginia; and Concord,
Massachusetts
Barrel about 1705; Lock about 1777;
Stock about 1777
Iron, steel, cherry
Overall Length: 85⅛"; Barrel Length
50"; Bore: ¾" (about .75 caliber)
Gift of Dr. Joseph C. Merriam. A104

which required allegiance to the British crown from its members. Among the congregants were many who became Loyalists, including Ame and Elizabeth Cuming. Caner left with the British Army Regulars, as did the Cuming sisters, but had little opportunity to prepare. *"I had not time to bring off any of my effects,"* Caner wrote to the Bishop of London in April of 1776, *"except Bedding and Cloaths & a little provision. Before we left the Harbour I had noticed that my Library worth above 200 Ster. [£200 sterling] was plundered & my Household Goods worth at least 500 more thrown into the streets & either carry'd off or demolished."* Among the goods thrown into the street was a bottle, probably filled with Madeira wine, that Henry Caner had acquired two years after coming to King's Chapel [no. 68].

With the departure of the British Regular regiments from Boston, the Continental Army under the command of General Washington departed as well and of course they took their arms with them. This left the stock of weapons in the province depleted and the Provincial Congress made provision to start replacing them. A musket fitted with a Rappahannock Forge lock may represent the sort of arms this effort produced [no. 70]. The musket was given to the Concord Antiquarian Society with the history that it had been carried at the North Bridge by Josiah Merriam (1726–1809) of Concord. The barrel is old enough to have been involved in the North Bridge fight, but not the lock or stock. The barrel is English and dates to about 1705. It is marked on the upper flat of the barrel *"JOSEPH MERIAM"* for blacksmith Joseph Merriam (1677–1750), the father of Josiah Merriam. Joseph Merriam's house still stands at Merriam's Corner, the site where the attack on the returning column of Regulars began. The lock is marked *"Rapa / Forge"* for the Rappahannock Forge gun manufactory established by John Hunter in Virginia in 1776. The lack of a butt plate and the presence of a wooden ramrod on the Merriam musket suggests that it would not have been fit for service in the Continental Army but may have been one of those made for the use of the militia. The trigger guard is a replacement for an iron trigger guard, which may itself have been a replacement.

After the Siege of Boston, the wartime campaign that involved the greatest number of Concord soldiers was the action at Saratoga in New York. In what was supposed to be a coordinated attempt to cut New

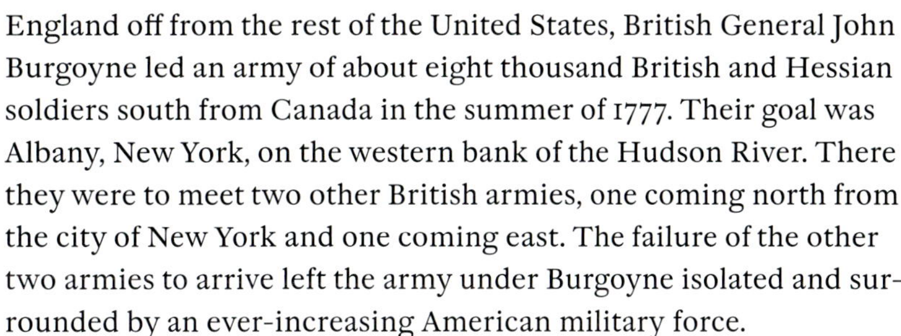

England off from the rest of the United States, British General John Burgoyne led an army of about eight thousand British and Hessian soldiers south from Canada in the summer of 1777. Their goal was Albany, New York, on the western bank of the Hudson River. There they were to meet two other British armies, one coming north from the city of New York and one coming east. The failure of the other two armies to arrive left the army under Burgoyne isolated and surrounded by an ever-increasing American military force.

In response to the threat posed by the movements of the British forces, Massachusetts had drafted one sixth of the militia into the Continental Army. Each militia regiment was given a quota that their colonel had to fulfill either through volunteers or conscription. Concord and Acton sent sixty-three volunteers. On October 7 the Burgoyne-led army lost a decisive battle and retreated to Saratoga, surrendering there on October 17, 1777 [nos. 71 and 72]. British general John Burgoyne and American general Horatio Gates signed a surrender document called the Saratoga Convention, which called for the surrendered forces, numbering over five thousand, to be marched to Boston and from there sent back to Europe. The British and German troops marched from Saratoga over the Green Mountains of Vermont and down the Connecticut River valley through Deerfield, Massachusetts, then east through Worcester to Cambridge. The march took three weeks. Hannah Winthrop, whose husband John was the Harvard professor of natural philosophy (physics), on November 11, 1777, wrote a letter to Mercy Otis Warren (in the collection of the Massachusetts Historical Society) describing vividly the arrival of what was termed the Convention Army in Cambridge:

> To be sure the sight was truly Astonishing, I never had the least Idea, that the Creation producd such a Sordid Set of Creatures in human Figure — poor dirty emaciated men, great numbers of women, who seemd to be the beasts of burthen, having a bushel basket on their back, by which they were bent double, the contents seemd to be Pots & kettles, various sorts of Furniture, children peeping thro gridirons & other utensils. Some very young Infants who were born on the road, the women barefoot, cloathd in dirty rags.

Because the terms of the Saratoga Convention were never agreed to by the Continental Congress, this unfortunate army was to spend years marching from one place of confinement to another until the remnant was finally released in 1783.

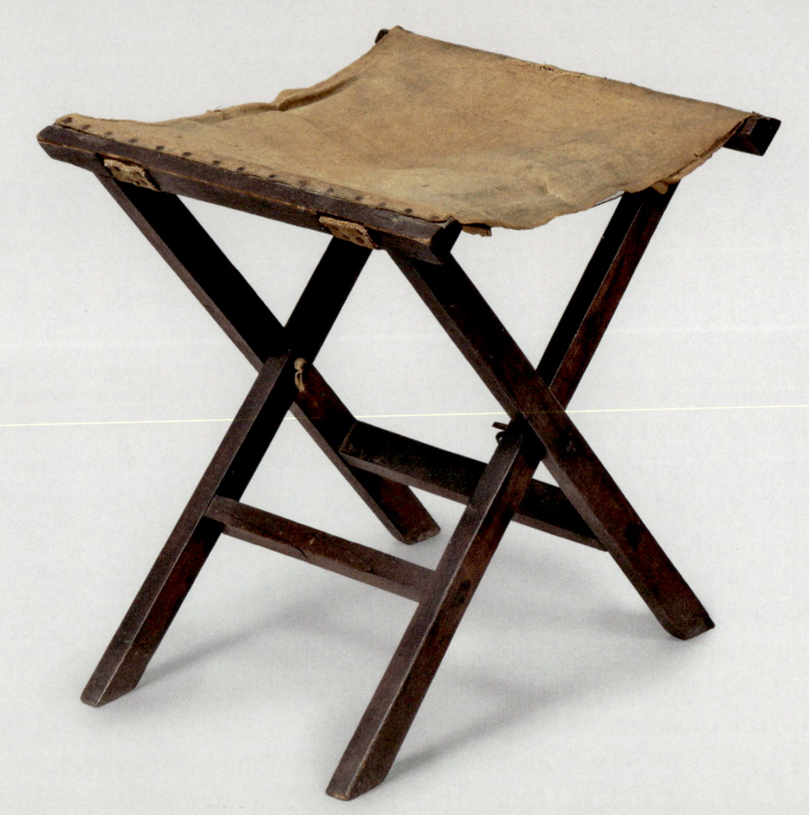

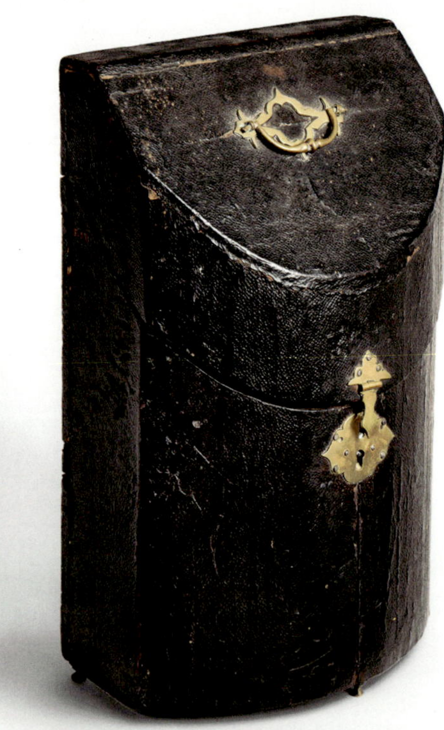

71. CAMP STOOL

England, 1765–1770
Walnut, linen
Height: 20⅜"; Width: 18⅛";
Depth: 16½"
Gift of Cummings E. Davis. F2075

A stool survives that was said to be the property of a Lieutenant Spiller who surrendered at Saratoga with General Burgoyne's army. Perhaps it was brought back by one of the sixty-three Concord and Acton men who responded to the call for troops to support the Northern Army in September 1777. There is no Lieutenant Spiller included in the list of those captured, but it is reasonable to associate the stool with a British Regular officer. It is an example of what cabinetmakers called "campaign furniture." British army officers with the means could somewhat soften the hardships of war by purchasing for themselves specialized portable furniture that might include beds with curtains, chests, desks, portable liquor chests, looking glasses — almost anything appropriate for a genteel parlor might have an analog in campaign furniture. The use of furniture in camp indicated elevated rank, in much the same way that wearing a fine sword did.

Officers in the army wanted to be perceived as gentlemen. This stool comprises eight pieces of wood tenoned together into two frames that are hinged at the crossing with nuts and bolts. The seat bottom is a piece of linen canvas tacked into a rabbet cut into each of the two top rails and supported underneath by two canvas webs. George Washington used a camp stool of similar form with a leather bottom.

Tolman 1911, 375: "CAMP STOOL of Lieutenant Spiller, of the British Army, taken prisoner at the surrender of General Burgoyne in 1777."

England, 1760–1770
Shagreen, wood, velvet, printed
paper, gold braid, brass
Height: 12¹¹⁄₁₆"; Width: 7¾"
Gift of Cummings E. Davis. F921

Connecticut general Israel Putnam gave Eleazer Brooks a handsome fitted cutlery box whose contents would have allowed General Brooks to entertain other officers in a manner befitting elevated rank, social as well as military. The exact circumstances of the gift are not recorded but it was probably at Saratoga, the only occasion when the two distinguished field officers commanded divisions in the same campaign.

Tolman 1911, 205: **"KNIFE CASE, with six forks still remaining. Given by Gen. Israel Putnam to Gen. Eleazer Brooks of the Army of the American Revolution."**

The service of one Massachusetts militia company in guarding these marching prisoners is documented in an account made in January 1778. Titled "*A Muster Roll of Capt Ford, Company of Militia, now in Service of the United States for the Purpose of Guarding the Troops of the Convention Commanded by Col. Eleazer Brooks,*" [no. 73] the document lists four sergeants, four corporals, a drummer, a fifer, and fifty privates. The captain of the company was Cadwallader Ford, Jr. (1743–1804) of Wilmington, Massachusetts. Ford was captain of a Wilmington minute company that responded to the April 19, 1775 alarm.

An act of the Provincial Congress passed on December 6, 1776 directed the treasurer to issue more than £200,000 in notes "*for the payment of the bounty-money granted by the general court of this state to the soldiers raised by this state to be inlisted into the Continental service.*" "Continental service" refers to the Continental Army that had formed on July 2, 1775, on the arrival of General George Washington in Cambridge to take command of the minutemen and militia besieging Boston. The notes were to be "*printed on good paper, and a suitable border round the same; and when said notes are issued, a counterpart, indented, of each note, shall be kept by the treasurer.*" "*Indented*" refers to the wavy line cut in the left margin of the note that would match the stub retained by the treasurer as a means of discouraging counterfeiting. In the border of the note, which is not engraved but printed in letterpress, are the words "*BOUNTY NOTE.*" All the notes were for the value of £10.

On September 20, 1777, the Massachusetts General Court passed a resolution for furnishing firearms to the three thousand troops then being drafted for service in the Continental Army. Each soldier who needed one would receive "*one Fire arm and accoutrements, valuing the same at four Pounds ten Shillings, taking the Receipts for the same to be returned into the Commissary General's Store when Discharged from the Service.*" Some of the bounty notes, including the one shown here, [no. 74] were used as receipts for those firearms and accoutrements, which included a bayonet and cartridge box. The receipt states that Captain Jonathan Winslow acknowledges receiving a firelock and accoutrements valued at £4 10s. The cancelled signature of the receiver general, Henry Gardner, indicates that this note was redeemed, either at the face value of £10 or for £5 10s, if the firearm was not returned.

France began supplying muskets to the American army in 1776 through the efforts particularly of Benjamin Franklin. At first in small numbers and somewhat clandestine, the trickle of arms became a flood

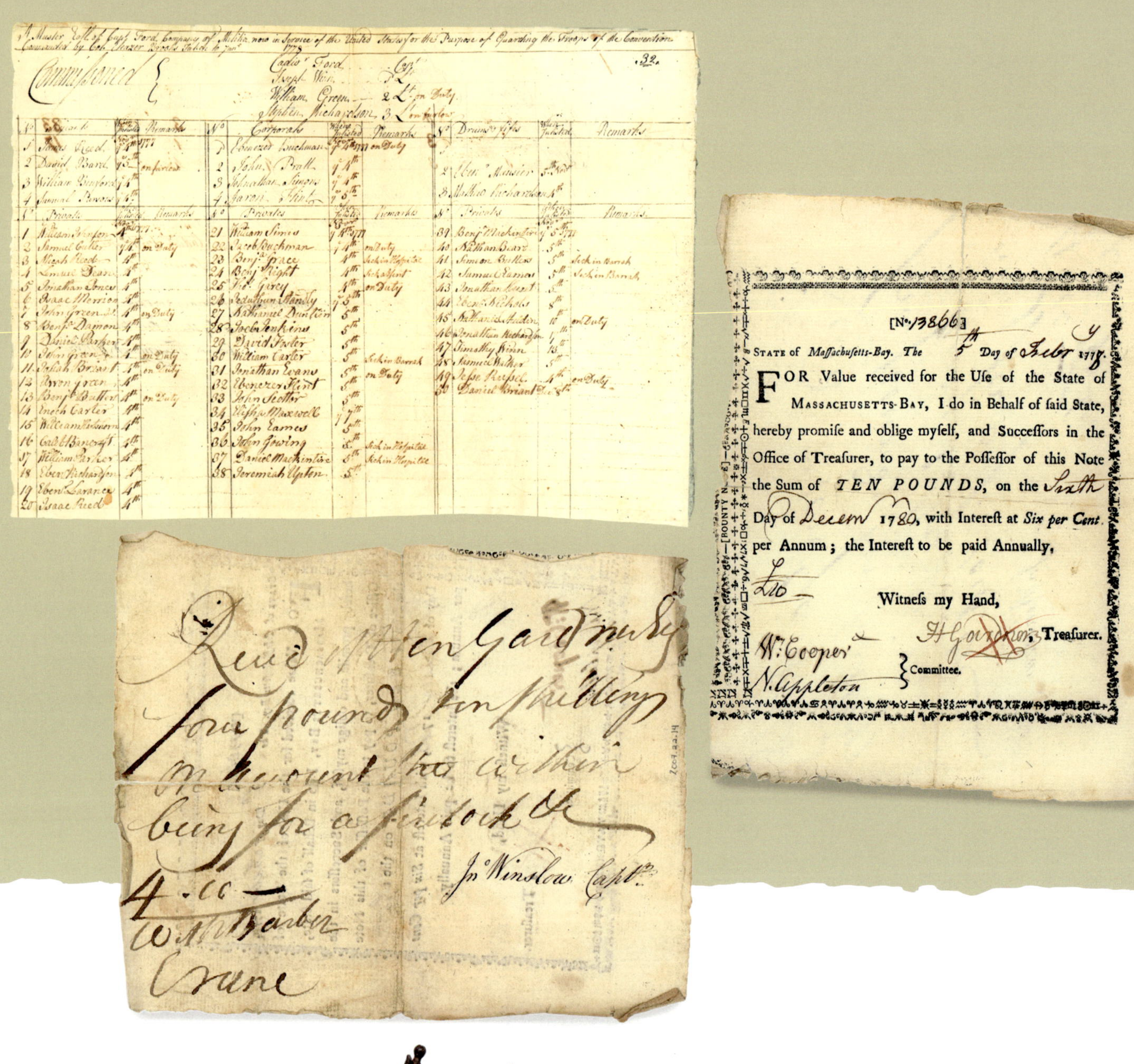
[N.º 13866]
STATE of Massachusetts-Bay. The 5th Day of Febr 1779
FOR Value received for the Use of the State of
MASSACHUSETTS-BAY, I do in Behalf of said State,
hereby promise and oblige myself, and Successors in the
Office of Treasurer, to pay to the Possessor of this Note
the Sum of TEN POUNDS, on the Sixth
Day of Decem 1780, with Interest at Six per Cent.
per Annum; the Interest to be paid Annually,
£10
Witness my Hand,
W. Cooper
N. Appleton
Committee.
H Gardner Treasurer.

73. MUSTER ROLL FOR THE COMPANY OF CAPTAIN CADWALLADER FORD

Cambridge, Massachusetts, 1778
Manuscript on paper
Height: 10⅝"; Width: 15⅜"
Concord Museum collection. 2023.20.1

74. TEN-POUND BOUNTY NOTE

Massachusetts, 1778
Letterpress and manuscript on paper
Height: 7¹⁸⁄₁₆"; Width: 6⅜"
Gift of the Cummings Davis Society.
2007.22.14

"Rec'd of Henry Gardner Esq / four pounds ten shillings / on account the within / being for a firelock &c. / Jno Winslow Captn"

75. MODEL 1763 / 1766 MUSKET

Charleville Armory
France, about 1770
Steel, walnut
Overall Length: 60"; Barrel Length: 44¾"; Bore: ⁷⁄₁₀" (about .70 caliber)
Mrs. Eleanor Gardner Cook. 1995.11

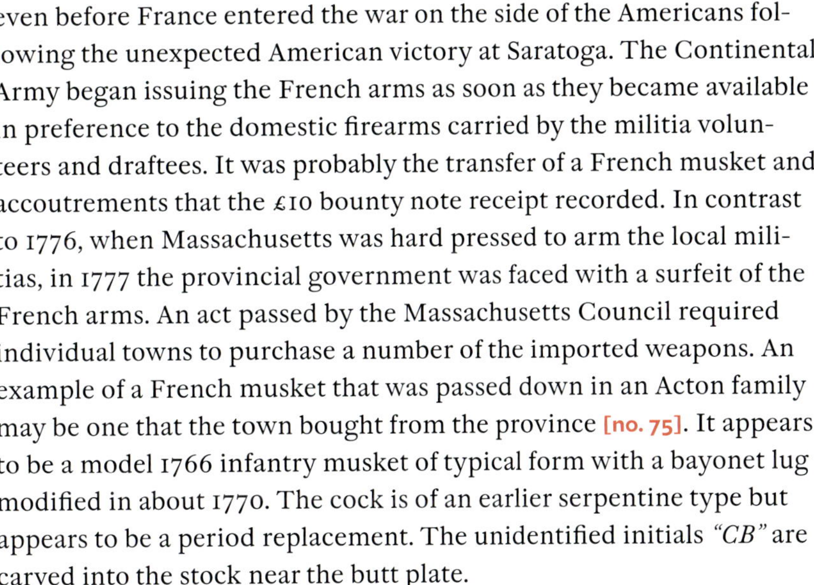

even before France entered the war on the side of the Americans following the unexpected American victory at Saratoga. The Continental Army began issuing the French arms as soon as they became available in preference to the domestic firearms carried by the militia volunteers and draftees. It was probably the transfer of a French musket and accoutrements that the £10 bounty note receipt recorded. In contrast to 1776, when Massachusetts was hard pressed to arm the local militias, in 1777 the provincial government was faced with a surfeit of the French arms. An act passed by the Massachusetts Council required individual towns to purchase a number of the imported weapons. An example of a French musket that was passed down in an Acton family may be one that the town bought from the province [no. 75]. It appears to be a model 1766 infantry musket of typical form with a bayonet lug modified in about 1770. The cock is of an earlier serpentine type but appears to be a period replacement. The unidentified initials *"CB"* are carved into the stock near the butt plate.

Four more years of combat lay ahead, but the entry of France into the conflict proved to be decisive. In October 1781 a combined American force commanded by George Washington and French force commanded by the Marquis de Lafayette surrounded the army commanded by British general Charles Cornwallis at Yorktown, Virginia. Cornwallis surrendered an army of about the same size as that captured at Saratoga.

Although negotiations would continue for two more years, the war was effectively over. The Treaty of Paris, concluding the conflict, was signed in September 1783. On December 23, 1783, General George Washington resigned the commission as Commander in Chief of the Continental Army granted by the Continental Congress in May 1775, and the American army disbanded. In turning over the sword representative of command to Congress, George Washington self-consciously emulated the example of Lucius Quinctius Cincinnatus, a quasi-historical figure from the Roman Republic who came to represent the ideal of the soldier-citizen-farmer. Cincinnatus had retired from a consulship in Rome to a farming villa in the provinces, farming being the only occupation considered honorable by the Romans. In a crisis, the Roman Senate persuaded Cincinnatus to become Rome's tyrant. Cincinnatus resolved the crisis and promptly resigned the tyranny, returning to the plow, much as Washington resigned the command of the victorious American army and returned home to Mount Vernon.

American Brigadier General Henry Knox is given credit for proposing in May 1783 a fraternal organization — the Society of the Cincinnati — composed of the American and French field officers who had served under George Washington. Henry Knox had served throughout the war with distinction, successfully completing the mission to transport the fifty-nine cannon that helped end the Siege of Boston, and participated with General Washington in many of the major engagements of the war. A cake plate from a tea service that belonged to Henry Knox features the emblem of the Society of the Cincinnati [no. 76]. The plate, which has been broken in two and repaired, is inscribed with the gilt initials *"HK."* Other surviving pieces from the Knox service bear the initials *"HLK,"* for Henry and Lucy Flucker Knox (1756–1824). The decoration on the plate is also inferior to the other extant pieces in the set, which survive in a number of collections, suggesting that it was made later as a replacement piece.

The founding document of the Society of the Cincinnati, called the *Institution*, articulates the mission of the Society as a benevolent effort to sustain the national independence achieved through the Revolutionary War, to maintain the friendships that grew up among the officers who helped achieve it, and to provide for any among them, their widows, or their children who might become indigent. Membership was meant to be hereditary, passing to the first-born male in subsequent generations. Mild as that purpose appears, there were nevertheless objections raised almost immediately from several quarters. In an undated draft (collection of Lincoln Public Library, Eleazer Brooks Scrapbook) of the report of a committee appointed by both houses of the Massachusetts legislature in 1783 to "inquire into the existence, nature, object & probable tendency" of the new society, Eleazer Brooks listed some of the perceived difficulties.

The committee considered the Society *"unjustifiable"* and potentially *"Dangerous to the peace & Liberties of the united States in general & this Commonwealth in particular."* The first objection was that the Society was self-created, not regulated by any constitutional authority, and

China, after 1790
Porcelain with overglaze enamel
decoration and gilding
Height: 2"; Width: 8"
Gift of Mr. Cummings E. Davis. C522

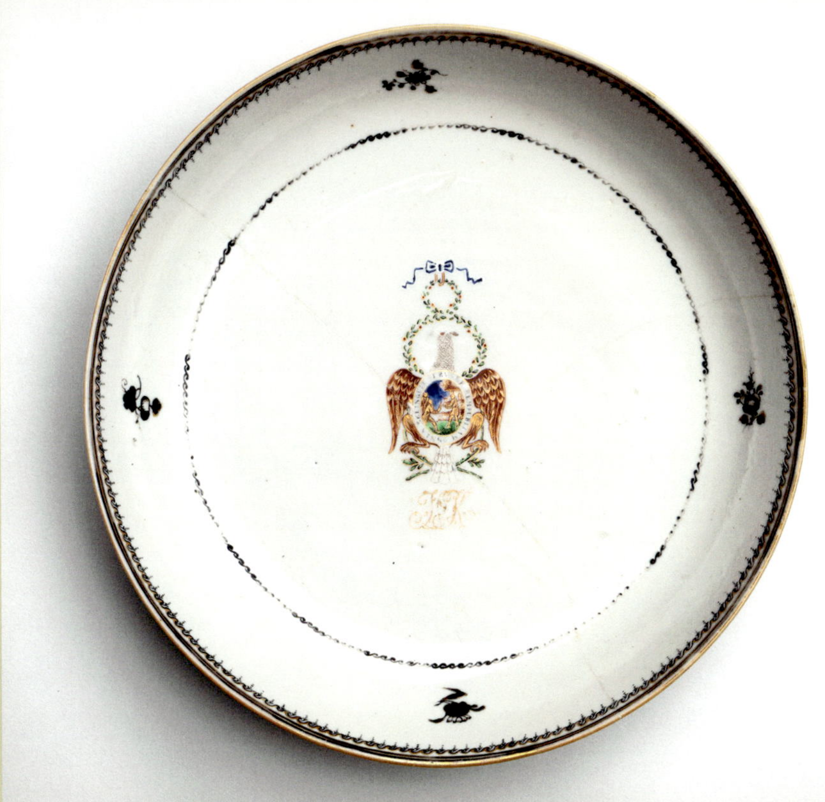

assumed the right to make its own laws, a charge almost identical to that leveled in 1774 by General Thomas Gage against the Provincial Congress. The committee also objected to the circulation of letters among the state branches of the Society that was proposed in the *Institution*, much as the British government had objected to the committees of correspondence. The plans to raise money for the support of indigent members was also seen as a threat, because there was no limit to how much could be raised. The Society *"Savours too much of ostentation,"* the committee felt, and because it was hereditary it threatened to develop into a hereditary nobility *"contrary to the Spirit of all republican governments."* The final objection was that, considering the reputation of the members, George Washington prominently among them, the Society was *"Likely to Succeed & Consequently more likely to become Dangerous in future."* The fears of the committee, born of the recent American experience of fashioning an opposition government, coupled with a recognition that tyranny is as possible in a republic as it is in a monarchy, turned out to be unfounded. The Social Circle in Concord, a local organization in some ways reminiscent of the Society

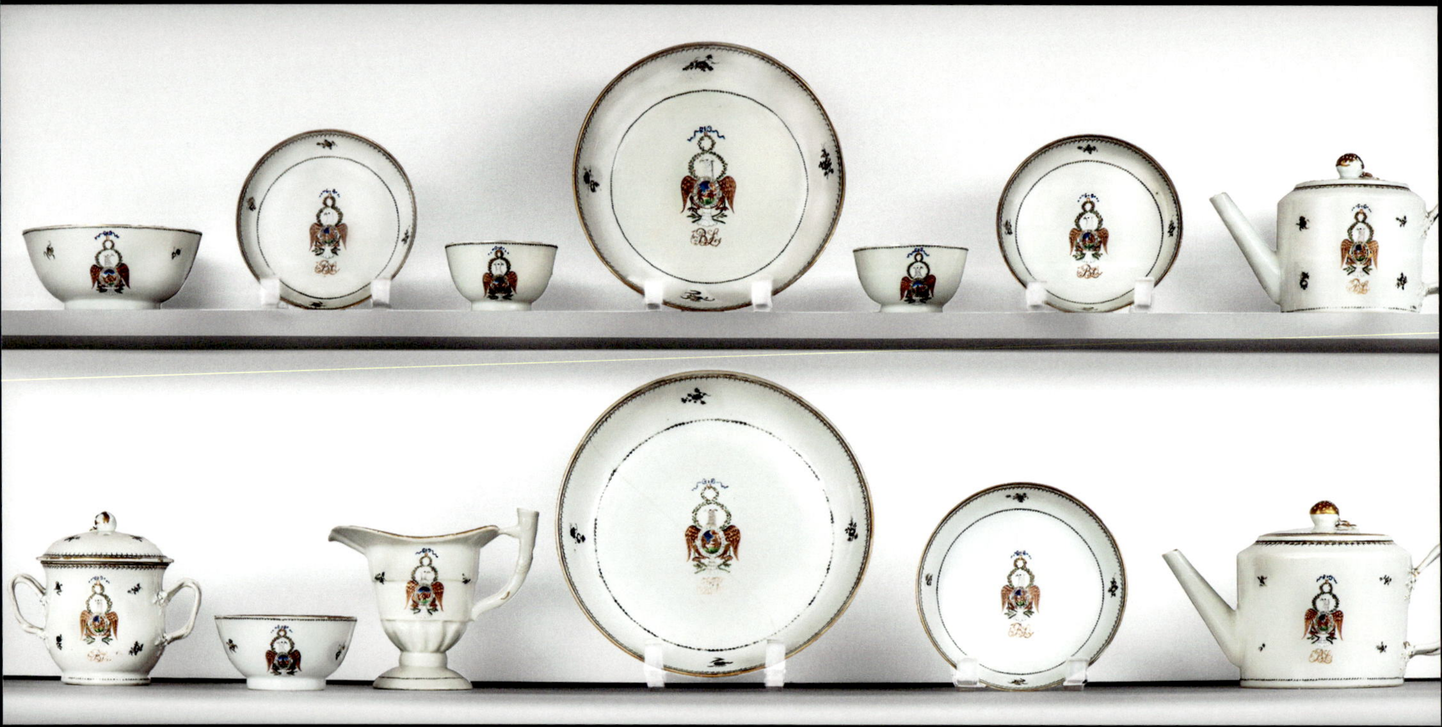

77. PARTIAL TEA SERVICE

China, about 1790
Porcelain with overglaze enamel
decoration and gilding
Height of largest teapot: 5½"
Gift of the sons and daughters of
Dr. William Lincoln Smith (Hilda
Smith Hollis, Benjamin Lincoln Smith,
Farnham Wheeler Smith, Philip Loring
Smith, Elizabeth Farnham Johnson,
Donald McRuer Smith). C788

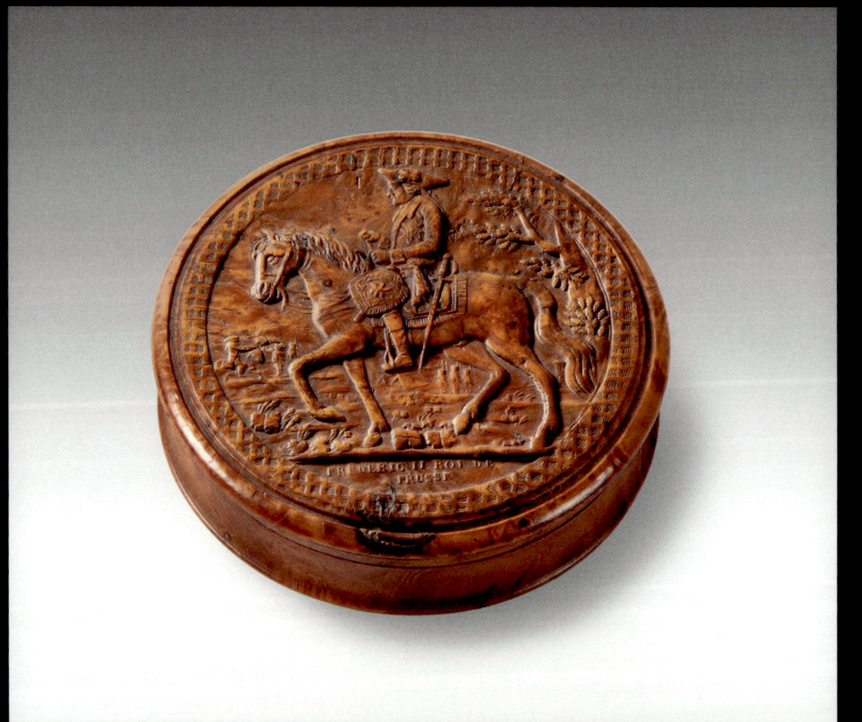

Design after David-Nicolas
Chodowiecki (1726–1801)
France, 1780–1790
Walnut, tortoise shell, silver
Diameter: 3⅜"
Gift of Mr. Stephen Lincoln Smith.
Per2338

A handsome snuff box testifies to the esteem in which George Washington held Benjamin Lincoln. A silver plaque attached to the tortoise shell interior reads: *"Presented by Gen'l Washington to Gen'l Benjn. Lincoln."* The lid is embossed with an equestrian portrait in a technique called "ecorche," which involves pressing the steamed inner bark of a walnut tree in an engraved die, much like stamping a coin. The image is identified as *"FREDERIC II ROI DE PRUSSE"* for Frederick the Second, King of Prussia, often referred to as Frederick the Great. George Washington viewed Frederick as the exemplary model of the modern soldier-statesman, a figure like Lucius Cincinnatus worthy of both admiration and emulation. In the background is a scene of a military encampment. The design was the work of David-Nicolas Chodowiecki (1726–1801), a Polish-born graphic artist and prominent member of the Berlin Academy.

of the Cincinnati, formed in 1782. Its stated mission is: *"To strengthen the social affections, and disseminate useful information among its members."* Among the Social Circle's first set of members were five who had been at the North Bridge: Joseph Hosmer, Samuel Jones, David Brown, Reuben Brown, and Emerson Cogswell. Twelve others in that first group of twenty had served in the military during the Revolutionary War. Unlike the Society of the Cincinnati, membership in the Social Circle is not hereditary. As members die or move away from Concord their vacancies are filled by election.

The Henry Knox tea service is one of nine that Samuel Shaw (1754–1794), secretary of the Society of the Cincinnati, had produced in China in 1790 as gifts to friends, which Shaw recorded in a letter (collection of Historic Deerfield). Another of those services, made for Benjamin Lincoln (1733–1810) of Hingham, survives relatively intact in the Concord Museum, comprising twenty-eight pieces of the original forty-five or so [no. 77].

The Lincoln tea service includes a large and a small teapot, their lids with strawberry finials; a slop bowl for used tea leaves; a sugar bowl, its lid with a gourd finial; a helmet-shaped creampot; a cake plate; a berry dish; five cups with four saucers; and six larger cups with six saucers. Three pieces from this service are in the collection of the Porter-Phelps-Huntington House, three in the collection of the Society of the Cincinnati, and there is a cup and saucer in a private collection. The principal decoration is a rendition of the Order of the Cincinnati, the badge designed by Pierre-Charles L'Enfant, the engineer who designed the layout of Washington, D.C. One side of the Order features the motto of the Society of the Cincinnati, *Omnia Relinquit Servare Rempublicam* (He Gave Up Everything to Serve the Republic).

Benjamin Lincoln was chosen secretary of the Provincial Congress when it first gathered in Salem in October 1774 and served in all three congresses. A brigadier general in the Middlesex County militia in 1776, Lincoln was commissioned a major general in the Continental Army in 1777 [no. 78]. Wounded at Saratoga, General Lincoln was captured at Charleston in 1780 and exchanged for a captured British officer. Evidence of the high regard the Commander-in-Chief had for General Lincoln is the fact that George Washington chose Benjamin Lincoln to receive the sword of surrender of the British Army at Yorktown.

A NOTE ON SOURCES

The goal of *Eyewitness to Revolution* was to allow the items in the Concord Museum collection to each tell their part of the story. In sympathy with the inherently first-person nature of material culture objects, the sources for those stories are in large part the words of participants.

Those words principally come from the 1838 edition of the *Journals of Each Provincial Congress*, which includes the journals of the committees of Safety and Supplies, the resolves of the Massachusetts county conventions of 1774, and the depositions of participants on April 19, 1775, taken by order of the Provincial Congress; the journals of the Continental Congress; and the Acts and Resolves of Massachusetts. The contemporary vantage is also abundantly present in the Harbottle Dorr newspapers at the Massachusetts Historical Society, readily accessible on the Society's website. The letters of Thomas Hutchinson and Francis Bernard, published by the Colonial Society of Massachusetts, combine the official viewpoint with the personal in a unique fashion. The *Diaries and Letters of William Emerson* (1972) edited by Amelia Forbes Emerson provides another voice of an engaged civic leader. The vivid voice of one of William Emerson's parishioners is present in Amos Barrett's 1825 memoir of April 19. Frank Warren Coburn's *The Battle of April 19, 1775* is a fine narrative and the 1922 edition includes in an appendix the muster rolls of many of the companies engaged. In addition to these sources, the compilation heroically assembled by Vincent J.R. Kehoe in time for the Bicentennial, *We Were There* (1974), draws together and helpfully points the reader to a tremendous array of first-person accounts from official military reports, as well as journals, depositions, and letters.

SPECIAL THANKS

I am pleased to have another opportunity to thank the governance of the Concord Museum for making scholarship an institutional priority. My thanks to former director Tom Putnam for initially approving the project, and I wish to thank Lisa Krassner for allowing me the time and for gathering the support to accomplish the book. My thanks to Jessica Desany for help with collections records in general and for wrangling images in particular, and to Eden Piacitelli for attending to myriad related details. The content of this book benefits from years of collaboration with Susan Foster Jones and Jenny Gratz on the methodology of object-based learning. My thanks to Reed Gochberg generally for a fierce engagement with the subject and specifically for working on the enabling grants as well as reading and improving portions of the manuscript. The sine qua non for this publication is Allison Shilling who has confidently shepherded it from its inception with enthusiastic good cheer.

Robert Gross, author of *The Minutemen and Their World,* has been my de facto professor of Concord history for over forty years, an inestimable advantage I hope I have exploited. My sincere thanks to Bob for reading and commenting on an early draft.

Joel Bohy has for nearly two decades provided me with a vivid introduction to the living historian's habit of considering history, particularly military history, from the first-person vantage, which tends to highlight the documentary value of objects. All my descriptions of the objects in this book are informed by examination and discussion with Joel over the years, though the errors are still my own.

My thanks to Beth van Duzer generally for discussing the project informatively from the very beginning and particularly for focusing on the service records of the people associated with objects in the collection. The breakfasts at Helen's with Bob, Joel, and Beth were a highlight of this project.

Of a long list of those whose work I have found particularly helpful I would like to note John Hannigan, John Tyler, Toni Norton, and Amanda Lange.

My special thanks to Julia Collins for editing the text and to Rick Rawlins for designing the book, and to Puritan Press, Inc. for printing the volume.

My thanks as well to Gerald W.R. Ward for reviewing a late draft editorially, to Frances Pulver for proofreading the galleys, and to Diane Brenner for preparing the index.

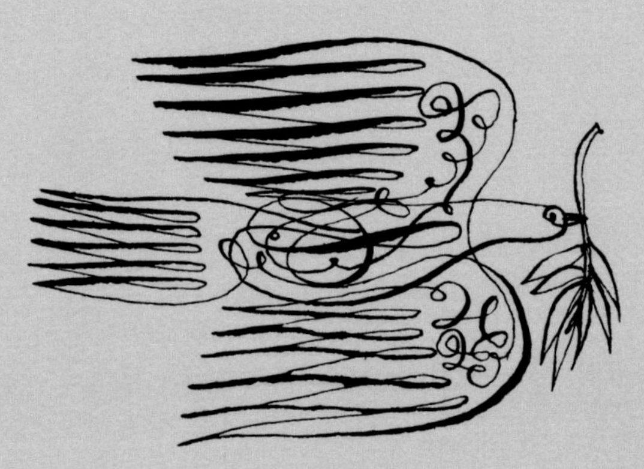